More Praise for *Why Talking Is Not Enough*

"This is a clear and practical presentation of how to bring spiritual principles into everyday relationships. Susan Page presents essential information that will help every couple create more love and harmony in their life."

—**Barbara De Angelis**, author, *How Did I Get Here?*

"I love this book! It is truly a treasure. Susan courageously shows us why we need to stop talking about problems and start taking loving action. She clearly describes the actions we need to take to create loving, spiritually growing relationships. If you are having problems in your relationship, or you want to make your relationship even better than it is, read this book!"

—**Margaret Paul**, coauthor, *Do I Have to Give Up Me to Be Loved by You?* and *Healing Your Aloneness*; and author, *Inner Bonding* and *Do I Have to Give Up Me to Be Loved by God?*

"This exciting new book is a gem. It is one of the best presentations I've ever seen of how to bring spiritual principles into everyday relationships. Page is not talking about meditating for a weekend but about how to live your spirituality every day. This wonderful book presents a shift in consciousness that will help couples have a great relationship for a lifetime. I strongly recommend this book for all couples and singles who want to be the best possible partner they can be, now and in the future."

—**Howard J. Markman**, coauthor, *12 Hours to a Great Marriage* and *Fighting for Your Marriage*

"This book describes an entirely new way for intimate partners to relate based on spiritual principles. In clear, simple language, Susan Page offers practical concepts and experiments that can improve your relationship in no time at all."

—**Kathlyn and Gay Hendricks**, authors, *Conscious Loving* and *Spirit-Centered Relationships*

"This book is like the Buddha channeled by Ann Landers! As a pastor, I have given away many copies of this book to people struggling in intimate relationships—and I've used it in my own marriage. There are many classics of spiritual wisdom and many nuts-and-bolts self-help books on relationships. Susan Page brilliantly combines the two. Her gift is to translate spiritual ideals into practical, understandable, and eminently achievable goals for everyday living in Spiritual Partnership. Read it, apply the lessons, and transform yourself and your relationship."

—**The Rev. Fred Small**, senior pastor, **First Church Unitarian, Littleton, Massachusetts**

Why Talking Is Not Enough

Eight Loving Actions That Will Transform Your Marriage

Susan Page

JOSSEY-BASS
A Wiley Imprint
www.josseybass.com

Published by Jossey-Bass
A Wiley Imprint
989 Market Street, San Francisco, CA 94103-1741 www.josseybass.com

Jossey-Bass books and products are available through most bookstores. To contact Jossey-Bass directly call our Customer Care Department within the U.S. at 800-956-7739, outside the U.S. at 317-572-3986, or fax 317-572-4002.

Jossey-Bass also publishes its books in a variety of electronic formats. Some content that appears in print may not be available in electronic books.

Library of Congress Cataloging-in-Publication Data
Page, Susan.
   Why talking is not enough : eight loving actions that will transform your marriage / Susan Page.
      p. cm.
   Includes bibliographical references.
   ISBN-13: 978-0-7879-8370-3 (cloth)
   ISBN-13: 978-0-7879-9529-4 (paper)
   1. Marriage. 2. Love. 3. Married people—Psychology. 4. Married people—Conduct of life. 5. Spiritual life. 6. Communication in marriage. I. Title.
   HQ734.P175 2006
   646.7'8—dc22   2006000527

Printed in the United States of America
FIRST EDITION
PB Printing   10 9 8 7 6 5 4

Contents

PART THREE

Seeing Spiritual Partnership in a Broader Context

For Cathi and Steven
Guadalupe
Tim
and Aurora
who have transformed my life

Introduction

Slight shifts in imagination have more impact on living than major efforts at change.
— THOMAS MOORE

Welcome to a journey of discovery and, most important, to Eight Loving Actions that will improve the quality of both your relationship and your spiritual journey, whether that is inside or outside a specific religion.

Whether you are married or not, these Loving Actions will be useful for you.

- If you are a happy and well-adjusted couple, this book will offer you new language to clarify and inspire the ways you are already loving each other, and some new ideas that are more effective than what you are doing now.

- If you are troubled and having difficulty with each other, even if one or both of you are considering ending your relationship, you'll find insights that can create permanent change—quickly.

- If you are single, the Eight Loving Actions will help you in any new relationship that might come along and in all the relationships in your life: family, friends, and work.

Chapter One gives you an overview of what I call Spiritual Partnership, which differs in two major ways from conventional ideas about marriage. First, Spiritual Partnership uses Loving Actions instead of communication as the primary tool for resolving conflicts and enhancing love; second, Spiritual Partnership shifts your focus from making changes in your partner or your relationship (over which you have little control) to making changes in yourself (over which you have complete control).

Chapters Two through Nine present Eight Loving Actions, which are a new way of "doing" your relationship. They include such ideas as freeing you from the myth that you have to solve the problems in your relationship before you can be happy. They help you manage negative emotions and move directly toward more pleasure and happiness. They give you a way to balance the giving and taking in your relationship, more than you would ever have thought you could achieve by yourself. These Loving Actions give you the power to make your relationship harmonious and loving, even if all your problems aren't solved. They offer you explicit ways to be more accepting and compassionate toward your partner and to elicit these attitudes in return. And they do all this without asking you to learn new communication skills.

The chapters in Part Two offer you an optional "program" for putting Loving Actions to work, answer common questions, and provide several practical strategies. Part Three gives an in-depth definition of *spiritual*, describes the origins of Spiritual Partnership, and puts it in historical context.

An Invitation to Use the "Experiments" in This Book

Throughout the book, I offer optional "experiments." You certainly aren't required to do them in order to understand and use Spiritual Partnership in your relationship. But the experiments offer you an opportunity to work with the material you are reading. They will be useful if you are working through this material with your partner or with a friend or as part of a support group. Often they serve as a kind of summary of foregoing material.

If you choose to use this book as a do-it-yourself workshop, the experiments offer you a structured, systematic process for integrating all the material in the book into your life.

I encourage you to use a notebook or journal so that you can keep all your experiments together. Whenever you do an experiment, date it. Part of the value of these experiments is repeating them after several months and comparing your results to earlier versions. In fact, consider not only dating each experiment but also making a few notes about what is going on in your life at the time.

I deliberately use the term *experiment* because I never intend any particular outcome from any of the exercises I suggest. This aligns closely with my general philosophy of life: if you treat everything you do as an experiment, you will never fail, for your only goal is to gather data, to learn something new. No matter what the outcome of the experiment—even if you found you didn't want to or couldn't do it—you will have learned something interesting about yourself. The only requirement is that you do the experiment *and then reflect, at least briefly, on what you learned by doing it.* You learn, not just by doing something new, but by doing something new and then reviewing what you did and what you learned. Without reflection, any learning is diminished, even lost.

Step One: Your Relationship Now

To begin our process together at the beginning, I invite you to start your journal with this experiment, a general assessment of your relationship. If you plan to do any of the experiments as we go along, you will need to do this first one, because future experiments build on it.

EXPERIMENT 1

Assess Your Relationship

1. On the first page of your journal, write a paragraph that is a completion of this sentence: On a scale of 1 to 10, right now in this moment, I rate my relationship _____ because . . . (Remember to record the date and a few notes about what is going on in your life right now.)

2. In your journal, draw a line across one page, from left to right, in the middle of the page. Above the line, list the reasons you are happy to be together with your partner, the strengths of your relationship, the qualities you love in your partner and your relationship, and the things that work well. What makes you happy?

   Below the line, list the difficulties, the aspects of your relationship that are not fun, the problems, the challenges, the incompatibilities, the areas in which you could improve—in short, anything that causes friction or unhappiness.

   How much time do you spend above the line, and how much below the line? Write percentage figures over on the right, just above and below the line.

   Give these lists careful attention, as we will make use of them later in the book.

Don't worry about what number you chose to describe your relationship. Whatever your number, and whatever your level of commitment to your partner, your use of Loving Actions will help you.

The Eight Loving Actions that are the heart of Spiritual Partnership work well if you feel committed to your partner and are fully invested in making your relationship the best it can be. Your devotion to your partner will strengthen your commitment to making the Loving Actions work in your life.

If you are ambivalent about your relationship and not certain of your commitment to it, experimenting with the Loving Actions is an effective way for you to gain more information about yourself and your partner and how you are together. Observing what happens when you use Loving Actions will help you make a decision about whether to move forward with your relationship or to leave it. For the vast majority of couples I have worked with, their use of Loving Actions moves their number up the scale. Even if it is already at 10, it moves up to 10+. If you use these actions sincerely and your number moves down, it could well mean that you are not with your true spiritual partner. This is useful information for you.

My Wish for You

As I explain more thoroughly in Chapter Fifteen, I have developed and honed these Eight Loving Actions over many years of working with couples in workshops and trainings all around the world. I have seen couples make changes that range all the way from subtle shifts to seemingly miraculous transformations. My only regret is that I can't be with you when you read this, to hear firsthand what happens when you try one of the Loving Actions, to encourage you when you encounter frustrations, and to celebrate with you when you make a change that makes a difference.

I invite you to be in touch with me by e-mail (susan@susanpage. com). I would love to hear how your use of the Loving Actions is affecting your relationship and which new ideas are most useful for you. And I do respond to e-mails.

Remember that the Loving Actions do not require extra time on your part. They are simply a new way of doing what you already do. And the really great part is that they don't require the cooperation or even the participation of your partner! But they do require commitment and focus. Just know that I am with you in spirit and cheering for you every step of the way.

My very best wishes to you! I hope you find this book as exciting to read as I have found it to write, and that it creates welcome changes in your day-to-day pleasure, your passion, your commitment, and your feelings of love.

Acknowledgments

My first debt of gratitude is to the many couples whose stories I tell in these pages, who were willing to experiment with something different and stay with it until it made a difference. Thank you for so generously staying in touch, for sharing your success with others, and for all those follow-up interviews. Your joy and excitement are what compelled me to write this book.

My gratitude to my editor, Alan Rinzler, is immeasurable. He saw the potential in this project, and his vision and commitment brought it to life.

Sandra Dijkstra has been my business and literary partner for twenty years; a more supportive, skilled, and tenacious literary agent I cannot imagine.

Glenda Robinson and Susan Harrow generously shared their expertise and compassion at crucial moments.

Richard Morrison's general support of my work and clever contribution mean a great deal to me.

Wendy Bichel, Kathleen Cummings, Kirsten Dehner, Leah Feldon, David Garfinkel, Michael and Jean Gerber, Malcolm Lubliner, Monica Maass, Kathleen McCleary, Adam Mitchell, Doug Robinson, Jerry Rothman, Lulu Torbet, Stephanie and Jay Vogt, and Patrice Wynne have provided special friendship and support.

I am grateful to Golda Clendenin, Bob Davidson, Bonnie Davis, Naomi Epel, Anita Goldstein, Susan Goldstein, Paul and Jan Hammock, Melinda Henning, Carolyn and Michael Hittleman, Fran May, Victoria Nerenberg, Roseanne Packard, Amanita Rosenbush, Harriet Sage, Susan Schwartz, Neil Tetkowski, Dorothy Wall, Ellen Weis, and Gordon Whiting for making contributions that became a part of this book, and to Jenny Davis, Beverly Nelson, and Richard Trumbull for their support after reading the manuscript.

My own spiritual partner, Mayer, supports me and my writing every day in more ways than I can enumerate here. He made this book possible, and I adore him!

PART ONE

What Is Spiritual Partnership?

CHAPTER 1

Introducing Spiritual Partnership

S piritual Partnership is a new model for couples, a different understanding of the purpose of loving relationships and how they work. It does not require that you be religious or part of an organized religion, or that you maintain a spiritual practice. As you will see, *spiritual* is different from *religious*. It simply means that you align with "spiritual" values, as we define them here.

Spiritual Partnership expands the possibilities of what you can experience with each other as a couple. No matter what the status of their relationship before they began to practice Spiritual Partnership, many couples who engage in this kind of relationship report greater ease between them; freer, more passionate love; and less focus on areas of conflict. Most important, they experience increased inner strength and personal peace and well-being.

For example, Jan was exasperated because her husband, Terry, was extremely controlling when it came to their money. He complained every time Jan spent money on anything, even essentials. Jan tried every communication skill she could find. She expressed her own frustration, she suggested possible compromises, she declared ultimatums, she tried to understand what was behind Terry's anxiety. Their fights escalated, and the tension in their household increased.

Then Jan learned the principles of Spiritual Partnership and began using Loving Actions. She stopped trying to solve the problem. She moved directly toward creating a pleasant atmosphere in their family. She found ways to meet the family's needs without upsetting Terry. She found actions that conveyed to Terry that she had compassion for his anxiety, instead of trying in vain to change it.

Within a week of her changes, Jan felt back in charge of her own life and experienced personal power she had not felt for years. The atmosphere in their house transformed; the tension between the two of them melted away. Terry was still anxious and controlling about money, but Jan had found ways to manage these qualities rather than fighting against them.

The changes Jan made are the ones we will learn thoroughly in this book. First, in this chapter, we will lay the foundation on which the Loving Actions of Spiritual Partnership are built. We will learn:

- The historical context of Spiritual Partnership
- What we mean by "spiritual"
- Why communication has failed so many couples
- Exactly what a "Loving Action" is
- The new way that change happens in Spiritual Partnership
- How to make your relationship a spiritual practice

How Spiritual Partnership Fits Historically

If we were to divide modern relationships into three historical stages, with Stage One being the classic 1950s model of homemaker and breadwinner, the second stage would be our rebellion against the inadequacies of that model. In Stage Two, we struggled to achieve equality between partners and a broader range of acceptable relationship lifestyles.

In the past forty years, we have focused a great deal of attention on equality and fairness in our relationships, on better communication and conflict resolution techniques. Although not every individual marriage has achieved these ideals, the model of equality and fairness in relationships is widely accepted and practiced.

We are ready now for Stage Three, in which we will build on and incorporate the equality and fairness we achieved in Stage Two and move beyond it. In Stage Three, the emphasis will be on love and spiritual depth.

When my husband taught ceramics, he would draw on the blackboard a figure that looked like an hourglass. The bottom half of the hourglass, he would say, is learning the basics. You follow all the rules carefully to achieve competence at designing, throwing, glazing, and firing a pot. Then he would point to the middle of the hourglass and say, "This is the pinnacle of mediocrity." Your ceramic pots are competent, but they are not imaginative, individual, magical; they don't yet transcend the ordinary. However, it is only when you have mastered fundamental skills and achieved this pinnacle of mediocrity that you can burst through to levels beyond that to express your true individual creativity.

In our brief history of relationships, we hover today at the center of the hourglass, the pinnacle of "equal, fair, open relationships with good conflict resolution skills." These are important values, but if we stop with them, we risk limiting our relationships to the ordinary. Now that human endeavor has advanced to a time in which spiritual consciousness is rising, we understand that love is not limited to passion and good communication alone, but can include a spiritual dimension as well.

It is that spiritual dimension that we will explore in depth in this book, and it is for that reason that I have chosen to call Stage Three couples *Spiritual Partners.*

Spiritual Partnership is *not* simply a bigger and better version of the fair and equal relationships we have valued for years. Spiritual Partnership is qualitatively different. You are about to discover some methods and techniques for resolving differences that I strongly suspect you have never tried before. You will not be invited to sit down with your partner and talk things out. Instead the focus will be on what it means to love and on highly specific ways that you can put your love—love for yourself and love for your partner—into action.

What Do We Mean by *Spiritual*?

Spirituality is a widely used term, and we all know vaguely what we mean by it. I need to be precise about what I mean, however, because my understanding of the term *spirituality* underlies everything in this book.

I offer a comprehensive, in-depth definition of spirituality in Chapter Fourteen, but I don't want to delay getting us into the practical aspects of Loving Actions by giving the full definition now. So I offer here an abbreviated definition that we can use as we get immediately into the heart of what Spiritual Partnership is and how it can transform your relationship. You can refer to the full definition in Chapter Fourteen whenever you feel a need for it.

First, I believe that spirituality is a natural and universal element of our lives that we choose to move toward or to ignore; that it is possible to be more spiritual, less spiritual, or not spiritual at all. A case can certainly be made that because we are all made up of mind, body, and spirit, everyone has a spiritual dimension, and that it is not possible to be "nonspiritual." But I have chosen to use *spiritual* to mean "being aligned with your spirit" or "choosing spiritual values." You can choose a spiritual approach to your relationship, for example, or a nonspiritual approach. So spirituality is not an automatic part of a relationship but rather a commitment, an act of will.

EXPERIMENT 2

What Is Spirituality?

Before reading further, you may want to take a few minutes to define spirituality for yourself. In your journal or in a conversation with a friend, answer these questions:

1. What do you mean when you use the term *spiritual*?

2. Do you consider yourself to be a spiritual person? Explain your answer.

To be spiritual, I submit, is to recognize your connection to the universe and to everyone and everything in it, *and to strive each moment for the thoughts and actions that will increase and not decrease this connection.* Your spiritual journey is your own personal journey

- **From isolation to connection.** We are not separate from one another, but one with the universe and everything in it. Anything that moves you toward connection is spiritual; anything that moves you toward separation or isolation is not spiritual.

- **From your conditioned personality to your authentic self.** Each of us consists of layers of beliefs and behaviors that obscure our pure, authentic self. "Spiritual" means moving toward authenticity, toward who you really are.

- **From fear to love.** Love is a gentle, powerful force, too often overwhelmed by fear, which appears in many disguises. Our spiritual task is to recognize how fear stops us, and to progress through it so that love can move freely in our lives.

- **From sleep to consciousness or awareness.** The only true prison is the one we each create with limited consciousness. To be spiritual is to stay curious about our own areas of blindness, of limited or inaccurate vision, and to be open to new awareness.

- **From control to surrender.** You can't control the universe; instead, be open and receptive to what it offers.

- **From restlessness to inner peace.** As we become more connected, authentic, loving, aware, and receptive, we will experience deep inner strength and radiant joy.

If a spiritual person is one who is moving toward connection, authenticity, love, consciousness, receptivity, and inner peace, then a spiritual practice, such as your relationship, is any behavior that brings you into increasing alignment with the you who embodies these qualities. In other words, *spirituality is bringing yourself into closer and closer alignment with your highest self.*

How Spiritual Partnership Is Different

There are two major ways in which Spiritual Partnership differs from Stage Two relationships.

In Spiritual Partnership,

1. Loving Actions replace communication as the primary tool for problem solving and relationship enrichment.

2. Your focal point shifts from your partner and your relationship to your own spiritual path.

Let us now look in depth at both of these significant differences.

Difference 1: Loving Actions Replace Communication as the Primary Tool for Problem Solving and Relationship Enrichment

Stage Two relationships rely on a fundamental principle that we are now ready to rise above: that the skills we use in the marketplace—such as negotiating, bargaining, and reaching agreements—will work in love relationships. They won't. The purpose of the marketplace is to win, to gain advantage over others. The purpose of love is to love. They are two different universes.

For decades, we have been relying heavily on elaborate rules for sharing feelings, negotiating, and even "fair" fighting. When you have a conflict, what can you do? Find time to sit down and talk it over with each other, argue, negotiate. What else is there? When you want to feel closer, you have an honest conversation. Tell your partner what you need to feel loved. Listen to your mate's deepest feelings.

I want to be very clear that I am not against communication skills! Couples who know and use them are likely to have a far better relationship than couples who don't. Knowing that your partner has truly understood and accepted a painful, joyful, or sensitive feeling you have is a deeply moving and bonding experience. Resolving a conflict using excellent communication skills can be joyful rather than painful. In fact, if you are reading this and you don't know how to use "active listening" or what an "I" statement is, the best primer I know for basic, extremely important communication skills is the classic book that as far as I know invented those terms: *Parent Effectiveness Training* by Thomas Gordon. Even though the book is written for parents, especially Chapters Two and Six are a superb explanation of fundamental communication skills, which are useful for every relationship in your life! Spiritual Partnership builds on these skills.

But communication can also *cause* problems, and, because communication skills are a limited tool, relying on them may restrict your potential as a couple. Loving Actions open up whole new frontiers for your relationship.

Why Talking Is Not Enough

There are four ways in which communication can be problematic or limiting as a relationship-enhancing tool:

1. Your partner may be unavailable, unwilling, or even unable to talk. If the two of you are depending entirely on communication and have no other tools available to you, when your partner simply won't talk or listen, you may feel stuck, maybe even utterly frustrated, with nowhere else to turn.

2. In many couples, one partner is better at communicating than the other. So when you use communication, you are relying on a skill that puts you on an unequal playing field from the very start, puts one of you at an automatic disadvantage, and creates frustration for the other. Relying only on communication will exacerbate this problem, not solve it. It will be like trying to remove your finger from one of those woven finger traps by pulling harder and harder and only trapping yourself worse.

3. A third problem with relying exclusively on communication to solve problems and create closeness is that communication skills

are high-level, difficult skills that most people have not even begun to master. Effective communication does not come naturally to most people. In fact, what we seem to be born with instead is a natural tendency to use poor communication:

- To become defensive when attacked
- To offer an immediate solution when someone cries or complains
- To blame the other guy when there is a problem instead looking at our own role
- To gloss over feelings instead of acknowledging them
- To ask indirectly for what we want
- To criticize others more often than we affirm them

All these extremely ineffective communication patterns are ubiquitous. Unlearning them and replacing them with effective skills is work that most people never have the opportunity or interest to do.

When communication is done badly, it exacerbates the original problem, creating more confusion, frustration, and anger than ever. *Poor* communication doesn't solve problems; it creates them!

4. The really giant problem with communication is the hidden agenda it so often brings with it. When two people sit down to communicate about a problem, what they are really trying to do is get the other person to see things their way, and to change.

Trying to solve a problem by getting your partner to change is by far the most common problem-solving approach there is. Yet it is the worst possible method! It is neither effective nor spiritual because (1) it never works and (2) it does not honor your partner. As we shall see, Loving Actions do work, and they do honor your partner.

As we said, *good* communication between two people who love each other and who treat each other in a spiritually mature way is a valuable tool and a great pleasure. One major difference between Stage Two relationships and Spiritual Partnership is this: *in Spiritual Partnership, good communication is a goal you strive for, not the means you use to get there*. Good communication flows naturally when you have become Spiritual Partners through the use of Loving Actions. As we shall see in detail in Chapter Twelve, good communication is the natural *result* of a highly evolved, thriving intimate relationship.

Loving Actions

If we are going to replace the old tool of communication with a new approach, let's find out more about it. What are Loving Actions?

A Loving Action is an intentional behavior that

- Is motivated by a desire for spiritual growth
- Is unilateral
- Requires discipline, an act of will
- Is experimental

The good news is that deciding to use a Loving Action does not require you to change the way you feel. You can't order your feelings or emotions around anyway. All you have to do as a Spiritual Partner is decide to try an experiment, even if you don't feel like it, to try a new action or behavior. Hoping that your feelings will change or waiting until you feel like changing your behavior is only a way of digging yourself deeper into your unpleasant feelings. But changing your behavior as an experiment, even when you don't feel like it, can definitely lead to a change in your feelings. In other words, you will never feel your way into new actions, but you can act your way into new feelings.

We can best understand each of the four characteristics of a Loving Action by looking at an example.

Lyle had gone to great lengths to plan a surprise for his wife, Wendy. An old friend of hers, Deb, was coming to town. Lyle arranged for Wendy to meet him at a restaurant at six o'clock, where Deb would also be waiting.

At a quarter to six, Wendy called Lyle on his cell phone to tell him she wouldn't be able to make it.

Working late, usually unexpectedly, was a pattern of Wendy's that caused a lot of friction between the two of them. In the past, Lyle's pattern was to get a righteous tone in his voice and to lecture Wendy about how inconsiderate she was and how this just couldn't continue. He kept looking for ways to convince her that she was being selfish, that he too had legitimate needs, and his frustration would escalate, because he felt there was nothing he could do to make Wendy change her ways.

Wendy loathed the way Lyle became paternalistic with her, and she felt misunderstood and unsupported. She couldn't help these work crises, her work was important, and she contributed a lot of income to the family. She needed some slack.

But Lyle had recently begun attending a Spiritual Partnership group, so he decided to experiment with Loving Action 3, act as if, which we will learn in Chapter Four. Lyle was upset, but he deliberately acted as if he were loving and understanding, as an experiment. He asked Wendy, in an interested way, what was going on at work. While she was talking, he had a chance to pull his thoughts together; he realized that the surprise would be just as much fun if he and Deb waited until Wendy came home later. Then Lyle wished Wendy good luck with her project, said "I love you," and told her he'd see her later.

Lyle and Deb had a lovely time getting to know each other better, and later at home, they all had a wonderful time with the surprise.

So in what ways was Lyle's behavior a Loving Action? Let's see:

1. *Lyle was motivated by his desire to grow as a spiritual person.* He knew from his own meditation practice and from spiritual tapes, books, and speakers that the spiritual path would be to return to a quiet mind, to let his inner calmness prevail rather than to react out of habit to this circumstance.

"It's not what happens to you, but how you deal with what happens to you," said the voice in his head. He got a vision of the Dalai Lama and Jesus and knew that they would not be all torn up inside, angry, helpless, and out of control at Wendy's behavior. He wanted to be a stronger spiritual person, to be more loving and accepting, and to do something that would move him in the direction of connection to Wendy, not separation from her. He realized that even if he did not *feel* that way, he could choose to *behave* that way.

2. *Lyle's action was unilateral.* He didn't announce his decision to Wendy. He didn't ask for her cooperation. He didn't worry about whether his action was "fair." He moved completely beyond who was right and who was wrong to a different realm entirely by asking, "No matter who is right and who is wrong, what can I do to make a difference?"

The hard part of taking a unilateral action is that you have to do all the work by yourself. But the great part of it is that you *get* to do it all by yourself! You can skip altogether the monumentally difficult step of having to secure cooperation from your partner! Suddenly, all the cards are in your hand. You don't have to wait until your partner "gets it" or until your partner cooperates or agrees or until your partner changes. Being able to affect the situation all by yourself gives you enormous freedom. It empowers you! It gives you power, not over other people, but inner power, inner strength. It lets you out of the prison of being at the mercy of someone else.

All Loving Actions are unilateral. They may even have a kind of secret quality about them, as though you are a little elf or angel who did a good deed but will never tell. Sometimes you may never reveal your Loving Action to anyone. You certainly can, of course, and may want to if you are in a spiritual support group or if you and your partner are on a spiritual journey together.

But the point is, a unilateral act is its own reward. Lyle did not need to tell Wendy what he did to salvage their evening in order to elicit her praise or to feel even better about himself. He knows inside himself that he had the courage and discipline to take a Loving Action and that it brought him everything it promised: he became stronger in his spiritual life, and he single-handedly turned a potential fight into a pleasant evening.

3. *Lyle's action required discipline and an act of will.* There is a reason spiritual "practice" is not spiritual "theory." Spiritual growth is about making difficult choices and then practicing them over and over. Eventually they will become less difficult and even more natural than doing things the old way. Spiritual growth is about turning back the strong tide of habit and conditioning. It is about overcoming laziness and apathy.

When you are climbing a mountain, you won't reach the summit if you give in to the voices that say, "Hey, it isn't worth all this hard work. Just turn around and go back down. So what if you don't get to the top?" Part of spiritual work is staying disciplined, keeping yourself motivated, because the work is hard and the rewards sometimes seem dim and remote (although that is less true when relationship is your spiritual path, for in your relationship, the rewards are sometimes more immediate, as they were for Lyle).

4. *Lyle's action was an experiment.* The outcome was not predetermined, but open ended. Lyle needed to try acting as if, but he had no idea what the result of his action would be. It was an

experiment. The goal of his action was simply to see what would happen.

Lyle didn't say, "I'm going to act as if I'm not angry so that Wendy will feel guilty," or "I'm going to act as if so we can have a good evening," or "I'm going to act as if because then Wendy will appreciate me more and maybe even see the error of her ways." He undertook the experiment *without knowing what the outcome would be,* just like a scientist working in a lab. He may have had an hypothesis about what would happen, but until he conducted the experiment, he wouldn't know whether his hypothesis was correct. He acted as if because he knew this was one spiritual choice he could make. Now he would watch carefully to see what would happen.

No Loving Action can ever fail, because it is always an experiment, and the only goal of an experiment is to gain new information. When you try a Loving Action in a relationship, maybe you will discover that you feel different inside; maybe your partner will respond more warmly toward you; maybe your partner will become angry and hostile; maybe you will feel worse than you did. Whatever happens, you will have learned something. The more consciously you engage in your experiments and the more carefully you observe the results, the more you will learn. This learning is the substance of spiritual growth.

So again, a Loving Action is a specific unilateral act of will that is motivated by a desire for spiritual growth and undertaken as an experiment, the results of which will be carefully watched and factored into future experiments.

Loving Actions have two functions. First, they give you a taste of what it is like to be a fully evolved spiritual person. Second, they help you to become one. An evolved spiritual person in Lyle's situation would have such a highly developed inner calm and peace of mind that he would never have been thrown off balance by Wendy's behavior in the first place.

Lyle isn't there yet, but by deliberately adopting spiritual *behavior* as an experiment, he gets to experience something of what it would be like to be a spiritually evolved person. Also, he moves forward in his spiritual journey because his Loving Action is one more effort at spiritual practice. After years of acting as if and engaging in whatever other spiritual practices he is doing, Lyle will have the quiet mind and inner strength that are the goals of spiritual practice.

Loving Actions Require Leadership

Whenever you use a Loving Action, you are voluntarily offering leadership to your relationship.

A leader is someone who agrees to watch over not only his or her own needs but also the needs of everyone in the group and of the group itself. A good leader promotes the goals of the whole group, not just his or her own personal goals, and wants the whole group to succeed. Above all, a leader takes initiative in order to accomplish these goals, both by setting a good example and by supporting each member of the group.

Reread that last paragraph, applying it very specifically to your relationship.

If you are a natural leader, this role will be easy for you. If not, this will be a excellent opportunity to push yourself, to reach outside your comfort zone, and to increase your skills and self-confidence. The Eight Loving Actions will give you specific ways to lead. For now, it is important just to see the concept that using Loving Actions is a form of leadership, which, all by itself, is a substantial contribution to your relationship.

Leadership is not fair. Often the leader has to do extra work. But the leader also receives the satisfaction of guiding the group to success. How often have you been part of a department or class or committee and had the feeling, "I could have done a much better job of leadership myself!" Here is your chance to do that—in your very own relationship.

If both you and your partner are using Spiritual Partnership together, then you will both be providing leadership at different times. Very often, however, one partner is more inclined to provide it than the other. If you are the one who seems to care more about the quality of your relationship or to experience problems more often, you have the opportunity to make an impact by voluntarily taking a leadership role. Or if you are undertaking Spiritual Partnership by yourself without involving your partner, you can enjoy the role of uncontested voluntary leadership.

Another way to talk about spiritual leadership is that the spiritual leader is the "big" person in any interaction. Being the "big" person means that you voluntarily take the high ground. You make a sacrifice. You say to yourself, "The relationship is more important than whether or not I get my way this time." You put your ego in the backseat for the time being and don't worry about being acknowledged for what you do. Being the "big" person may mean that you give up being right or making sure your partner knows you are right. You become more interested in good results for the relationship than in either "winning" or receiving praise.

My friend Erin, who is a real estate agent, was working with a family who found their ideal dream home but felt it was beyond their means. Erin knew that in the current fast-paced market, within a year they would feel they had gotten a bargain, and she encouraged them to stretch their limit. She told me that she quietly gave up her own commission, though the family never realized this.

"I didn't need the money," she told me. "And they really needed that home!"

Erin was the "big" person here. She made a sacrifice, an unselfish gesture. She took pleasure in her good deed and didn't need any recognition for it.

Every time you adopt that attitude in your relationship—and the Loving Actions will help you do it—you will reap enormous rewards.

Being the "big" person means that you avoid getting caught up in the most immediate action and take one step back so that you can see the whole "game" you are a part of. Then you have the choice: simply not playing the game or maybe even inventing an entirely different game. Leadership is the simple switch from, "Why won't you *talk* to me about this? I really don't feel we can spend the money!" to "Look, here we are arguing about money again. Let's go get some ice cream. I'm sure this thing will work itself out."

Lyle was exercising leadership and being the "big" person when he deliberately decided to act as if he were not angry, even when, inside, he felt anger and frustration.

The great thing about deciding to provide leadership in your relationship is that you gain power—not power over your mate, but inner strength and confidence. You suddenly realize you have far more control over life in your relationship than you had thought.

The Purpose of Love Is to Love

Our culture has not taught us to love openly and freely, and the idea of unilateral acts of love may seem naive and, well, unfair. Because most of us were parented imperfectly and have been through painful "love" experiences in our adult lives, we have few models for spiritually informed love. Instead, we turn to the model we have learned so well in the capitalistic marketplace. We think of our relationships as a contract that has to be fair and have built-in safeguards. We bargain with each other for better results for ourselves.

EXPERIMENT 3

Try Actions Instead of Words

Even before you have learned any specific Loving Actions, watch for an opportunity in your relationship to act instead of talk. Think of something you want to convey to your sweetheart. Maybe it is a compliment or an appreciation. Maybe it is a request or a complaint or criticism. Now, just for fun, see if you can figure out a way to convey this message with some kind of action instead of words.

In your notebook, write down exactly what you tried and how you felt the experiment worked or didn't work.

But marriage is simply not about gaining or winning, and the rules of the marketplace will never work there. Marriage and loving partnerships are for something else altogether: they are for learning how to give and receive love. That's all. Loving Actions are not bargaining chips. When you offer them freely, with no strings attached, you will experience them in return, no matter what the response from another person is, because you will be experiencing your own strong and loving self.

Suppose you act lovingly, and your partner does not respond in kind. You have still been loving, in accord with your spiritual practice, and your kind, loving behavior is its own reward. Does the Dalai Lama stop behaving with compassion and acceptance because the Chinese still occupy Tibet?

To live in accord with spiritual values is to live by choice and awareness rather than always to be in reaction to the people around you.

Chances are that the marketplace rules of negotiating and communicating have not produced desired results in your relationship anyway. Stop and think for a minute. What is the biggest source of conflict in your relationship? How far have you come in resolving it by using communication?

If you choose to bring your spiritual practice into your relationship, your only question will be, "How well can I love this person?" You are not loving as a strategy to gain certain specific results, but the "results" of love are likely to be richly rewarding.

Behaving lovingly toward your partner is not a vague concept; this book will show you exactly how to do it. For most people, Loving Actions are easier to learn than complex communications skills, and they have much more far reaching and long-lasting effects. The rewards of loving go far beyond the very best you can achieve using the old rules. The couples I studied for my second book, *The Eight Essential Traits of Couples Who Thrive*, were thriving precisely because they focused on loving each other, in a spirit of good will, not in a spirit of "Am I getting my fair share?" While couples around them were busy negotiating with each other, these couples were learning better and better how to love, exactly what you will learn in this book.

Focusing on love rather than on negotiation makes a staggering difference. All the assumptions change; all the rules change; all the ways of measuring results change. You may feel some resistance to this new idea. I will address some of the most common hesitations and questions about it in Chapter Eleven. But the only way to find out whether Spiritual Partnership is right for you is to try it.

So the first major difference between Stage Two relationships and Spiritual Partnership is the change from communication to Loving Actions as the primary method of relationship enrichment and problem solving. Now let's look at the second major difference.

Difference 2: Your Focal Point Shifts from Your Partner and Your Relationship to Your Own Spiritual Path

Most of us try to solve our relationship problems by using every means possible to persuade our partner to change.

> *If only you would clean up your messes after you! This is a reasonable request, it's fair, and it's easy for you to do.*

> *Look, I'd like just one compliment a week. Is that too much to ask? Just one time, tell me I look nice or that you enjoyed the meal I prepared.*

> *It isn't fair for you to talk on the phone so much every evening. It leaves no time for us. You've got to find a way to cut down. It's only fair.*

> *There you go criticizing me again. I hate this. Are you ever going to learn that your criticisms hurt me? They will never change me anyway. Just lay off!*

Asking your partner to change is the most common relationship problem-solving technique in the world—and the least effective.

Change will happen in your relationship when you use a spiritual approach, but not because you engineer it. It will happen on its own, naturally, not in a forced or artificial way. Change will come from a deep place, and it will endure. When you try to change your partner, you are leaving spirit out of your relationship. Remember what Thomas Moore said: "Slight shifts in imagination have more impact on living than major efforts at change."

In Chapter Eight, where we discuss the power of acceptance, we will see in detail how change *does* occur within Spiritual Partnerships. For now, we need to see that change does not happen when your focus is on your partner and your problems.

There are two major drawbacks to the age-old technique of trying to change your partner: (1) It doesn't honor your partner, and (2) though it may create a temporary, Band-Aid solution, it will never truly work.

Trying to Change Your Partner Doesn't Honor Your Partner

Each of us has a little flame deep within us. All of life is an effort to keep that flame burning brightly. The flame is our self-love, our inner strength, our happiness and sense of well-being. Every time you interact with your intimate partner, you are either throwing sand on your partner's flame—or breathing fresh oxygen on it to make it glow brighter. A love relationship should be all about brightening and supporting the inner flame of the person you love. We have somehow acquired the illusion that if we throw enough sand and water on our partner's flame in the guise of being "fair" or of offering "suggestions" (usually criticisms) or of insisting on change, we will both end up happier.

Trying to get your partner to change is always a way of dimming his or her flame. It is not supporting or loving. It doesn't honor the precious person your partner has spent all these years becoming and is still trying to become.

Your partner has a right to be sloppy or controlling or absent-minded or workaholic or selfish or habitually late or rude to his parents. These may be personality characteristics that displease you, but your partner doesn't have to change them for you.

For one thing, your partner's "faults" were probably there when you fell in love with this person. Either love blinded you to them, or the very same quality you once loved has transformed itself in your own eyes. What you originally saw as generosity, you now see as careless spending. What you originally saw as strength, you now see as arrogance. The iconoclasm you loved now seems weird to you. The ambition you so admired has turned into workaholism, or the free spirit you adored has now become a lack of ambition.

Your partner has personality tendencies, a family history, and difficult past experiences. He or she didn't just spring from whole cloth, ready to satisfy your images of love. Your partner has images too, and has a right to those.

Women often want more expressions of affection and affirmation from men. They want to feel more adored and to experience more intimate moments.

Men's ideal is often the precise opposite of this. Men love to relax into a relationship and not feel they always have to be taking care of it. They like "parallel play," relaxing together while they both are reading, or puttering in the garage knowing their loved one is inside on the computer.

You have a right to what you want, but so does your partner. So you may not end up with everything you want. This is not a problem; it's a fact of life. Badgering your partner to change will only create discord, upset, and distance between the two of you. It is the opposite of loving, honoring, and supporting this person you love.

Trying to Change Your Partner Will Never Be Effective

When you keep mentioning that your partner is late or sloppy or inattentive, or even if you negotiate constructively and sweetly for change, the message you are conveying to your partner is, "You are not quite good enough the way you are. I would love you more if you would change." So your partner's experience is, "I'm being assaulted, criticized."

It is actually a *healthy response* for your partner to feel inside, "I'm not a bad person. I'm fine just the way I am. I love myself, even if you can't love me the way I am."

When you criticize a relatively healthy person, you actually trigger that person's self-protective instincts and probably make the person even more likely to behave in the way you don't like, whether this reflex is conscious or unconscious. If you have a partner who acquiesces to your every desire and never stands up for himself or herself, then you have an even worse problem. You should be grateful for a partner who is trying to maintain personal integrity in the face of your criticisms or requests for change.

"But," you may say, "I'm trying to persuade my partner to be more organized or more thoughtful or more competent *because I know it would be better for him or her*, as well as better for the relationship. I'm trying to be helpful!"

Help is help only when it is perceived as help.

A person is not likely to change a deeply rooted personality trait for you. If the trait is something your partner doesn't like in herself or himself, then the more you convey your love and create an atmosphere of acceptance, the safer your partner will feel to risk experimenting with changes. Change happens when you accept and support your partner, not when you criticize. We will see many examples of changes taking place in an atmosphere of support as we discuss specific Loving Actions.

To reiterate then, trying to solve a problem by getting your partner to change doesn't honor your partner and doesn't work. Nevertheless, most couples keep trying to change each other for years and years, because it is the only thing they can think of to do.

Spiritual Partnership invites you to try something entirely different.

Spiritual Partnership Suggests a Different Focus

In Spiritual Partnership, you stop putting attention on your partner and start putting it on yourself. Your actions arise out of your own desire to become a more spiritually developed person. In Spiritual Partnership, relationship work is inner work.

Always view your relationship as an opportunity for you to move toward the spiritual person you would like to be: to become more connected with your true self, more connected with your partner, more authentic, and more loving.

In Spiritual Partnership, you are not asking, "How can I resolve this problem? How can I get my needs met here? How can I convey what I need to my partner?" Rather, the question is always, "If I am going to behave in accord with my highest spiritual self, what will I do right now?" The Eight Loving Actions will offer you some very specific answers to that question.

In Spiritual Partnership, it doesn't matter what is going on with your partner; it matters only how *you respond to* what is going on with your partner. Your work is to pay attention to yourself, to learn what you can about yourself, and then to provide spiritual loving leadership. When you use this approach, you will automatically move both yourself and your relationship forward.

"This Is About Me"

In one of my groups of eight people, Sharon became very annoyed with Tim, a man in the group who was not her partner. Tim was an advanced student of yoga. He talked about yoga all the time and even sat in our group in yoga positions. Sharon felt that he was "showing off" and that his self-centered behavior was disruptive to our group. She wanted to get him to look at his inappropriate behavior, and she thought the rest of us should join her in this effort.

However, every time Sharon spoke to Tim about his yoga, I would say to her, "Sharon, where is your charge about this coming from?" I would invite her to look at exactly what her feelings of annoyance were and to see what she could learn about herself from this irritation. Sharon hated my interventions; she wanted me and the group to support her in conveying to Tim that he was insensitive and arrogant. But we all helped her see that Tim had a right to be who he was and that Sharon's feelings were offering her an opportunity to learn something *about herself.* Why did she find his behavior to be so upsetting? "This is not about Tim," I would tell Sharon. "This is about you."

It took Sharon several weeks to understand what I meant when I said, "Sharon, this is about you." In her view, Tim was being glaringly disruptive.

Gradually, as Sharon became willing to look at the reason for her upset, it developed that she had practiced yoga herself in the past, but had let her practice lapse and felt pangs of regret about it. Tim was evoking this regret. When Sharon discovered how strong her regrets were, she found a way to fit yoga back into her schedule.

Whenever you find yourself annoyed with your partner, remember the phrase, "This is about me." As a Spiritual Partner, you want to ask not, "Why is my partner doing this dumb thing?" but rather, "Why do I have such strong feelings about what my partner is doing? Where does this big 'charge' in me come from? What can I learn about myself from this incident?"

The way to "fix" whatever you don't like in your relationship is to stop worrying about what your partner is or isn't doing, and go within. The answers to your conflicts, to your longings and dissatisfactions, are not out there in someone else or some other situation. Everything you need for peace and happiness is within you, and that is where your relationship work has to start.

EXPERIMENT 4
This Is About Me

Think of something your partner did that annoyed you, an incident where you clearly felt your partner was insensitive or thoughtless.

Now, just as an exercise, try to think of any small way in which you might have contributed to this incident. What was your role?

This can be a powerful experiment. Take it seriously and take your time with it. Write about it in your journal or talk with a friend.

"If you focus only on yourself all the time, isn't that pretty selfish and self-centered?" someone once asked me.

Spiritual attention to self, which moves you toward connection with yourself and with others and toward authenticity, is completely different from inappropriate selfishness, self-involvement, or narcissism, all of which lead away from connection and authenticity. When you pay spiritual attention to yourself, this should not be apparent to other people. Paying attention to your own spiritual journey leads you in the direction of love. It means that you stay aware of your highest spiritual aspirations and act out of them.

. . . [I]f you take good care of yourself, you help everyone. You stop being a source of suffering to the world, and you become a reservoir of joy and freshness. Here and there are people who know how to take good care of themselves, who live joyfully and happily. They are our strongest support. Everything they do, they do for everyone.

—Thich Nhat Hanh

A deeply held belief in this society is that relationships are hard work. Many people experience this to be true. What's sad is that most people spend their whole lives doing the *wrong hard work*, trying either to change or to put up with their partner. This is futile and frustrating hard work. Becoming spiritual, waking up to your true self and your deepest desires, learning how to operate from love and empathy—*that* is hard work, but it leads somewhere! It takes you beyond the hard work! It is the kind of hard work that is enormously satisfying and that makes your relationship into the one you wanted in the first place.

Spiritual Partnership is learning how to do the *right kind* of hard work! The "work" is on your own spiritual path, your own journey to connection, authenticity, love, and inner peace. And as a bonus, your work on that journey will enhance your relationship more than anything else you can do.

Your Relationship as a Spiritual Practice

We are not used to thinking of our relationships as a spiritual practice. When we think of a spiritual practice, we usually mean something like meditation, prayer, religious practice, reading of sacred scriptures, journal writing, dream work, or developing a connection with a spiritual teacher.

The supposition throughout this book is that you can make your relationship itself an active part of your spiritual practice. If you already have a spiritual practice, you are invited to add this to it; if not, your relationship is a fine place to begin a spiritual practice. Just as you might learn how to meditate and then engage in the "practice" of meditating for many years, in this book, you will learn about Spiritual Partnership and be invited to practice it for many

EXPERIMENT 5

On Changing Your Partner

1. Look back at the list you made below the line in Experiment 1, the problem areas in your relationship. Choose one problem.

2. First, in your journal, write a sentence or two about how this problem could be eliminated if your partner would be willing to change.

3. On a scale of 1 to 10, with 1 being "Never happen" and 10 being "Extremely likely," give the scenario you wrote in point 2 a number that expresses how likely it is that your partner will change in this way.

4. Now, with regard to this same problem, write, "The reason I react so strongly to [your partner]'s behavior is _____."

5. Assume that your partner will never change with regard to this behavior. Do you think you could ever change your reaction to this behavior? Explain your answer.

years. With meditation, Spiritual Partnership, or any other spiritual practice, all along the way you will learn more about yourself and your relationship to the divine, discover your resistance to spiritual growth and move through that resistance, and ultimately become a happier and more loving person.

Relationship is probably the most powerful spiritual path that exists in the world today. It's the greatest tool that we have. Our relationships can be the fastest and the most powerful route to the deepest truth, if we know how to use them.

—Shakti Gawain

Some spiritual groups create special circumstances to help them focus their spiritual practice. For example, the San Francisco Zen Center maintains a mountain retreat center where students are invited to become part of the staff. As they clean the rooms, garden, prepare meals, and put fresh flowers everywhere, they are "practicing" being mindful and reverent. I know of a Gurdjieff study group whose members volunteer in a high-stress kitchen for long hours on "practice" weekends so that together they can pay close attention to the feelings and behavior that this stress evokes.

Many families use the common spiritual practice of pausing for a moment of gratitude before eating. One woman told me she asks each of the children in her soccer carpool to say what they learned in practice that day and what they hope to improve on at the next practice. This is a way of making the soccer game a form of "spiritual practice"—that is, playing soccer with a specific intention to move toward self-improvement.

Spiritual Partnership is simply the act of treating your relationship as a real-life laboratory for spiritual practice. Your relationship evokes certain emotions and behavior that you can pay attention to and learn from. In improving your effort to "do" your relationship in accord with spiritual values, you will automatically be improving your relationship.

The term *practice* has a dual meaning when used in the phrase *spiritual practice*. It means vocation or way of life, the way a doctor practices medicine. But it also means learning by doing. If you practice being loving, nonjudgmental, accepting, and forgiving in all of your life, then when you are faced with a difficult situation, you will be more likely to respond in a spiritual way, because you will be practiced.

One advantage of using your relationship as a spiritual practice is that it does not require extra time; instead, it means making small changes, one at a time, in activities that you are already doing every day. You won't have to set aside several hours for you and your partner to do contrived exercises. There are no long written questionnaires, no self-tests. Except for a few experiments I will suggest from time to time that might involve meditation or journal writing, you won't need to set aside extra time every day. You will need discipline, but not the kind that takes extra time.

Spiritual Partnership can change your relationship very quickly. Most couples experience positive changes as soon as they decide to practice it in a deliberate way. The *spiritual* goals of your journey— such as deep self-knowledge or an expanded capacity for compassion and forgiveness—may be achieved gradually over many months and years, but wonderful changes in your *relationship* are likely to appear right away.

Spiritual Partnership at Work: Karen and Al

Karen and Al were in love and had a solid relationship, but a big problem was beginning to undermine all of this: since Karen got a troublesome new boss, Al kept trying to convince her to quit her job.

When Karen came home at night, exasperated and wanting to tell Al the outrageous things this new boss had done, Al wouldn't listen. Instead, he also became critical of Karen.

"You just lack the courage to make a change," he would tell her. "Don't be so afraid. Just leave. This company doesn't own you. Take a break. Get back to the writing you're so eager to do."

Karen didn't agree that they could manage without her income, even for a short while, and there was much that she valued about her job. At first, Karen and Al carefully tried to use all the communication techniques they had learned. But Karen was better at using them than Al was, and she would become furious when Al, although he was trying hard, didn't listen, wouldn't accurately reflect back what she had said, interrupted her, and made "you" statements instead of "I" statements. Now they were arguing, not only about the job but also about their communication process! And they each seemed to become more deeply entrenched in their positions.

Al had heard about one of my ongoing groups and decided to learn about Spiritual Partnership. When he arrived at the first group, he felt angry and stuck. He thought that he was being truly supportive of Karen and had no idea how to proceed.

I suggested to Al that he experiment with the spiritual practice of using restraint, the fourth Loving Action, which we will learn in Chapter Five. He made a pact with himself that for two weeks, he would refrain from making any negative, critical, or demanding comments to Karen.

After one week, he returned to the group with this report:

> The atmosphere in our house changed completely overnight. At first, we were just quiet. About the third day, I was struck with the realization that, while I had been blaming Karen for all of our recent problems, in fact I was the cause of all the upset. When I simply didn't say anything, the arguing disappeared. I still thought she was wrong, but we were being nice to each other again. We both loved this.

Over the next weeks, as Al began to use several other Loving Actions, such as acting as if, acting alone, practicing acceptance, and practicing compassion, he had a second major insight: he saw that Karen had a right to her position. He moved from thinking that Karen was wrong to seeing that both of their points of view might have validity. This too was a revelation to him.

As Al practiced compassion (Loving Action 8), again over a period of weeks, he began to look behind Karen's position to the person Karen was. He realized that Karen's father had quit a job once, catapulting the family into a period of poverty and chaos. He saw that security was an extremely high priority for Karen. He began to feel compassion for her and to accept that she was doing what was right *for her.* As a deliberate act of will, he stopped making any suggestions to her about her work life.

The epilogue to this story is that, after eighteen months, Karen was promoted to take the place of the boss who caused her so much trouble. She created flex-time scheduling for her whole department, allowing her to work four days instead of five, and she rented a small cabin to use as a writing studio, where she unfailingly spent that fifth day every week.

When Al began to focus on his own spiritual behavior and stopped trying to solve the problem, the distance that had threatened Karen and Al's happiness was gone.

Which Comes First: Spirituality or Relationship?

I am often asked this question: In Spiritual Partnership, which is more important: each individual's spiritual growth, or the relationship? Which comes first? The answer is, the two are so intertwined that it doesn't matter.

For example, one of the Loving Actions we will learn is to practice restraint, as Al did. If your partner yells at you and you can think quickly enough to be quiet and then to respond later in a nondefensive way, you will have put a spiritual value into use at the same time that you will have made your relationship a more pleasant place to be. Your relationship gave you a chance to act spiritually, to nourish your soul; and your spirituality gave you a chance to improve your relationship—both at the same time.

So, in your own mind, view your relationship as a way to work on your spiritual life, *or* think of your spiritual life as a way to work on your relationship, whichever works for you. In Spiritual Partnership, love and spiritual growth support each other.

Why Is Relationship a Good Place to Practice Spirituality?

In a rousing presentation I was fortunate to attend, the spiritual writer Iyanla Vanzant told us, "If you want to test your spirituality, fall in love. You can be as spiritual as Buddha when you are by yourself."

Relationship is an excellent place to practice spiritual values because you can be certain that they will be tested there. It is in your relationship that you are most likely to feel isolated, to revert to the worst aspects of your personality, and to experience anger, fear, and confusion. So, right then and there, you will have an opportunity to work on these spiritual challenges. Close relationships tend to magnify both your strong and weak points, so you can get a really good look at yourself if you are paying attention. And you can watch your spiritual "experiments" actually making a difference.

Spirituality is not more and more principles you learn; it is a quality you gradually achieve. Nowhere is it more satisfying to achieve that quality than in your relationships with the people you love.

How Spiritual Practice Deepens Connection

If relationship provides a perfect opportunity to practice spirituality, the reverse is also true: a more spiritual you will be able to practice relationship at its very finest. Your soul has the power to love far, far beyond what your personality is capable of. The more attention you pay to your soul—that is, the more you are motivated by your deepest inner stirrings—and the more you become your most authentic self, *the more you will be able to connect with your partner at a deep level.*

Often it is a relationship itself that brings you in touch with your authentic self. When you invest yourself in a person and pin hopes and dreams on a certain relationship, you are automatically making yourself vulnerable. It is in the nature of love that you become dependent on your lover in certain ways. Even though a certain amount of dependency is completely healthy and normal, it can be frightening. This fear is part of the authentic you. Don't run from it because it feels strange and unpleasant; welcome it. Vulnerability always presents you with an opportunity for spiritual growth.

The you that is more real and less "conditioned" almost always feels vulnerable when it first comes out after being buried for a long time. First you feel the vulnerability, the fear, the shame, the sadness. But if you are part of any relationship in which you can experience being fully accepted and loved for the person you truly are, vulnerability and all, you will get to experience the profound pleasure of relaxing into your real, unadorned self. In that state, you are totally lovable. Others are likely to be drawn to you, to feel love for you, and to feel deeply connected.

Now imagine having an experience like that with someone you already love. Locating and then sharing your deepest pockets of fears, regrets, low self-esteem, or shame requires courage, but it moves you toward greater authenticity and deeper connection with the one you love.

So relationships are a good place for you to focus on your spiritual journey because they give you concrete opportunities to become more authentic. And the relationship you will create as a result of your spiritual work will be deep and genuine.

A Quick Recap

Let's review what we have said in this overview of Spiritual Partnership.

1. Many couples are ready to move to a new level of intimate partnership because humanity has progressed to a point where we are aware of spiritual values and have the option of operating from them. (That much of the world is engaged in a rebellion against spiritual development does not change the fact that these frontiers have been opened up and are being richly explored by many.) Many couples are ready for Stage Three relationships, or Spiritual Partnership.

2. Spiritual Partnership will build on and expand the fairness, equality, and good communication that are the ideal of Stage Two relationships.

3. Two fundamental differences separate Stage Two relationships from Spiritual Partnership.

4. The first difference is the move from communication to Loving Actions as the primary tool for conflict resolution and relationship growth. We looked at four limitations of communication as the only tool available to couples. We learned that a Loving Action is a specific unilateral act of will that is motivated by a desire for spiritual growth and undertaken as an experiment, and that the use of Loving Actions requires a willingness to take a leadership role in a relationship. And we saw why it is important to move beyond communication and negotiation in our love relationships, because this model of relating is based on the values that govern the marketplace, whereas love is a different universe altogether. The purpose of love is to learn better and better how to give and receive love, and love is its own reward.

5. The second difference separating Stage Two relationships from Spiritual Partnership is the shift of focus from trying to change your partner and your relationship to gently coaxing yourself to change by paying attention to your own spiritual aspirations. As a Spiritual Partner, you view your relationship as a spiritual practice,

an opportunity to put your spiritual values to work minute by minute, day by day. You are always asking, "If I am operating in accord with my highest spiritual values, what will I do now?" These spiritual values include moving away from separation, habit, fear, limited awareness, control, and restlessness, and moving toward connection, choice, authenticity, love, consciousness, surrender, and inner peace.

EXPERIMENT 6

First Impressions

In your journal, write your answers to these questions, or discuss them with your partner or a friend.

1. After reading only this chapter, what appeals to you about Spiritual Partnership?

2. What questions or skeptical thoughts do you have about it?

3. What does not appeal to you?

Now we are ready to learn the Eight Loving Actions that will give you highly specific, easy-to-use experiments that automatically guide you to behave in accord with spiritual values. Let's begin the journey!

Loving Action 1

Adopt a Spirit of Good Will

I n the extensive interviews with thriving couples that I conducted for my second book, *The Eight Essential Traits of Couples Who Thrive*, I found over and over one outstanding quality that separated couples who thrive from couples who don't.

It wasn't that happy couples all came from stable, loving homes. It wasn't that happy couples all had excellent communication skills. What happy couples had that set them apart was a spirit of good will.

What Is Good Will in Your Relationship?

Good will is an overall feeling of generosity toward your partner. It is the attitude, "I am on your side, no matter what. I am your ally, not your adversary." When you approach a situation with a spirit of good will, it means you value your relationship far more than whatever problems were caused by this one small incident. You are willing to acknowledge that your partner's annoying habit or point of view, even when you don't agree with it, might have some validity *for him or her.* You realize that positive, spontaneous acts of thoughtfulness are important expressions of love. You understand that love has nothing to do with fairness. Love is love. The more you give it away, the more you receive.

What Is the Purpose of Your Relationship?

Ask yourself, "What is the purpose of this relationship? What are my goals for this relationship?"

Is your purpose to get your partner to be more considerate or less controlling?

Is your purpose to get the living room painted light green when your partner wants to leave it white?

Is your purpose to be sure your partner takes fair responsibility around the house?

Probably not. Most likely, your overall, guiding purpose is to create a relationship that supports you both, that makes your burdens lighter because you don't have to carry them by yourself. It is to enjoy your lives together, to keep alive the love and excitement that brought you together in the first place. Your purpose may be to nurture your love so that it overflows beyond the two of you, enabling you to champion those who need you, your children, your other passions in the world.

To operate on a foundation of good will is to keep the true purpose of your relationship in mind, especially in times of stress or conflict. It means keeping the difficulties you encounter in perspective. In the grand scheme of things, how important are they really? It means believing you can work through even the most difficult challenge. When the current stress or obstacle is long behind you, will your love have been strengthened or diminished by it?

The answers depend on your ability to maintain a spirit of good will toward your partner, instead of a spirit of "Am I going to get my needs met? Am I going to get my fair share?" (Of course you have to pay attention to those needs also, as we shall see in more detail, but only in a general atmosphere of good will.)

EXPERIMENT 7

The Purpose of Your Relationship

In your journal, complete these sentences. If you like, discuss them with your partner or with a friend.

1. The purpose of our relationship is . . .

2. Our goals as a couple are . . .

3. I lost sight of our purpose recently when . . .

Good Will Surpasses Being "Right"

When your relationship operates on a foundation of good will it means that even when you are angry and you know you are right, you can be reasonable, you can be "nice."

Gail and Jeff were both exhausted one evening, and they got into an argument. Jeff was late for a meeting, so right at the height of Gail's tirade, he slammed the door and left. Gail was furious and felt dismissed and abandoned. She was sobbing.

About five minutes after Jeff left, he pulled over, took out his cell phone, and called Gail. "I'm still angry," he told her, "but I love you. I'm sorry I left so abruptly. We'll talk when I get home. I know we will work this out. Don't worry."

Jeff wasn't worried about who was right or wrong in this conflict. His good will prevailed, even when he was angry. If this had been a couple in which there was little good will, I can imagine this fight might have escalated, with much name-calling and blaming and bad feelings being carried around for days.

Alice, a participant in one of my groups, told me that just the idea of good will turned her marriage around.

> As soon as I heard the idea, I saw right away that I didn't have any good will. If I wanted the window open at night and Peter wanted it closed, all I could think about was that I needed to protect my interests. I spent a lot of years learning how to be assertive and how to "get my needs met." I blamed Peter for everything, but the truth is, I was never generous or thoughtful— or even kind, really. No wonder he wasn't being nicer to me!
>
> Now, in a situation like that, I actively think about good will. It's not that I always give in at all. It's that incidents that used to create a fight are just nothing now. I let things roll off my back. I'm much kinder to Peter now, and it pays off incredibly every single day. We don't go around anxious that we are not going to get our fair share. The idea of good will has transformed our relationship.

Good Will Supports You, *Not Just Your Partner*

Good will sounds as though it is designed to help the other person, but in fact, extending good will toward another person is one of the kindest things you can do for *yourself*. A kind or generous gesture toward another person puts you in control of a situation, eliminates conflict, and lets you experience the pleasure of giving to someone you love. Operating out of good will is a way of providing loving leadership for your family.

And good will can actually solve problems.

Although she knew it was minor in the grand scheme of things, Julia tried in vain to get Mike to put away his newspapers and magazines after reading them. The dining room table and the couch always seemed to be cluttered, no matter what she did. Mike said he never felt like he was really finished reading, and besides, he didn't view reading material as clutter. He would make a halfhearted effort after they talked, but then revert to his old habits. Julia felt thwarted.

Then, one day, she had a long conversation with a woman who was upset because her husband was gambling more and more. Julia became aware of how lucky she felt to be with Mike, and how many things she adored about him. She made up her mind to view the messy newspapers as a little reminder of how much she loved Mike, and to view cleaning them up as a little love ritual, a secret gift to herself.

In a spirit of good will, Julia yielded, and the problem disappeared.

The term *good will* actually covers a range of specific behaviors, such as

- Being grateful for what you have
- Emphasizing the positive traits in your partner
- Accepting your partner just as he or she really is
- Tolerating the aspects of your partner that you wish you could change
- Practicing thoughtfulness and generosity

The Loving Actions will give you specific ways to incorporate all these qualities into your relationship.

Good Will Is Not Codependency

Good will goes against the grain of much of what we have been taught. This country was founded on an ethic of rugged individualism and watching out for number one! Also, in the last several decades both the women's movement and the recovery movement have encouraged us to identify and take care of our own needs. Above all, we must avoid the dreaded "codependency."

The pendulum needs to swing back now. We must balance our hard-won self-care and independence with a willingness to be thoughtful, gracious, and generous.

Let's be clear that good will has nothing to do with being codependent. Codependence means attempting to do for other people work that they must do for themselves, as when you try to "help" someone stop drinking. Or it can be behavior that actually encourages someone else to continue dysfunctional behavior, as when you call in sick for your friend who is too drunk to go to work. There is a huge range of generous, loving, kind, thoughtful, giving behavior that is in no way whatsoever related to codependence.

Good will is not about "giving in" or losing your feeling of control. It is not about becoming a doormat and letting your partner determine everything. Quite the opposite: an act of generosity comes from a self that is so strong and well developed that it can easily tolerate not getting its way. A deliberate decision to make a kind gesture is *empowering*.

Even when you are not feeling strong, engaging in deliberate acts of generosity will help you build your inner strength and will help you develop your growing spiritual self. When you "think good will," you will begin to experience more compassion for your partner. You will become more forgiving and more able to see a different point of view. You will start to recognize that your partner is doing the very best he or she can and that your love and support—far more than your nagging or your watching out mainly for yourself—will expand your partner's ability to do well and to love you back.

Good will is definitely part of a spiritual approach to love. And it is also high on the list of effective strategies for good relationships. John Gottman, who studied couples in a laboratory setting, also encourages couples to develop a spirit of good will.

"Turn toward your partner, instead of away," he says. Also, "Let your partner influence you."

What a concept! Let your partner's needs and desires have an impact on you. It is profound advice! Especially coming out of the decades when all the emphasis seemed to be on getting your own needs met.

"Do I Have to Be a Saint?"

You may be thinking to yourself right now, "This is never going to work in my relationship. I've been giving in all along, and it does nothing. Besides, it doesn't sound fair. If I show 'good will,' my partner will just take advantage of me. I don't think I can do it anyway; I'm not a saint."

The Eight Loving Actions give you highly specific ways to practice good will; you will see that it is not a vague concept. A spirit of good will underlies all the other Loving Actions we will discuss.

In his "Treatise of Human Nature," the eighteenth-century philosopher David Hume wrote this about love:

> 'Tis plain, that this affection, in its most natural state, is deriv'd from the conjunction of three different impressions or passions, viz., the pleasing sensation arising from beauty; the bodily appetite for generation; and a generous kindness or good-will.

How has it taken us so long to learn this wisdom? Let's not miss it this time around.

EXPERIMENT 8

Adopting a Spirit of Good Will

Think of something about which you and your partner are feeling stress or are in conflict.

If you adopt a spirit of good will toward your partner, how will this affect your situation or your relationship?

Write about this in your journal or discuss it with a friend.

You can see that Loving Action 1 does not require any extra time on your part. It's an idea that may give rise to a change in your behavior or in your approach to a certain situation. It's an attitude. Remember that what separates happy couples from unhappy couples is, to a great extent, their ability to base their relationship on a foundation of good will. They view each other as allies, not adversaries. Couples who thrive have a spirit of good will toward each other; troubled couples are missing this key trait.

The next seven Loving Actions will help you develop your spirit of good will.

CHAPTER 3

Loving Action 2

Give Up Problem Solving

Most couples believe, "If only we could solve our problems, then we could be happy together." The opposite is actually true: if you focus first on being happy together, your problems will diminish.

I've heard people say so often, "We have problems; therefore we don't feel good together." But what is far more likely is, "We don't feel good together; therefore we have problems." Problems are not the *cause* of unhappiness in marriage; they are the *symptoms* of unhappy marriage.

The traditional approach to improving marriage is to work on resolving conflicts and differences, to *focus on problems* as though the road to happiness is *through* the brier patch of problems. Sadly, this strategy has left many couples hopelessly stuck in the brier patch.

Loving Action 2 invites you to try using the opposite approach: always focus *first* on creating a harmonious atmosphere and a spirit of good will between the two of you. Only then, within this harmonious atmosphere, should you ever begin to resolve conflicts or solve problems.

In his book *Divorce Is Not the Answer,* psychologist George Pransky used this metaphor: if you have a sore on your arm, the last thing you should do is poke at it, dig around in there, examine it more thoroughly. You'll make it worse! Instead, you should create a gentle, healing environment for the wound and allow it to heal itself.

Relationship problems should be treated the same way.

Most Problems Can't Be Solved

Usually, "working" on problems *won't solve them*. Why? Because most marital problems can't be "solved." When your problems are based on fundamental differences in personality or values, there is no "solution," and the search for one will increase your frustration and drive you farther apart.

> All the greatest and most important problems of this life are fundamentally insoluble. They can never be solved, but only outgrown. This "outgrowing" [requires] a new level of consciousness. Some higher or wider interest appears on the horizon, . . . and the insoluble problem loses its urgency. It is not solved logically in its own terms but fades when confronted with a new and stronger image.
>
> —Carl Jung

Jung has an elegant way of describing the very core of Spiritual Partnership: focus primarily on your own spiritual growth, and the "new level of consciousness" you will achieve will transform everything, including what you thought were problems in your relationship.

Problems Are Really Facts of Life

Many relationship problems aren't truly "problems" at all; they are facts of life. If you label something as a problem, you imply that it has a solution. If you label it a fact of life, you understand that you simply need to learn to live with it, to "accept the things you cannot change," as the Serenity Prayer says.

Learning to accept what you can't change is an important aspect of spiritual growth. It will not only create an atmosphere of harmony in your relationship but also expand your awareness and open you up to new possibilities. As the Dalai Lama says, "If you intend that your relationship with your husband or your wife become harmonious and loving, that intention will open you to new perceptions." That is a deeply profound statement. And remember, "new perceptions," expanded awareness, and higher consciousness are key parts of spiritual development too.

A conflict or problem in your relationship always represents an opportunity for spiritual growth, not an opportunity to solve the problem. Train yourself to think, "What can I learn about myself and about us from this conflict?"

I do not mean to be glib about conflict in relationships. Your current conflict may seem insurmountable to you. My point here is that the Spiritual Partnership approach to problems is fundamentally different from the old "conflict resolution" model and that the spiritual approach is not only more enlightened but also more effective. It is what Thomas Moore means when he says that change is more likely to happen as a result of "slight shifts in imagination" than because of "major efforts at change."

All couples have problems. But when you focus most of your attention on the problems because you have the illusion that if you focus on them, you will solve them, then pretty soon all you have is problems. The weakest, most dissatisfying parts of your relationship will be receiving all your attention, leaving little time for fun, affection, and mutual support. "Problems are like goldfish," says psychologist George Pransky. "The more you feed them, the bigger they get."

One man who wrote me a letter several weeks after our workshop together said this:

> What attracted me most of all was the idea that the solution to improving my relationship with my wife did not involve "sitting down and communicating." I can't tell you what a relief that was. I had a newfound hope and confidence, and experienced the most peaceful sleep I've had in years.
>
> If I had the unenviable task of picking just one of the many valuable tools and ways of thinking that [Spiritual Partnership] offers, it would be the idea that *"You can be happy together even if you don't solve all your problems."* Again, what a relief! [These ideas] helped me to keep trying new things but to retain a spirit of experimentation and be open about the results. . . . Now, when some irritating problem resurfaces, I remind myself what my real goals in this relationship are: intimacy, support, and pleasure.

The Spiritual Approach to Problem Solving

Think of an ongoing problem that plagues your relationship. Or the problem you happen to be dealing with right now. Are you having a power struggle over something? Is your partner too controlling?

Do you disagree about something? Does your partner have certain traits that feel annoying or even intolerable to you?

Does it surprise you to hear that the best way to "solve" the problem is to ignore it?

It probably does, because most of what you have heard before is about how to talk so that you will be heard, how to negotiate with your partner, how to "fight fair," how to work at understanding your partner, how to find time to sit down and talk.

Spiritual Partnership has a different approach. Spiritual Partnership suggests that you prepare a special meal for your sweetheart this evening, or take him or her out to a cozy restaurant—*even if you don't feel like it*, just as an experiment.

Find an unusual way to say, "I love you," such as writing it in shaving cream on the mirror or making a heart-shaped pancake. Write your loved one an unexpected little love note. Bring home a CD or book that you know will delight your honey. Give your partner a sincere compliment. Plan a surprise erotic evening. Make reservations for a B&B in the country for this weekend. Have your partner's favorite friends over for Sunday brunch. Surprise your partner by "giving in" on some difference you are having now, not with any anger or victim feeling, but as a gift you freely decide to give.

If you are short on ideas, buy a copy of Greg Godek's book *1001 Ways to Be Romantic* and find something thoughtful to do for your sweetheart every day. Even ten minutes with that book will inspire you.

If you have been feeling deprived in your relationship, maybe the best way for you to feel better is to do something wonderful for yourself. Take a vacation day from work and treat yourself to a day hiking, shopping, or going to a spa. Plan a special lunch with a good friend. Hire someone to take care of lingering household projects.

That's it. That's the spiritual approach to solving the problems in your relationship. Deliberately create a harmonious atmosphere between the two of you, *even if all of your problems have not been solved.* Just think: you don't have to solve your problems in order to be happy!

Above all else, don't focus attention on your problem. Don't discuss it. Don't try to solve it. Don't focus on how frustrated you feel about it. When you start to think about it or feel anxious or hurt, allow yourself to replace those thoughts in your head with something very pleasant to think about. If your partner brings it up, gently and unobtrusively change the subject. Remember that focusing on your problem is not likely to solve it. If you had a solution to your problem, it wouldn't be a problem!

What If You're Furious?

If your problems are familiar, fairly minor glitches in your otherwise loving bond with each other, this Loving Action will feel liberating to you and will be easy to do.

But suppose right now you feel terribly distant or upset or betrayed or furious. This is painful; I've been there too, and so has every other intimate partner at one time or another. I'm not suggesting it will be easy, but now is exactly the time for you to muster up your willingness to try an experiment, *even if you don't feel like it.*

In Spiritual Partnership, you are not at the mercy of your feelings. Your feelings and emotions will never change if all you do is sit and feel them. But if you are willing to experiment with a new *behavior*, your feelings might change—in ways you can't possibly imagine before you experiment with the new behavior. In any case, you will learn something about yourself and your partner.

The spiritual journey is difficult, remember? You are climbing a steep mountain in bad weather, not sauntering along a level path in the summertime. You have to care about your spiritual growth. You have to be willing to try something that you've never tried before, even if it seems impossible, even if it sounds absurd.

What are your excuses?

I just can't bring myself to do anything nice right now. I'm too hurt.
My partner won't even notice anything I do.
It's just too corny.
Anything I do will backfire on me.
This is so unfair. I already do all the giving.
I already do all those nice things. We are beyond that.

You may truly believe in your excuse. That's OK. Just suspend it for the sake of this experiment. The harder this challenge to "create an atmosphere of harmony" seems to you, the more important it is for you to try it.

If you are in the midst of a very troubling and painful episode in your relationship and "moving toward pleasure" sounds absurd and simplistic to you, consider this: What are your alternatives? You can separate or even terminate the relationship. Are you ready to do that? If so, look seriously at that option and take a first step in that direction. If not, you can maintain distance, perpetuate the tension sadness, anger, or hurt you are feeling. That may work for a while.

Or you can table this problem. When it arises, put it off until later. And have the courage to do something generous and loving that you know will make your partner smile—or, better yet, laugh— and that has the possibility of making the two of you feel a good flow of warm energy between you. You may find that when the problem arises again, you will have "outgrown" it.

Remember that this is an experiment. It can't "fail," because no matter what happens, you will have learned from it. There is no wrong outcome. Just try what you now know is the spiritual alternative, and carefully observe the results. Pay attention.

Remember that focusing on and trying to solve your ongoing problems won't eliminate your problems and won't make the two of you happy. Giving up problem solving will free up time in your relationship and will transform negative energy into liveliness, warmth, and love. Don't worry about the problems you are now setting aside. Trust that as you give your attention to Loving Actions, the problems will take care of themselves. As you expand your consciousness about your relationship and create new experiences for the two of you, your "problems" will transform, and you will outgrow them.

In the meantime, deciding to enjoy each other is its own reward.

Give Up Being Right

In addition to giving up problem solving, Loving Action 2 invites you to give up something else that may be causing problems in your relationship. I invite you to give up the heavy burden of being right.

In Stage Two relationships, there was a lot of emphasis on who was right and who was wrong. We believed that if the partner who was wrong would be willing to admit this and change, the problem would be solved and harmony would result.

In Spiritual Partnership, we recognize that being right is both divisive and irrelevant. Instead of asking who is right and who is wrong, the Spiritual Partner asks, "No matter who is right or wrong, what can I do to ease this situation?"

Being Right Gets You Nowhere

In a given situation, you may in fact be right about your point of view. For example, your partner should be more helpful around the house. Any reasonable person would agree with you. But as a Spiritual Partner, you need to understand that being right will never get you anywhere. Your point of view may be accurate, but it is useless.

Name an ongoing problem in your relationship.

EXPERIMENT 9

Give Up Problem Solving

1. Make a new list of everything you consider to be a problem or a negative aspect of your relationship.

2. Next to each item write either a "T" for "Tolerable" or "DB" for "Dealbreaker."

3. Now consider not discussing or working on any of these problems at all for the next two weeks.

4. For now, make an agreement with yourself that you will not discuss any of these problems for one day.

5. Think up one action you can take to create harmony in your relationship: a favor for your mate, a surprise, a special treat. Do this *even if you don't feel like it*, just as an experiment.

6. Make a note in your journal about what you did and how it worked out. Remember, avoid anticipating any particular outcome. Just note what actually does happen.

I'll pick the biggest problem Ellie and Jack have as an example, but throughout this discussion, I suggest you substitute your own problem.

Jack says: Ellie is involved in way too many activities. She goes out almost every evening. I love our cozy evenings at home, and I don't think it's fair for her to leave me alone so often. All I ask is a little moderation.

Ellie says: I feel like Jack wants me to stop the rest of my life. He should see how much these activities mean to me. When am I supposed to see my women friends? He never appreciates how much I do give up so I can be home more. No matter how much I do, it's never enough.

Jack is right. So is Ellie. And the way they have been dealing with this problem for years now is to use Stage Two methods. They listen to each other, discuss the problem, argue about it, and negotiate it. They even see each other's point of view. Ellie sort of likes that Jack wants her home more. Jack admits that he likes Ellie's gregarious nature and admires her community involvement. Jack gives a little. Then Ellie gives a little. But the problem remains, because deep inside, Jack still believes he is right. And deep inside, Ellie still believes she is right. And neither can convince the other.

In your own relationship, what are you absolutely right about? Your partner should be more affectionate, should help more with household tasks, should stop nagging and criticizing you, should be less controlling? Pause now and pick one thing that you know you are right about. Do you have something in mind?

First understand: I am not suggesting that you are not right. Let's stipulate that you *are* right about your analysis of this problem. Probably any reasonable person would agree with you.

But as a Spiritual Partner, what you need to understand is that although being right may make you feel good, it is counterproductive for your relationship. In fact, insisting on your point of view is counterproductive in four ways:

1. Being right is a dead end. It will never move you forward.

2. Being right prevents you from expanding your vision.

3. Being right keeps you helpless.

4. Being right doesn't honor your partner.

Being Right Is a Dead End

Being right is the booby prize of life, because you do get to be right, but that is all you get.

- You don't get to feel closer to your partner.
- You don't get to allow your partner to feel closer to you.
- You don't get to solve the problem.
- You don't get to reduce the conflict and upset in your relationship.

All you get is to be right. It's a dead end.

When you insist on being right, you are signing up for an endless tape loop. How likely do you think it is that your partner will suddenly one day just roll over and say, "Yeah, Honey, I see your point. I guess you've been right all these years. And I've been wrong."

Being right is useless.

Insisting That You Are Right Prevents You from Expanding Your Vision

What if there is an off chance that you have your whole problem figured out wrong or that there is a dimension you are not seeing? What happened to Don and Sarah was a good example of this.

Sarah was upset with Don because he rarely made conversation with her. When they first got together, they talked intensely all the time, and Sarah loved this. But now, Don was always either reading or watching TV. He didn't want to talk about movies they saw, friends and family, or even his work. He just gave her one-sentence answers.

Sarah approached this problem by trying to convince Don that she was right, that what marriage is about is staying in touch on a day-to-day basis, sharing ideas, and enjoying casual conversation. Don didn't disagree, but he felt annoyed by what felt to him like nagging and criticism. He would make small efforts to make conversation occasionally, but only to try to appease Sarah.

After several years with little change in this situation, Sarah and Don had occasion to visit Don's sister, who lived two thousand miles from them. Sarah and Don had married later in life, and Sarah had never met this sister.

The household was chaotic. Radios and TVs were going on everywhere. Two teenagers and their friends took over various common rooms. Dogs barked and required attention. Neither Don nor Sarah could take it for very long. "This is exactly what my house was like growing up," Don told Sarah.

The incident opened Sarah's eyes. She also knew that Don's mother, who was now dead, had been an extremely invasive woman. When Sarah put these facts together, she began to see Don's quiet as a way of protecting himself from chaos, of carving out some privacy for himself. She saw how precious privacy would be to him. She even saw herself as a shadow of Don's overly intrusive mother. Something inside her shifted. She saw how inappropriate it was for her to take Don's reserve personally; she felt herself wanting to help protect his quiet.

Sarah didn't exactly let go of her position, but she softened. Her vision expanded.

Shortly after the visit, Sarah mentioned to Don that she could now see why quiet was so important to him. And she stopped talking about it as though hers was the only correct position. When there was quiet in the household, she decided to relax and enjoy it herself. She began to see an evening at home as a little retreat for herself, a welcome respite from her hectic days.

What Sarah found over a period of time was that as she herself became more quiet, Don started to talk more!

So another problem with insisting that you are right is that there are often several "right" ways to look at a situation, and your right way is only one of them. Being right may be keeping you from expanding your vision.

Being Right Keeps You Helpless

Usually your "right" view of the situation is that the problem is your spouse's fault. When you think about your own relationship problem, it probably starts out, "My partner won't . . ." or "My partner is too . . ." or "My partner isn't . . ."

If the only solution to the problem is that your spouse needs to make a change, you've put yourself in a terribly weak position. Because you have no control over what your spouse does or doesn't do! You can rant and rave and flail about, but it will gain you nothing. Or you can sulk in silence, feeling betrayed, cheated, and angry. Those are about your only alternatives, and neither of them achieves anything that you want.

But you still have that precious booby prize: you are right. And when you talk it over with your friends, they will agree with you. Poor you: your partner is so controlling, so thoughtless, so indifferent. Everyone agrees you are right. But you are helpless to do anything about it.

Being Right Does Not Honor Your Partner

As you are trying, always in vain, to get your partner to admit to being wrong, the indirect message you are consistently giving him or her is, "You are not good enough the way you are. I would love you more if you would agree with me. You are not okay." You are actually indirectly diminishing your partner all the time, instead of offering support and love. By insisting on your point of view, you give your partner a reason to withdraw from you, when what you would truly like is more closeness. You are creating separation, the nonspiritual direction, instead of connection, the spiritual path. You may view the problem as your partner's fault, but by harping on it all the time, *you are the one who is creating the distance!*

Being right is the booby prize of life. But it is actually worse than a booby prize. It is more like the monkey's paw, because it brings you nothing but pain.

What to Do When You Know You Are Right

But you *are* right. So how can you just give that up?

Here's the secret: no one is suggesting for a second that you are not right. You probably are. All we are saying is that being right makes absolutely no difference to anyone. It is irrelevant. And one of the least effective and least spiritual things you can do in your relationship is to keep insisting that you are right and to keep making your partner wrong.

In Spiritual Partnership, instead of asking who is right and who is wrong, you ask, "No matter who is right or wrong, what can I do to make a difference?"

What can you do?

There is always a Loving Action that will be appropriate. We have already seen that you can adopt a spirit of good will and that you can stop trying to solve the problem and do something sweet for your partner. We will soon learn six more Loving Actions that are possibilities. Choosing a Loving Action brings you far better results than insisting that you are right ever will.

Being Right as a "Defense"

For some people, being right is their defense, the personality trait that they have assumed to protect themselves from feeling foolish or

EXPERIMENT 10

Relinquish Being Right

1. Select a problem from your list in Experiment 1, or choose a conflict you are having right now with your partner.

2. With regard to this problem, who is right and who is wrong? In your journal, write "_____ is wrong about _____."

3. Now write, "No matter who is right, the way I could make a positive difference, in a spirit of good will, is _____."

4. If what you wrote in 3 is something you are willing to do, do it. Make a note in your journal about what you tried and how it turned out.

unseen or left out. Being right all the time is a superficial way of saying, to yourself and to everyone else, "See, I'm a great person. I'm very knowledgeable, and I always have the right answer. Aren't I clever? Aren't you impressed?"

When you use being right as a defense, you don't stop with being right about conflicts with your partner; you are right about religion, politics, current events, family history—everything. You will often contradict others, add the correct information in every conversation, and even go out of your way to point out to people when they have been wrong.

If you (or others) notice this tendency in yourself, as with every other personality characteristic, just start paying attention to it. Begin to catch yourself doing it. See how you feel after you have corrected someone or added additional correct information. See if you can catch yourself before you are about to correct someone, and try being quiet this time. See how that feels. That's all spirituality requires of you. Pay close attention and see what happens. This is the route to your authentic self, to self-love, and to connection instead of separation.

So try this: Give up all attempts to solve your relationship problems. Don't discuss them at all with anyone. Instead, focus on creating a harmonius atmosphere in your home, in whatever creative ways you can think of, *even if you don't feel like it.* And when you catch yourself insisting that you are right, ask yourself, "No matter who is right and who is wrong, what can I do to relieve this situation?"

These are spiritual approaches, moving you toward connection and helping you to discover a new side of yourself. And you may notice immediate changes in your relationship.

CHAPTER 4

Loving Action 3

Act as If

Acting as if is one of the most powerful Loving
Actions we will learn. Let's say your partner, Janice,
shows up late for an appointment, for the fourth
time in a row. You are angry and frustrated, and of course you will
express this to Janice. "How can you do this to me again? This is
going to mess up my whole day. I even called to remind you. I just
don't understand why you can't get it together. Damn, this makes
me angry!"

But here is one of the great keys to success in life, a closely guarded
and little known secret: *you don't have to behave the way you feel.*

You have a choice. You can *feel* angry and frustrated inside and
acknowledge your feelings, but *behave* in a loving way. Not as a thinly
veiled disguise. Not as a passive-aggressive strategy (being nice with
a big fist right behind your smile). Nor as a manipulation. But as a
deliberate, spiritual exercise.

What would Buddha do in this situation? Or Jesus?

They would already have a well-developed inner calm and a
larger perspective or "consciousness" that would help them realize
how minor this incident is in the grand scheme of the world. Instead

of wanting to be right ("I was on time! You are the bad person here; you are the one who blew it!"), they might be in touch with compassion for Janice. Maybe they would be thinking, "I've done things like this myself. I know how bad it feels. She must be upset with herself, too. I know she is trying to work on this problem and would really like to be on time."

They would know that moving toward connection is the spiritual choice. They would understand that the relationship is more important than this incident or than changing Janice into someone who is always on time. They might give Janice an earlier time next time, or bring a book with them, accepting that Janice will be late.

Of course most of us are not there. We have not spent the last thirty years fasting and meditating so that nothing upsets us. But we can learn by deliberately simulating what we think the spiritual response would be, *even if we don't feel like it*. If you superimpose spiritual behavior onto a situation as a conscious experiment, you will give yourself a taste of what it is like to be more spiritual, and gradually, over time, you will help yourself get there.

For example, let's say you would like to feel nonjudgmental, but you don't; you are filled with judgments. Do you have to wait until nonjudgmental feelings arise spontaneously? No. *Behave* in a nonjudgmental way and see if the new feelings you hope for follow.

Putting Acting as If to Work in Your Relationship

Of course, like all spiritual disciplines, acting as if is not always easy to do. It requires enormous effort, especially at first, and especially if your feelings are very strong. But the more you do it, the easier it becomes. You will like the feeling of being in control instead of at the mercy of everything going on around you. And you will like the results.

From Separation to Connection

Acting as if is a Loving Action because it will make a difference in your relationship. It is also an exercise that will help you grow spiritually: as you pay attention to how you feel when you do it, acting as if will expand your consciousness, help you separate your personality from your authentic self, help you become more loving, and increase your self-love. Acting as if is a move toward connection and away from separation. As you become more experienced, you will definitely feel happier more of the time, because you will not be at the mercy of other people's behavior.

Always behaving exactly the way you feel is not conscious or deliberate. Rather, it is a knee-jerk reaction, like an old tape being flipped on. Once that reaction has kicked in, you are not part of an "experience"; you are part of a familiar old tape just running itself again.

You probably always become angry when Janice is late, or when _____ (substitute your own ongoing relationship problem). We already know what that produces. You get to be right and to make Janice wrong. You get to feel distant from Janice and angry at her. You make it hard for Janice to feel warm and close toward you. Maybe your frustration (because you can't get Janice to change) will hang around for a few days. Then you'll feel better, then she'll be late again, and the whole cycle will repeat itself. Probably for years.

Think about a problem in your own relationship. You have no doubt tried the same approach over and over (probably trying in some way to get your partner to be different), and every time you repeat the same behavior, you actually still hope that something might change! It never will, because it is always true that when you keep doing the same thing, you'll keep getting the same results.

Trying Something New

Acting as if gives you something brand new to try. Something that may never have occurred to you before.

And when you try something new, you might get new results! No guarantees here. Remember, every time you act as if, you are conducting an experiment. Don't be attached to any particular outcome. You have no idea what will happen. Just pay close attention to the results.

One possibility is that your partner's response to you might change. Never act as if as a manipulation, but just watch the results. Janice's chronic lateness is far likelier to change if you keep the atmosphere between you warm and stop blaming her than if you go off on your anger every time she's late, just as you always have. People are more likely to change in an atmosphere of love and support than in one laced with criticism and anger. By acting as if, you provide leadership and engage in a creative act of love.

A second possibility is that your own feelings might actually change. That's what happened for Karen.

Karen and Chad didn't fight very often, but when they did, it always took Karen days to feel good again. The arguments left her feeling belittled, frustrated, and helpless.

After learning about acting as if, Karen determined to try it after her next argument with Chad. They argued one Sunday morning about whether or not to buy a new rug. One more time, Karen felt as though Chad insisted that he was right and had no regard for her opinions or feelings. The familiar anger and frustration set in. Unfortunately, the two of them had planned a whole day together taking their niece to the zoo.

Karen decided to act as if she felt just fine. Even though she was actually on the verge of tears, after a little time and with great effort she made a cheerful, normal-sounding comment to Chad: "I think I'll take this blanket in case we want to sit by the lake after the zoo."

"Yeah, that's a good idea," replied Chad.

After fighting off tears but continuing normal-sounding conversation for another five minutes or so, Karen found that she actually began to feel better inside. The longer she continued her experiment, the better she felt. Her mood shifted. The anger actually abated, and they went on to have a very pleasant afternoon.

Acting as if is not new; it has been around for a long time, but we have underused it and have failed to recognize it as a spiritual practice. Remember Anna in *The King and I*? When she felt afraid she whistled as a way to fool those around her. But, she goes on to sing, "When I fool the people I fear, I fool myself as well." She acted as if she were brave and had no fear at all, and her own feelings transformed.

The strategy of changing your feelings by acting the way you want to feel is a fundamental principle of the new science called Neuro Linguistic Programming. To change your feelings or your "state," change your physiology. It's the same principle that is involved when you are feeling blue and you go for a run or take a bike ride, and afterward your mood has changed.

Stories of Acting as If

Let's see how acting as if worked in several real-life situations.

When Ed and Nancy left for a two-week vacation in Italy, Ed had just been laid off from a job in an accounting department of a Fortune 500 company and was considering taking a job with a nonprofit agency devoted to AIDS research. Nancy thought this was a big mistake. They felt a great deal of tension over this and had had several fights. On the plane on the way over, they read and just kept their distance. Nancy told me,

At first, I felt like we should talk about the job and the fact we'd been fighting so much lately and see if we could get to a better place. I didn't want to spend the whole two weeks feeling rotten about him. But it never seemed like the right moment, and I kept putting it off. Then I remembered "act as if." Right away, it was a huge relief. I started to relax and focus on having a good time. When we arrived at our gorgeous Tuscan villa, we were both so impressed, we got sort of playful and giddy as we began to unpack. The tension we had been feeling seemed gone. I let go of the whole problem and focused on having a good time, and on all the things I adore about Ed. I was amazed at how quickly and easily it worked. Over dinner, I began feeling very loving toward him. By the next day, we were feeling as close as ever and having a wonderful time.

I never brought up the job issue again. He took the job, and while I thought he'd be out of there in six months, he's now been there two years and loves it.

A woman I interviewed, Charlene, told me this story:

Acting as if works well for me with sex. Often when Michael wants to make love, I don't always feel in the mood. I used to say no a lot, and he'd be upset and it would become a big deal. Now, I act as if I'm in the mood, and it doesn't take long for me to really be in the mood. I act as if in a spirit of good will toward Michael, because I really do want to give him what he wants. Now that I know it works, it's not hard to do. I virtually never say no to him anymore. Michael is so happy about the change—and so am I!

A two-career, two-child couple I interviewed for my second book have a similar attitude. They call their policy "mood schmood," meaning that if they waited until they felt in the mood, they might not ever make love. They act as if they are in the mood and soon enough, they are.

Peter also had a revelation about his sex life when he began to act as if:

> I've always had a clear fantasy about what I wanted in sex, and when I married Kelly, I thought she was everything I wanted. But we had a baby right away, and things really changed. I was pretty sad about it, and I would talk with her, but it just made her feel bad. She would just say, "I can't be what I'm not." I lost interest too. I was very skeptical about acting as if. [Peter resisted our suggestions in the workshop for almost the full eight weeks.] But finally, I decided to act as if she were the sexy lover I imagined. She loved the change in me. The big difference was, I was not judging her; I was just being me to the fullest. She became more and more responsive. I saw that I needed to let go of my ideas of what she ought to be, and just be who I wanted *me* to be. I am so grateful that we have our sex life back now. It is right for who we really are, not some fantasy I had in my head. I feel now that sex is truly an expression of our love for each other.
>
> I was very surprised that this experiment changed anything. I found out that *thinking about* doing something is very different from *doing* it. I was certain that nothing would change after the experiment. I was so wrong.

Acting as if can work very well when you apply it to your own moods, even if you are by yourself. Anne told me this:

> When I get up in a blue mood or come home from work tired and cranky, I have learned not to talk about it and "milk" it.

When I hear myself make a bitchy remark, I'll just turn around and make a cheerful one. I act as if I feel good. Then either my blue mood continues, but I'm not forcing those around me to suffer through it, or the mood fades away and I start to feel better.

I didn't believe in acting as if at first because it seemed to contradict the philosophy I was raised on, that it's healthier to express emotions, to examine them thoroughly and not to sweep them under the rug. I can still do that when I think it's appropriate, but now I have a choice, and I have been able to brighten up a lot of my own days.

Of course it is appropriate to examine your feelings sometimes, and to allow a blue mood to come over you. Our dark sides have much to teach us. But when acting as if is one of your tools, you have a choice about when you want to go deeper for yourself and when you want at least to behave in a brighter way to see what happens.

Guidelines for Acting as If

Acting as if simply means choosing "nice" behavior, *even when you don't feel like it*. It means not allowing your feelings to dictate how you will behave, but instead, by an act of discipline and will, motivated by your desire to become a more spiritual person, *choosing* how you will behave. When you act as if, you are no longer at the mercy of your feelings or your mood. Here are some tips:

1. Start small. You can act as if you are a loving, adoring spouse, even if you don't feel that way, for just five minutes, for a half hour, or for one evening a week.

The next time something upsets or angers you, think about acting as if. Try it for just one minute.

Recently, as I returned to my car because I knew my parking meter would be running out, I saw a meter maid writing out a ticket.

"Wait! I'm here. The meter just ran out!" I cried out.

But she wouldn't tear up the ticket. I don't do well when I have no control over what I consider to be a dumb situation. I felt my face flush, my heart start to race. But because I'm writing about spiritual behavior every day right now, the thought "act spiritually" went through my head. I took a deep breath. And then I smiled. Not a sarcastic smile. It was an act-as-if smile. I couldn't bring myself to say anything nice to the meter maid, but at least I didn't say anything nasty to her. I kept smiling. By the time I was driving away, I was thinking, "So a parking ticket, so big deal."

2. You can also act as if, not in response to a situation, but as a proactive way of taking initiative or providing leadership.

Try directly creating the feeling you wish you had in your relationship. What do you want from your partner? Do you wish he or she were more demonstrative? Do you wish you had fun more often? Would you like more thoughtfulness, more romance?

Create these activities yourself. Ask yourself, "How would I behave if I were a totally loving spouse?" You might do favors for your partner. You might greet him or her enthusiastically when you come together at the end of the work day. Maybe you'd fix your partner a drink and suggest a little cocktail hour.

What do you wish you could do with your partner? Don't wait.

As one workshop participant told us after two weeks of experimenting with acting as if, "It's so easy to get affection; just give it."

3. Don't be discouraged if your feelings or your mate's responses don't change quickly and dramatically. Patiently proceed with acting

like a loving spouse on a regular basis, even if it is just for a few minutes at a time, even if you see no direct results or changes. Pay attention to what is happening inside you.

Remember, in the midst of a difficult incident or a time when you feel very bad, you cannot change your *feelings*. They are simply there. You feel angry. You feel afraid. You can't make your feeling go away by an act of will. Nor can you change the other person who is part of this situation, as we have already discussed.

But you do have control over your own behavior. You can make a deliberate choice to act as if you feel good. And when you do, you open up a whole range of new possibilities.

4. Be prepared for voices of resistance within you.

My partner doesn't deserve this loving behavior.

This is too one sided. I shouldn't have to be nice.

This is too fake. I can't pretend I feel loving. I don't!

It is okay for these voices to be there. Just don't let them win. Talk back to yourself. Be your own cheering section.

You can do it.

Remember, this is for your own spiritual growth.

If you never experiment, you'll never move forward.

As Dan Millman observes in *The Way of the Peaceful Warrior*, "Old urges will continue to arise, perhaps for years. Urges do not matter, actions do."

5. Actions matter. When you are trying to create a happy, safe atmosphere in your marriage, actions are what will make this happen. Apathy won't help you. Talking won't make any difference. Blaming will keep you stuck for years. Only new behavior, even when you

don't feel like doing it, will make changes start to happen. As we've said, you will never feel your way to a new way of acting, but you can absolutely act your way to a new way of feeling.

If Acting as If Makes You Feel Anxious

One woman told me,

> The difficulty I have with acting as if is that it sometimes literally makes me anxious to behave in ways that run directly counter to how I feel. Acting as if makes me feel like I'm abandoning myself.

If you feel anxious, realize that your anxiety—or any other form of resistance to acting as if—is a gift to you, because it is a window into your authentic self. Rather than running from the anxiety, gently allow it to be there. See how much you can tolerate. What is your anxiety telling you about yourself? This is all an integral part of your experiment. It's precisely the reason you are doing the experiment, to learn more about yourself. Just keep paying attention and let the results unfold.

Experiment. Try going back to behaving in accord with your real feelings. Does that feel better to you? Is it less anxiety producing? What results? You don't always have to act as if. Maybe sometimes it is not right for you.

But definitely try acting as if again in a few days, even if it is just for a short while. Keep paying attention to how you feel.

You might also take the time to write in your journal about your anxious feelings. Describe them. What other situations evoke anxiety for you? Are there any similarities? Engage in dialogue with your anxiety. Ask it what purpose it serves for you, and see what it says back.

When Very Troubled Couples Act as If

I have seen this one spiritual tool, acting as if, transform even the very bleakest of relationships. The following is just one of many such stories.

Becky and John had been married ten years, and there was little left of their marriage. Becky came to one of my groups, thinking she would get support for leaving John. She had a list as long as her arm of the qualities she didn't like in him. He was controlling. He never discussed anything with her. He was rough with the children. She actually didn't like him very much at all. What puzzled us in the group was that other people seemed to like John a lot, and he didn't sound like the bad fellow as she described him.

I suggested to Becky that she act as if she felt loving toward John for just five minutes during one evening. For several weeks, she reported that she couldn't bring herself to do it and was filled with excuses. Trying to make it easier for her, I suggested that she try just giving him one genuine compliment. The next week, she reported this:

> On Saturday morning when he returned from soccer with our son, I said to him, "Thank you for taking Sam to the soccer game. I appreciate what a good father you are, and all the interest you take around all this soccer stuff." Of course it surprised him to hear this. He did give me a little look, not quizzical, but more like a smile. And that night while we were watching TV, he reached over and gave me a little kiss on the cheek. That really got my attention.

Over the next weeks, Becky began to see that she was actually as big a part of the problems as John was. It was a stunning revelation to her.

He was controlling and too hard on the kids and self-centered,
but *I wasn't being a loving wife at all*. Why would he want to be
nice to me?

Becky began acting as if on a regular basis. She stopped making
John wrong about everything and began exhibiting a spirit of good
will more often. She was surprised at the differences she began to
see in John, and even more amazed at the feelings that began to stir
in her. Admitting these changes was a very difficult and courageous
act for her, and we gave her a tremendous amount of support.

When Becky started behaving as a loving wife and focusing on
John's strong points instead of his weak points, he was pleased and
began to respond in kind. Becky also started to take better care of herself in the relationship, and stopped depending on John for things
he would never provide. When I spoke with them a year later, they
were doing very well together. Becky said,

I didn't believe that I would ever feel so different about John.
He hasn't changed a lot. He's still controlling. I don't like that,
but now I stand up to him a lot more. I see that I have to take
care of myself. And that has made a big difference. I *like* John,
and I feel grateful for our relationship. Most of the time, we're
enjoying our life. And the children are so much happier!

Here is another marriage that was transformed when one of the
partners acted as if she felt loving even when she didn't feel like it.

Allison came to me quite distressed. Her husband, Ken, was part
of a group of four guys who had been backpacking together for years.
Two times each year, they took ten days to go off to the wilderness.
Allison had been stricken with polio when she was three and was
left with one very weak leg. She could walk, but with a severe limp

and only for short periods of time. She had been putting up with these trips for years, but now that they had three small children, she had reached her limit.

"It's so unfair!" she said to me. "You can't believe how hard it is for me to manage for ten days without him. He just doesn't care. All he ever says is, 'You knew about this when we got married.' The other three guys are all single! His situation is different. I feel like he just has to give this up for a few years. Eventually, he can take the kids with him or something. But every time he goes off like this, I get so angry, I feel like I want to leave him. He won't even talk to me about it. Where is his spirit of good will? It doesn't work for only one of us to have it!"

Allison was putting out her best effort under the Stage Two model of relationships. She insisted that she was right. Probably most of us would agree with her that Ken was being thoughtless and unfair, but being right did nothing for Allison except make her more frustrated. She had tried in vain to communicate with Ken and had focused endlessly on "the problem," believing that if Ken would help her, they could come up with a solution. One solution they had tried was to hire help for her while he was away, but they both felt bad about spending the money, and they couldn't find reliable people. Allison was riveted on the only solution she could think of: Ken needed to change. He had to give up or modify these trips!

After working for a time with Allison, I suggested that she try an experiment: to act as if she felt loving, even if she didn't. We talked in some detail about how she would do that and exactly what she might try.

Several weeks before the next backpack trip, Allison started asking Ken about it. Where were they planning to go? How much climbing would they do? What kind of food did they pack?

Ken was delighted. He took out maps and marked their route for her. He cooked up one of their favorite camp meals one evening. Allison was so interested in what she was learning and so surprised at how little she knew about what they did that she found she had more and more questions. Suddenly, they were talking more than they usually did, and enjoying it. Ken never said anything about the changes in Allison, but he obviously liked them. He even became somewhat affectionate with her, a habit they had lost in recent years.

The morning Ken left, Allison got up at 4 A.M. and cooked up a special breakfast. She gave Ken a big hug and told him to have a great trip. This was a huge contrast from previous trips when they would have a fight the night before and then Ken would steal off in the morning—alone.

I had been talking with Allison about taking more initiative to take care of her own needs also. She had a good friend who was a single mom with a big house, and they decided to have a great big "house party" for a few days. Her friend took some vacation days, they hired a high school girl to provide some entertainment for the children in the afternoons, and they interrupted all their usual routines and just hung out together. They took the children to the zoo one day and to a lake another day.

Then a most amazing thing happened: Ken phoned to say he was coming home early and that he wanted to take the whole family car camping if Allison was open to this. Allison didn't think she liked camping, but she hadn't done it for many years, and decided to go along with the idea. She ended up having a wonderful time, and was thrilled because it was the first activity they had done as a family for a very long time.

Of course, not all experiments work out so tidily. Yet this story is not unusual. Whenever a couple, or one member of a couple, is willing to try something new, even when it feels bizarre and is really difficult, new things happen!

Acting as if is one very concrete way to exhibit a spirit of good will. It's also a good way to stop focusing on a given problem or stress and to move directly toward pleasure. You can act as if for as little as thirty seconds or as long as several weeks. You can act as if with regard to one specific issue in your relationship, or you can act as if you feel like a loving spouse in general, and emulate the relationship you want to have.

EXPERIMENT 11

Act as If

1. In your journal, write your answer to this question: If you were completely in love with your spouse, totally adoring, how would you behave? You may want to write a paragraph or make a list. Let your imagination take over.

2. Go back to the goals you set for your relationship in experiment 7. What needs to happen in order for you to achieve these goals? Do you believe you have to solve certain problems first? Can you imagine having what you want in your relationship right now, by acting as if you have it?

3. Set a specific time—from five minutes to an evening or a full day—to set aside any tensions you are feeling with your partner right now and act as if you are a loving, adoring partner.

4. The next time you feel angry or hurt or have a conflict with your partner, make a point of trying to act as if. Look for an opportunity and try it. Acknowledge your feelings, but know that you do not have to act them out. You have a choice. Try something different this time.

5. Record what you did in your journal and how it turned out.

CHAPTER 5

Loving Action 4

Practice Restraint

According to my thesaurus, some synonyms for *restraint* are moderation, prudence, judiciousness, equanimity, self-control, poise, presence of mind, level-headedness, good taste, discrimination, and subtlety.

These are exactly the qualities we strive for in marriage and relationships. Composure. Coolness under pressure. Serenity. Inner peace.

The quest for these qualities requires discipline. But sometimes it isn't clear exactly how spiritual "discipline" translates into daily life. Loving Action 4 offers you highly specific opportunities to practice restraint and all those wonderful synonyms that go along with it. We will learn three specific ways to practice restraint: avoiding negative comments, avoiding defensive responses, and avoiding fights.

Avoid Negative, Critical, and Demanding Comments

Loving Action 4 is very specific: make a pact with yourself that for two full weeks, you will refrain from making any negative, critical, or demanding comments to your partner.

This assignment is easy to understand, simple, and direct. And extremely educational.

Virtually always, when people who have agreed to this experiment report back to me, the first thing they mention is how surprised they were to learn *how often* they make negative, critical, or demanding comments to their partners.

I strongly encourage you to do this experiment. Starting right now, and for two full weeks—mark it on your calendar—just agree with yourself that you will not make any negative, critical, or demanding comments to your mate.

I warn you, there is a learning curve.

The Learning Curve

If you are like most people I've worked with, you will at first realize that you have said something negative, critical, or demanding *after* you have said it. That is major progress. You are waking up! You are paying attention! You are expanding your consciousness about yourself.

Next, you may realize that you are saying something negative, critical, or demanding *as* you are saying it. Congratulations! You have moved to phase two. More progress.

Then, I hope, there will come a magical moment when you are on the verge of saying something negative, critical, or demanding, and you actually decide not to say it. You practice restraint.

This is spiritual growth. This means you have exercised your will and your discipline instead of living unconsciously on automatic pilot; you have been "spiritual"! You have just practiced moderation, poise, level-headedness, good taste, discrimination, *self-control*, and *presence of mind*. At the same time, you've done wonders for your marriage or relationship.

Operate from Your Inner Strength

After you are successful in practicing restraint several times, you may begin to feel a sense of accomplishment and a strengthening of your inner power. You will be more in control of your own behavior.

As you keep paying attention when you are tempted to make a negative, critical, or demanding comment, you will also learn what types of comments you tend to make. This can make an immeasurable contribution to your self-awareness and to your spiritual growth. What was motivating you to say what you were about to say? What was your remark going to accomplish? Are your negative remarks typically critical, controlling, whiny, sarcastic, invasive? Do you sound like your mother or father when you make these remarks? What can you learn by closely observing your own behavior and then choosing to modify it? I can't overemphasize the importance of what you can learn when you take this experiment seriously.

By the end of two weeks, you will experience the inner strength that comes from a sense of achievement and increased self-knowledge, as well as a difference in your household and your relationship.

Pay Attention to Your Offhand Comments

Many negative, critical, or demanding comments by themselves may sound fairly harmless. You may even think you are being helpful when you say them:

> *Honey, be careful. You're being too rough with Johnny. (critical)*
>
> *I didn't think your remark was very funny! It was rude! (negative, critical)*
>
> *Would you please stop talking about that! (demanding)*

Don't interrupt me! (critical, demanding)

If you hold the bagel this way, it would be a lot easier to slice. (control-
ling, invasive)

Don't follow that car so closely! (demanding)

But it doesn't take very many such comments in a row to begin to make your mate feel invaded, criticized, or belittled. And the remarks are, for the most part, completely useless. Your partner isn't really going to harm Johnny. She isn't going to stop making corny or crude jokes. The bagels will get sliced. He has for many years been arriving successfully at his destinations when you are not in the car.

But even when they are harmless and not very numerous, these kinds of statements bring down the energy between the two of you, ever so slightly. Pay attention. You'll see.

Reversing Negativity: An Example

Of course, for some couples, negative, critical, and demanding remarks are not so harmless. They make up the majority of all conversation.

Dennis came to me on the verge of leaving his wife, Mary.

> She's not affectionate, she's not warm and cuddly. She's too
> involved with her work, and she's always tired at night. I mean,
> why did she get married? She is supposed to kiss me when we
> both get home, cozy up in front of the fireplace. She's always off
> doing more work.

Dennis was receptive and wanted to make a change if he could. I asked him to try the experiment I've described here. After two weeks, he came back astonished.

I was spending a lot of time criticizing her. I had no idea of this. But I was always trying to prove to her how unaffectionate she was, and of course, this came out as criticism. And demands. And negative! I was being so negative. It took me a long time to truly stop, but by the end of this week, our household was much more peaceful, and I have made a discovery: I've seen something about myself I never saw before.

This is the discovery Dennis made: in his mind, the problems were all the fault of his wife, who just wouldn't get affectionate and lovey-dovey. But he found out that *he was actually the cause of all the upset in the relationship*. By criticizing her so much, he was making the relationship a very unpleasant place to live. He was pushing Mary away, when his desire was to bring her closer. It was he who needed to make a change, not Mary.

After Dennis discovered how liberating it was for him to stop his criticism, I encouraged him to begin acting as if he felt loving and adoring, behaving the way he wanted his wife to behave toward him, even when he didn't feel like it.

The result of Dennis's experiment is not surprising. Mary became more affectionate and more receptive to Dennis's affection.

That's not why Dennis made the change; he stopped all criticism because that was the spiritual thing to do. He experimented.

But he was amazed at the outcome of the experiment. Mary didn't magically transform into a totally different person; she had been raised in a repressive household and would never be completely uninhibited with her body. But she behaved more warmly toward Dennis. And Mary's strength was her high energy, happy and upbeat personality, and childlike playfulness. All those wonderful qualities had almost disappeared under Dennis's assaults.

Now they reappeared, and the two of them began enjoying each other's company much more.

Dennis still wishes Mary were more cuddly and sexy. But he adores her cheerfulness, and he single-handedly turned their relationship around, just by practicing restraint.

It is important to note that before this experiment, Dennis did not see himself as negative, critical, or demanding. He could not see beyond the obvious fact that he was "right"! "Wives should be affectionate," he would tell me. "Mary should be more loving." If he had continued trying to convince her of this, they would surely have ended up in the divorce courts. He might have won his precious booby prize by proving he was right (wives should be affectionate). But he would have lost his marriage.

Paying attention to your negative, critical, and demanding comments can open up wonderful doors for both your own spiritual development and your relationship. It requires a great deal of focus and paying attention. But the rewards can be enormous.

Instead of Criticizing, Think "Slago!"

Several years ago, I spent a day helping some friends move into their new home. Meredith and I were organizing the kitchen. Her husband, Cliff, was keeping his usual critical and controlling litany going, all directed at Meredith:

"Don't spend so much time sorting through that stuff. We'll never get finished. You are being way too fussy. It doesn't matter where stuff goes. Just put things away. You are so messy and unorganized, whatever you set up today won't last anyway."

Cliff is a very nice guy and extremely bright. I waited until Meredith ran out to get us some lunch and then I asked him if he minded if I gave him a suggestion or two. He was quite receptive. For about fifteen minutes, I explained to him about having a spirit of good will. I suggested that Meredith would probably be much more open to him if he made supportive rather than critical remarks, and I tried to show him how much negativity he was creating. I explained how much she needed his support with all the stress she was under. And I tried to show him that he was probably never going to change her, but might instead see her for who she really is and accept her. He seemed to take in what I was saying, and thanked me. (By the way, I had spent a lot of time giving Meredith suggestions too, about letting his comments roll off her back and "acting as if " she felt warm and affectionate toward him, especially by invoking her endearing sense of humor and joking with him more.)

A week later, Meredith phoned me. "Things are really different around here," she told me. "Cliff made up a little mnemonic about what you said: 'Slago: Supportive, Loving, Accepting, Giving, Open.' We go around saying 'Slago' to each other all the time now. It's sort of a joke, but he's really doing it. And so am I. I can't thank you enough for having that little talk with him. It has truly made a change."

Cliff probably still feels critical of certain aspects of Meredith's personality. But he saw right away the value of *behaving* more positively toward her, of restraining his criticisms and acting as if he fully supports her. Now she *feels* supported, so she is much warmer toward him. They will never "solve their problem" of her lack of organization or his desire to control everything, but they are happier together. They have learned to manage these differences.

What are the real goals in your own relationship? To solve some problem or other? To make over your partner? Or to increase your intimacy, mutual support, and pleasure? If they are these last goals, criticism and negativity will never get you there. Instead, think "Slago!" Slago sums up much of what we have learned in the first four Loving Actions.

Making Demands

Alex is another person who learned about himself using Loving Action 4. When he first heard about practicing restraint, he realized that he was demanding a great deal of his wife. On his own, he decided to reduce his requests. Rather than pestering her to find a time to cut his hair, he went out to get it cut. And even though he felt he wasn't good at buying his own clothes, he decided to begin managing that on his own. He found stores where the salespeople were helpful. His initiative completely eliminated two areas of negative energy in their relationship.

Alex never mentioned his Loving Action, and it was a couple of months before his wife even noticed the changes. But after she saw a haircut she didn't do and noticed a few new shirts, she expressed her surprise—and her gratitude. Alex was happy, not only because two areas of tension in his relationship were gone but also because his increased self-sufficiency felt great to him.

Two Suggestions That May Help

Practicing restraint by eliminating all of your own negative, critical, and demanding comments is not a small task. It requires a lot of vigilance. It may be useful for you to start by doing it for a specific limited time, such as one evening, or one Saturday. Here are two more suggestions that will help.

1. Before you begin the experiment of deliberately stopping all negative, critical, or demanding comments within your relationship, you may find it useful to ask yourself this question:

"What is it like for my mate to be loved by me?"

Actually talk with a friend about this or take a half hour and write your answers in your journal.

Put yourself in your partner's shoes. Think about your interactions in the last several days or weeks. What have you been like in the relationship? How do you suppose your partner felt about you? What contributions do you make in general? Are there ways you could brighten the life of your loved one? Are there behaviors you might let go of that would make you an easier person to be around? What is it like for your partner to be loved by you?

If you think your partner would be receptive, you might even want to ask him or her this question, sometime when you are both relaxed and in a talkative mood. You may become aware of something new that your partner does or doesn't like, something about which you had no awareness before you asked. If this conversation "raises your consciousness" or expands your awareness, it is spiritual growth.

2. A little "mantra" that is useful to some people as they practice restraint is this: "The relationship is more important than this one incident," or "The relationship is more important than [socks on the floor, my doing the dishes, that thoughtless remark, and so on]." One woman told me,

> That phrase comes up so often for me, and it is always on target. Most of the events I start to comment on are so trivial, and my comment won't change the situation anyway! I'm sure I say, "The relationship is more important than _____" to myself ten times a day now. It works with my kids too. What's most important is for everybody to feel good and be happy. Nagging or corrective "help" from me is going to spoil the good feelings. That sentence has a big impact on my family!

When you notice that you are about to make a negative or critical comment, if you can catch yourself, say the mantra to yourself instead.

If you, dear reader, do not act on any other specific experiment in this book, I encourage you to try practicing restraint. I know of no one who has seriously done this experiment and not learned from it.

Be Open Instead of Defensive

Now we move to a more advanced level of practicing restraint: learning to refrain from giving a knee-jerk defensive response when someone is being negative, critical, or demanding toward you. Refraining from making negative, critical, or demanding comments is a bit easier, because you are initiating the remarks. Avoiding defensive responses is harder, because you are usually caught off guard. But as you read here about alternatives to being defensive and you begin to pay attention, sometime soon you will catch yourself being defensive. That is an extremely important first step. Right then and there, you may be able to shift gears, as I suggest here.

Being defensive is a natural and normal response.

"I thought that was a rude remark you made to Mrs. Thomas."

"It wasn't rude, she wanted to know the truth. I was just being honest!"

"You never do anything around this house!"

"I do too! I swept the porch last night. I'm too tired when I come home. I do stuff on weekends."

"Can I tell you something I would like you to do when we make love?"

"You mean you don't like what I'm doing now?"

Defensiveness is as old as humankind. Someone throws a stone at you; you put your hands in front of your face to protect yourself.

EXPERIMENT 12

Ban Negative Comments

1. Mark your calendar for two weeks and promise yourself that for those two weeks, you will not make any negative, critical, or demanding comments to your mate. Don't expect perfection. Just keep paying attention. That's all.

2. Before you begin, give some thought to the question, "What is it like for my mate to be loved by me?" Write about this in your journal.

3. For the two weeks of your experiment, pay close attention. Listen to yourself. When you have a little victory or you realize something new about yourself or your relationship, make a note in your journal.

4. Memorize the phrase, "Our relationship is more important than _____." When you are about to say something negative, say this to yourself instead.

5. If you find the reminder "Slago" (supportive, loving, accepting, giving, open) useful, try thinking about it every morning as you get ready for your day. When you catch yourself being critical or negative, think "Slago" instead and then act on it!

Maybe you throw a stone back. This is the same thing we do with words: verbal assault, verbal self-protection. It is a survival instinct.

But, as we know, part of the spiritual approach to improving our marriage and relationships is becoming conscious of habitual behaviors and making a decision to change them if they are counterproductive. Defensiveness is usually part of your conditioned personality, not your authentic self. It is not loving, and it definitely creates distance and not connection. When you become defensive, even if the other guy started it, even if you are being unjustly accused, even if you are "right," you are escalating the hostilities. Spiritual practice requires you to be the leader, the "big" person. It requires you to exercise your will and discipline, to make a move toward connection, and to overcome bad habits.

Whenever you have any interaction with your loved one, whether you are being attacked or just having any kind of discussion or interaction, you have only two modes available to you: Is your heart open, or is it closed? The point of spiritual practice is to be able to keep your heart open to your partner as much as possible. Can you yield to your partner, moving with his or her mood, comment, opinion? Or are you resisting your partner, arguing back, becoming defensive and self-protective?

The Magic Sentence: "I Feel Defensive"

One way to start overcoming the bad habit of becoming defensive and closing your heart, especially when your partner is verbally assaulting you in some way, is to memorize the phrase "I feel defensive." The urge to make a defensive remark comes up fast, and it's hard to catch yourself before you do it. But if the phrase "I feel defensive" is right on the tip of your tongue, maybe it will fall out of your mouth instead of the knee-jerk "Yes I do!" or "I did not!" or "You're not so great yourself!"

"I feel defensive" is a noncombative comment. It buys you time to calm down and decide what to do next. It names what's going on without placing blame anywhere. You are simply telling the truth.

With the magic sentence, our preceding examples might have gone something like this:

"I thought that was a rude remark you made to Mrs. Thomas."
"I feel defensive. *(pause)* Let's see, you think that was rude?"

"You never do anything around this house!"

"I'm feeling defensive. *(pause)* You really think that? Let's talk about it. I'm open to looking at it."

Remember, it doesn't matter who is right or wrong about this. You may feel that your partner is outrageously wrong. The question is, can you use your leadership skills here? Can you put your desire for spiritual growth and for a loving relationship above your knee-jerk habit to defend yourself? Can you use the Loving Action of practicing restraint, thereby giving a gift to yourself and your partner?

The "Martial Arts" Response

The next level of nondefensive, peacemaking response to a verbal assault is to use the martial arts model. As you may know, in martial arts, when someone throws a fist at you, instead of throwing up your own arm and trying to stop it, which will probably hurt both of you (the defensive move), you can grab the fist and pull it, continuing in the direction of your opponent's momentum and pulling him or her off balance.

In conversation, a martial arts response, or continuing in the direction of your opponent's remark, would be to repeat the remark or ask about it, like this:

"I thought that was a rude remark you made to Mrs. Thomas."
"You thought it was rude?"

"We never go out anymore!"
"You feel like we never go out anymore?"

Another option is to respond in a way that seems as if you are agreeing with the remark, even if you actually aren't. At some later occasion, you may be able to bring the topic up and express your own, different opinion. But when someone is angry with you and all invested in being right, your trying to bring up another view then will only be contributing to negativity and bad feelings, and you will be passing up an opportunity to provide spiritual leadership, to de-escalate the hostilities. You can avoid disagreeing without actually agreeing either. For example,

"You never do anything around this house!"
"I know it seems that way. You do a lot of the work, it's true."

"We never go out anymore!"
(typical knee-jerk defensive response) "Yes we do! We went to the movies last night! We went out for dinner last week!"
(possible nondefensive, peace-promoting responses)
"You feel like we never go out anymore?" or
"It does seem like we never go out anymore" or
"We do enjoy it when we go out. I love to go out too."

Tina and Ron were recently visiting us for a few days from out of town, when they had a serious misunderstanding. Ron thought Tina was going to get up early and go for a run. Tina thought Ron was going to get up early with her. When Ron sauntered downstairs about 9:30, Tina was fit to be tied. Their conversation went something like this:

Ron: Gee, it felt good to sleep in. Did you go for your run?

Tina: Now I know what it's like to live with someone who doesn't keep his agreements!

Ron: Agreements?

Tina: I thought we were going to get up early! I just wasted this whole morning.

Ron: Was I supposed to get up early too?

Tina: You know you blew it. Don't sound so innocent. You are just so selfish. You only think of yourself! You're just being defensive because you know you're wrong.

Listening off in the corner, I knew this was the critical moment. I thought Ron would say something like, "I did not blow it! We never had an agreement that I would get up early. The last thing you said last night was . . ." and the fight would be on.

But Ron was brilliant. Here is what he said:

Ron: I'm being defensive because I'm feeling attacked. *(pause)* I am so sorry I misunderstood this. You must feel awful waiting around for me. I don't blame you for being angry. Honey, I'm so sorry you missed your run. That really makes me sad.

Ron didn't take Tina's bait. He didn't feel he needed to defend himself. He felt genuine empathy for Tina, in spite of her lashing out, and he decided to express that. Tina's anger toned right down, and we all figured out a way to redeem the morning.

Sometimes it takes several days to reverse your initial defensive response. I recall when a friend became angry with me because I broke a date with her. At first I was hurt and blamed her for not being more flexible. I felt she was deliberately trying to make me feel guilty. But after a few days, as I calmed down, I saw the validity of her position. I said to myself, "It doesn't matter who is right and who is wrong here. The relationship is far more important to me than this incident." I e-mailed her an apologetic note, which she appreciated. By letting go of being defensive, I mended my valuable friendship.

When Your Mate Is Controlling or Critical

One of the most challenging of all spiritual tasks is learning how to practice restraint when you have a nagging, critical, or controlling mate. If you have one of these, consider that the universe is offering you an extra-special opportunity to learn the Loving Action of restraint.

When your partner criticizes you or continually nags or harps away at you, it is of course tempting to fight back, to defend yourself, and, in fact, to work very hard at getting your partner to discontinue this behavior. Your partner is the "wrong" one, you will feel, for picking away at you all the time.

If trying to get your partner to stop this behavior has not worked for you, here is a new strategy that does not involve making your partner wrong or trying to get him or her to change.

Learn the phrase "This has nothing to do with me." Now, whenever your partner starts in on you, say it over and over *to yourself.*

The truth is, your partner's behavior probably does have very little to do with you. He or she has a natural tendency to be nagging, critical, or controlling and almost certainly behaves this way with other people besides you. The behavior is coming from your partner's own fears or perfectionism or insecurity and is not greatly affected by anything you do or do not do. If she is nagging you to lose weight and you do lose weight, she will probably start in on you about something else. Or if he is constantly telling you how to drive, he'll keep doing it no matter what you do behind the wheel.

If the nagging, critical, or controlling comments are habitual with your partner, they are not about you. You may be annoyed by them, but do not feel you have to defend yourself or change in any way. As much as you can, let the remarks slip off you, like water off a duck's back.

Sherry and Arthur were a couple for whom "This has nothing to do with me" worked well. Sherry was a backseat driver, but she didn't save her behavior for the car; she gave Arthur unsolicited advice about virtually everything he did. Arthur felt utterly frustrated when he came to one of my groups. Every attempt he made to persuade Sherry to stop not only was futile but usually ended in a big fight. His comment to me was, "If she thinks I'm so helpless, why did she marry me?"

I asked Arthur to observe Sherry's behavior with other people, and sure enough, he began to realize that Sherry backseat drove with everyone. Often her advice was actually quite good, and friends didn't mind it so much because they received it in limited doses. But it began to dawn on Arthur that Sherry was not singling him out for special treatment. She gave him advice, not because she thought he was inadequate or "helpless," but so that she herself could feel more in control. Her advice made her feel good about herself. It gave her the satisfaction (or the illusion) of helping other people. It had nothing to do with him! When he was able to stop taking her comments personally, he was much better able to let them roll off his back, to change the subject and move on. Sherry's controlling comments didn't change, but the atmosphere in the relationship was transformed because Arthur stopped making a crisis out of every remark.

The martial arts strategy we discussed earlier, of sounding like you agree even if you don't, can also be helpful with chronic criticizers or advice givers. You can respond by saying something like, "You are right; I wish I could be better," or "That's a good idea. Thanks," and then just go on your merry way. On your own, think through your partner's advice to see whether it has merit. If you can follow it or change what the person is critical about with no compromise of your own desires, then do it. But it is perfectly okay for you to go right ahead with your way of doing things if that feels better to you, as long as you are being reasonable. But then don't defend yourself. Simply don't engage with your partner. Just keep telling yourself, "This has nothing to do with me." It's one more way of practicing restraint, of taking leadership, of being the "big" person, thereby opening up more possibility for closeness, connection, and mutual enjoyment, the real purpose of your relationship, after all.

Becoming defensive is unenlightened, habitual, thoughtless behavior. Learning not to respond defensively is spiritual practice.

> If you think seriously about the true meaning of spiritual practice, it has to do with the development and training of your mental state, attitudes, and psychological and emotional state and well-being. . . . For example, if you find yourself in a situation in which you might be tempted to insult someone, then you immediately take precautions and restrain yourself from doing that. Similarly, if you encounter a situation in which you may lose your temper, immediately you are mindful and say, "No, this is not the appropriate way." That actually is a spiritual practice.
>
> —The Dalai Lama

Avoid Fights

The third aspect of practicing restraint is to stop destructive fighting.

Virtually all couples have arguments, lose their tempers, and become upset with each other from time to time. Fights are normal and certainly not a sign of a "bad" relationship.

EXPERIMENT 13

On Defensiveness

1. In your journal, list incidents or times that you can recall when you reacted defensively. It might be a big, classic fight you recall from some time ago, or small incidents from the last couple of weeks. If you can't think of any, start paying attention until you catch yourself being defensive. Then return to this exercise.

2. Next to each defensive incident you recall, write a nondefensive response you might have given.

3. Memorize the phrase "I feel defensive." For two weeks, associate the phrase with something you do every day, such as brushing your teeth, getting into your car, or turning on the dishwasher. Every time you do that activity, pause, close your eyes for just three seconds, and say the phrase to yourself three or four times. The idea is to keep the phrase in the front of your mind so that when an incident arises where it might be useful, you will remember it.

4. When you hear someone else being defensive, either with you or with some third party, to yourself say a sentence that would have been a nondefensive response. It might be "I feel defensive" or "Yeah, you could be right" or "That's an idea."

5. The first time you catch yourself *before* you make a defensive response and you actually make a nondefensive response, congratulate yourself. Record the incident in your journal.

Some fights are even useful and actually assist spiritual growth and move a relationship forward. Some fights may not be useful, but they are harmless.

Useful or Harmless Fights

A fight is useful when it helps clarify and convey true feelings. Maybe you are feeling uneasy but you aren't sure why. Or you know your true feelings, but you have been reluctant to express them to your partner. By letting the emotions fly, you may learn what it is that is truly upsetting you, and it is important for your partner to see how deeply you feel.

For example, Michael, a lawyer, had a difficult case and needed to work evenings until it was over. Jill tried to be understanding but found herself complaining about it now and then. Finally, one night, to her surprise, she erupted. As she went on for a while in great anger and with tears flowing, she discovered why she was feeling upset: she was deeply afraid that working nights would become a pattern for Michael that would continue forever. Further, she was feeling a great deal more strain over her lonely evenings than she realized. It was important for both of them to see all the emotion that was there and know exactly what they were dealing with. Jill's deep emotion was her authentic self speaking.

In this case, Michael helped make the fight useful for both of them, because *he did not become defensive*. He listened to Jill. He could understand that she was not blaming him; she was expressing her own feelings. Michael knew he did not need to "fix" the problem right then and there. He told Jill that he had had no idea she was having such a hard time and that he was really sorry. And he reassured her that he too did not want to make a habit of working evenings. This fight was definitely a move toward connection for both of them.

A good fight, with expressions of rage and anger, is a way for the body to discharge built-up energy and sometimes just feels good. Even though one or both partners may be very angry, at some level they both know that this is simply a good blowup and that it will pass.

Harmless fights are the ones that happen when both partners are exhausted, under stress, or even depressed. They bicker or complain. They are irritable or edgy. The next day, when they feel better, it all goes away.

Destructive Fights

The vast majority of fights between couples are destructive. They have no useful function. They create negative energy and leave the household in a doom-and-gloom atmosphere. Partners may say things that are truly hurtful or malicious. The people involved are *not* being authentic but are acting out of habit, exercising no control over their feelings. Most often the subject of the fight has little or nothing to do with the true source of conflict. No progress is made in resolving any problems. Because the partners are not paying attention, they are making no progress in their spiritual growth.

One easy way to tell whether a fight is useful or destructive is that useful fights happen only once, or once in a great while. Or a useful fight may happen in several stages over a period of weeks. It's the same fight, but each episode builds on the last, and progress is made each time. Also, in useful fights, you will be talking about your own feelings, not about your partner's behavior. Your partner's behavior may be contributing to your feelings, but what you are really talking about is your own feelings.

Destructive fights are the same fight over and over and over with no progress ever being made. The participants are not observing themselves or making any attempt to be conscious or to exercise choice. Destructive fights are characterized by habitual, thoughtless behaviors: blame, defensiveness, accusations, criticism, sarcasm, name-calling, insisting that you are right and your partner is wrong, and making yourself into a powerless victim.

The Solution

The spiritual remedy for destructive fights is to avoid them altogether.

This is not easy, because fighting can be addictive. When you are in a rage and your adrenaline level is up, it is hard to avoid the addictive stimulation and rush of adrenaline, to resist showing your partner how right you are or how he or she blew it again.

But the spiritual approach is to walk away.

You have a choice. You do not have to behave the way you feel. Pay attention. Bring consciousness to the situation. Discipline yourself to do something difficult. Be willing to experiment.

The way in which you walk away is critically important. If you throw in the last word and then rush out in a fit of pique, slamming the door, this is not spiritual. The ideal is to say, in as calm a voice as possible, "I'm very angry right now. I want to talk about this, but not when we are both so emotional. I'm going to leave so we can talk about this later when we are both calmer."

Then leave the scene altogether. Very decisively walk away.

If you are full of emotion, find a way to discharge that emotion *not* in the presence of your partner. Go for a run or a vigorous walk. Hit your bed: stretch your arms way over your head and, as you exhale, come down hard on that bed with your fists, over and over. Or call a friend and express your anger to a third person. This can work even if you get an answering machine—if this is a very understanding friend. You will feel better if you let your body discharge its buildup of energy.

One of the very best ways to calm yourself down is to let time pass. If you boiled over about something in the morning, chances are you will already feel less "charge" about it by afternoon. So, after you discharge your angry energy, find a way to distract yourself.

In the end, you may or may not choose to talk about the problem again later. If you were fighting about something that needs to be decided, such as where you will go on vacation or who's going to stay home with the children on Thursday evening or even whether or not you are going to have a baby, then you will have to resolve it later. But if your real fight is about who has more power in the relationship, for example, that issue will respond far better to unilateral Loving Actions than it ever will to long discussions. You'll never be able to resolve your power issues by discussing them; you probably won't even be able to agree on the problem, because you each see it from a different point of view. So instead of discussing it, choose a Loving Action and do that. Figure out what you need and figure out how you can manage that need on your own. And let your partner go ahead and be who he or she is.

I once attended a lecture on a particular type of psychotherapy. An audience member asked the speaker, "Will this method help us stop fighting?" The speaker replied, "The way to stop fighting is to stop fighting."

I agree. And avoiding fights is the spiritual path, too. Don't indulge your immature urges to punish your partner or get your way. Take your anger out on a pillow or a friend with a sympathetic ear, not on your partner. Your job is to nurture your own and your partner's sacred inner flame. Fighting will only dump sand on both of them.

Practicing Restraint and Spiritual Growth

Practicing restraint helps you learn how to pay attention. It helps you distinguish between your personality and your authentic self. And it moves you toward love and connection.

Truly, all you have to do is start paying attention. You will be able to hear yourself being negative, critical, demanding, defensive, or bellicose. When you do, that is a major first step. Just notice what you said. Notice how your remark made you feel. Notice the impact of your remark on those around you. If you can't stop yourself right away, don't worry. Just pay attention as you do it. Gradually, as you actually hear yourself, you may find that you naturally become less negative and defensive, because you yourself will find your negativity to be unpleasant. When you truly pay attention, change happens naturally, without having to be forced or engineered.

Most of us will never achieve perfection with any of these Loving Actions. Perfection is not the goal. Learning is the goal, always moving in the direction of greater connection, authenticity, love, consciousness, receptivity, and happiness. Practicing restraint is one good way to achieve self-awareness, self-control, and spiritual growth.

Meanwhile, you will create a much more harmonious and joyful household.

EXPERIMENT 14

Stop Destructive Fights

1. In your journal, list the last several fights you've had with your partner. Using the criteria we've discussed, label each fight "useful" or "destructive."

2. Next time you find yourself starting to become involved in a destructive fight, experiment with a spiritual leave taking.

CHAPTER 6

Loving Action 5

Balance Giving
and Taking

Fairness and equality are the bedrock of Stage Two relationships. In Stage Two relationships, marriage is strictly a 50-50 proposition. Both partners have to give and take equally for the marriage to feel good. In Stage Two relationships, there are many discussions about who is doing more work around the house. There are lists of duties and negotiations: "If you take Allison to soccer, I'll do the dishes." "You cook three nights, I'll cook four."

Bargains like these work well as long as both partners agree on the division of labor and show a spirit of good will.

However, when one partner feels mistreated and unable to negotiate successfully for change, the Stage Two couple runs out of options.

Envision a giant balance scale with your partner's contributions on one side and yours on the other. When you feel that the scales are out of balance and that you are giving more than your share, what can you do? In a Stage Two relationship, your only alternatives are to hold back on what you give to the relationship or to negotiate with your partner to give more. Neither of these is very satisfactory. Holding back on what you give is likely to make you feel resentful and does not flow from a spirit of good will. And we already know that badgering your partner to change lies outside the spiritual approach to relationship. It doesn't honor your partner, and it doesn't work.

A New Understanding of Balance

Spiritual Partnership opens up a whole new possibility to you, one that gives you full control over maintaining the balance and fairness that you seek. In Spiritual Partnership, you are invited to discard the balance scale with your contributions on one side and your partner's on the other and to replace it with a different scale. This one is right in front of you, and you alone have total control over it.

In a Spiritual Partnership this is the new scale. On one side is the amount you are giving to your partner and your relationship, and on the other side is the amount you are taking for yourself, the amount you are taking care of your needs in the relationship. The question you want to ask as a Spiritual Partner in your relationship is not

"Am I giving 100 percent and is my partner giving 100 percent?"

but instead

"Am I giving 100 percent, and am I taking 100 percent?"

In Spiritual Partnership, you have two big jobs: you need to stand up for and take care of your partner, and you need to stand up for and take care of yourself. Whatever *your partner* is giving and taking, your spiritual task is to accept that. Your partner is a given in this. What lies within your control is (1) how much and how often you take care of your partner, even if it is at your own expense, and (2) how much and how often you take care of yourself, even if it is at your partner's expense.

Evaluating the Balance in Your Relationship

Watching over the balance between giving to your partner and taking care of your own needs is challenging, ongoing work.

Each of us is usually better at one half of the task than the other. Are you someone who is very good at taking care of yourself, at meeting your own needs? Are you quite self-sufficient and decisive about what you want? Then your work will be to stand up for your partner more, to practice generosity and thoughtfulness, even if it may be at your own expense sometimes.

Or are you someone who is very good at taking care of others, at keeping peace, and at thoughtfulness and generosity, even though it may be at your own expense? Then your task will be to stand up for yourself more, to be assertive, to take initiative, and to act on your own, even though it may be at your partner's expense sometimes.

Let's look at an example of each of these two types of people.

Taking Care of Yourself

Jerry and Sabrina had been married five years when Sabrina came to a Spiritual Partnership support group. They were generally happy, and both adored their two children. Sabrina's major complaint was that Jerry did very little around the house. She came to the group carrying a copy of the book *The Second Shift*, the groundbreaking study by Berkeley sociologist Arlie Hochschild, which documented that although many middle-class two-career couples *say* they believe in equality and fairness, in fact these career women are still doing most of the child care and housework.

"I've negotiated with him to exhaustion," Sabrina told us. "He's willing, but his willingness doesn't translate into action. When he doesn't do his jobs, he apologizes. Big deal. I still have to do them."

We invited Sabrina to set up a Spiritual Partnership balance scale on a piece of paper. On one side, she wrote down all she gives to the relationship, a long list of tasks and attitudes, such as generosity and good will. On the other side, what she takes for herself, she could think of few items for her list. She felt love from her husband when he made an effort to spend time with her. She felt supported by his part of their income. But their time together, his contribution to their children and their home life, and his expressions of appreciation were too rare for her, and her scale seemed to her quite unbalanced.

We helped her brainstorm ways she could bring her scale into balance all by herself. It was a long, fun session with many ideas. After several weeks, Sabrina reported back that she had asked the housekeeper they had one day a week to come for three days and to prepare meals for the family. The housekeeper prepared extra food so that there were leftovers for the other days. Also, Sabrina announced to the family that she would not come home for the evening, including dinner, every other Tuesday night, that she would take those nights to visit with women friends. Jerry did not love this part, but we pointed out to Sabrina that it is sometimes okay for her to meet her own needs, even if it is at Jerry's expense, as long as she feels that her own giving-taking scale is still balanced.

By the end of our twelve-week support group, Sabrina was ecstatic. She told us she had her Tuesday nights booked up weeks in advance, that she adored having these times to herself to keep up with her friends. Being relieved of cooking was a huge weight off her shoulders. She found energy to cook special meals for friends more often. Jerry was thrilled with the changes too, because Sabrina's nagging and being upset were over. His evenings with the children became something very special for the three of them. And the big bonus was that from Sabrina's idea to take a night for herself, Jerry got the idea that they could do this for themselves, and they began scheduling a date night every two weeks for just the two of them!

Sabrina was a natural giver who needed to learn more about how to take care of herself.

Taking Care of Your Partner

In another group, when we all made our giving-taking balance scales, Barry found that he had almost nothing on the giving side of his. He was a painter and committed to his work as an artist, so his wife not only took care of the household, children, and meals but also provided most of the family income. Barry had come to our group for a different reason altogether, a worry about their sex life.

When we brainstormed with him, we first came up with all the obvious ways to give: flowers, dinner out, a love letter, a weekend away. But Barry knew what would really mean something to his wife: for him to spend more time with her son, his stepson. He took all of our suggestions and his own. As he reported back to us each week, we heard quite a few excuses, mostly that he didn't have the time to do what he had written on the giving side of his balance scale. He needed to learn that sometimes, giving means a certain amount of self-sacrifice. We encouraged him. By the end of our support group, Barry had done everything on his list, including making regular time every week for his stepson.

Barry felt good about all his changes, and what surprised him most was that the problem he had with his sexual relationship had greatly diminished. So often, sexual tension is a reflection of what is happening in the rest of the relationship.

Do you feel your relationship is unfair or unequal in some way? See if you can find a way to bring it into better balance without depending on your partner to change.

Finding Balance in a Power Struggle

The most difficult time to balance your own giving-taking scale is when you and your partner disagree on a life-changing decision on which it seems impossible to compromise. It may seem as though the two of you are in a power struggle.

Should we move to Chicago or not? Should we have another baby or not? Should I go back to graduate school or not? It seems as though you have to *either* give *or* take. It is hard to see a way to balance your own scale.

But even in these situations, balance is possible, and your own attempt to create balance will eventually lead you out of the impasse.

I recall a time years ago when I had come to the unhappy conclusion that I would either be thin and feel deprived and resentful all the time or be overweight but enjoy eating. Both paths made me unhappy, but I saw no alternatives. I saw only black or white, no shades of gray.

Then I read an article that to my complete amazement, shattered my tidy polarization. It presented me with a third choice: I could eat whatever I wanted, as long as I was eating because I truly wanted that food and not because I was tired or lonely or because everyone else was eating too or because it was time to eat. The food had to "hum" like a tune I couldn't get out of my head and not "beckon" like a bakery window or the smell of pizza, deliberately tempting me. I remember experiencing this insight as a true epiphany, dramatic and liberating. It was a third path I could not have imagined existed when

I was trapped in my polarization. The system worked well for me, and still does, all these years later—when I am disciplined enough to use it. When I first had that insight, I lost ten pounds!

In the same way that I was defeating myself by creating an inaccurate polarization, polarizing a conflict will also defeat you when you and your partner are facing what seem to be two mutually exclusive options. The more black-and-white you see this issue to be, the more entrenched you will each become and the harder it will be to allow a solution to emerge. Avoid making it into "my way or your way." You are looking for a win-win solution. Neither one of you is right or wrong. Together you are looking for the solution that is right for you both, for your family.

But how do you acquire the liberating insight, the third alternative, if someone doesn't hand you an article at the right moment? How do you solve a relationship problem that seems to have only two mutually exclusive solutions?

Amazingly, there is a way.

By yourself, take the initiative to depolarize your impasse.

Think about your giving-taking scale, the one over which you have complete control. On the giving side, you do all you can to develop empathy for your partner's point of view. On the taking side, you do yourself a favor by relaxing the urgency about your own position. Both of these strategies will reduce your own anxiety and create the conditions for an answer to emerge. Usually, if you can get out of the way, relax your need to control the outcome, and trust your process, decisions like this make themselves. They emerge. The answer becomes obvious. But only if you first soften the opposites and create the conditions for one or more alternative solutions to emerge.

Let's look more closely at the steps to depolarizing an impasse.

Develop Empathy for the Other Point of View

Begin by making an effort to understand your partner's point of view and why your partner might be holding it—even if this idea scares you, even if it makes you angry. Talking with a friend or writing in your journal, state the position exactly and then summarize your partner's arguments for it. Then ask yourself, what in your partner's background or present life might have led him or her to this opinion? In what ways do you respect your partner for holding this position? Can you accept that your partner holds this position, even though you don't agree with it?

Remember, you want more than anything for your partner to understand and accept your position. You try to do the same for him or her.

As you make progress in developing empathy for the other position, convey this to your partner. It does not mean you are acquiescing to the decision. You are showing a spirit of good will. You are softening the tension that surrounds this issue. And you are creating a space for your partner to do the same. When the other person no longer feels compelled to defend his or her point of view (because you have conveyed that you understand it), he or she may be able to relax the urgency about it and talk more freely about both sides.

Relax the Urgency of Your Position

Notice you are not being asked here to relax your position, not at all. Relaxing or letting go does not mean that you give up what you want; instead, it means you give up *your anxiety* about what you want.

Intention is desire with no attachment to the outcome. You still have your intention, which is a powerful force, and you still have your desire. But you also trust that the best outcome will emerge on its own; it doesn't require you to force or manipulate it. Keep your strong intention and relax.

The more you become attached to one outcome, the more you fear what will happen if you do not get it. Fear closes you down. When you are afraid, you become protective. You are less able to be open, to be flexible, to be creative. You help bring about a power struggle when you become certain that your own point of view is the only right one and you zealously cling to it.

To help you relax the urgency of your own point of view, talk with a friend or write in your journal. Ask yourself these questions:

1. With regard to the argument we are having, do I have my own inner conflict as well?

2. Is there any part of my partner's position that I would like for myself?

3. Am I really ambivalent in some small way?

4. On what parts of this conflict are we in agreement? (For example, often you may agree on the goals but disagree on how to achieve the goal. You both want to have a fun, relaxing vacation, but you want to hike in the mountains, and your partner wants to swim in the ocean.)

The final step you need to take to depolarize your conflict is simply to wait. Solutions need time to emerge. While you are waiting, you have to be willing to live temporarily in the realm of uncertainty, what Gestalt therapist Fritz Perls called the "fertile void." You may feel uneasy and confused. But remember, this void is fertile. If you are willing to tolerate emptiness for a time, you allow new possibilities to sweep in and fill the void.

The Giving-Taking Balance Scale at Work

In a fairly common type of power struggle, Timothy was offered a job promotion he very much wanted, but it meant that the family would have to move from Denver to San Francisco. His wife, Leigh, was completely against the move. She had a graphic design job she adored. The children were in good schools. They had friends and community and a great home. Leigh was participating in one of my groups when Timothy's opportunity arose. She was adamant about not moving and felt that all the arguments stacked up on her side.

Together in our group, we took Leigh through the depolarizing steps.

She could fairly easily state her empathy for Timothy's position. She knew how much the promotion meant to him. When she talked to him about this, he was appreciative. It was clear to him she had not relented on her position, but he felt moved by her understanding.

Then Leigh tried to soften the urgency of her own position.

Did she have her own inner conflict too? Did she have any hidden ambivalence on her own?

It turned out she did. She loved San Francisco and thought it could be very exciting and different to live there. She wanted Timothy to have his promotion. The extra money would help the family. She had a plan to someday go out on her own as a freelance designer, and this would be a chance for her to do that. Even her son was in favor of the move. He had spent several summers there visiting his favorite cousin.

Leigh took several weeks to wait and see what would happen. We encouraged her not to discuss it too much and not to feel compelled to make a decision just yet. Timothy agreed to go along with this plan.

The next time we discussed Leigh's decision in our group, she told us that she was more aware of her own conflict. Part of her was excited about the idea of moving. "I know what life in Denver is. I could keep doing this, or I could add a whole new adventure to my life. That's a compelling argument," she told us. "The other side of it is, I'm aware of all the loss that would be involved for me: friends, familiar routines, my beloved house, the garden club I've been in for fifteen years. But I know that with any change or risk, there is going to be loss. I can fly back to Denver whenever I want."

The couple finally did decide to make the move, and now Leigh adores San Francisco. She flies back to Denver often to see friends and is still able to remain somewhat active in the garden club.

Balancing Good Will with Self-Care

Balancing good will with self-care is the very heart of Spiritual Partnership. It is a way of providing leadership in your relationship, of resolving conflicts without talking about them, of exhibiting your spirit of good will. It's an ongoing, never-ending task, because you will always find yourself reverting to old habits, either giving in all the time or insisting on your way all the time. The more you strengthen your weaker muscle, the more you will appreciate the importance of it and the easier the balancing act will become. As you take initiative to give more or to take better care of yourself, you will reap great rewards in your relationship.

One of the secrets is to give up old, rigid ideas about fairness and equality. In the same way that you can get trapped into dwelling on who's right and who's wrong, which only leads to conflict, insisting on perfect fairness can also be a trap.

Remember that people's capabilities and propensities are different. For example, both of you may be giving 100 percent of your ability to express emotions. But your 100 percent may look like a gallon, and your partner's 100 percent may look like a teaspoon. Is that equal? Women tend to be demonstrative with affection and verbal affirmations, whereas men show their love by taking care of business, doing things around the house. How do you measure who is giving more? It's pointless and will only make you unhappy.

How do you measure the "fairness" of tasks that take different amounts of time and energy? For example, Barbara does 80 percent of the actual housework measured in time or number of tasks, but her partner's willingness to do all the grocery shopping and to wake up with the children on weekend mornings feels like way more than 20 percent to her. The rest of the housework feels easy to her, even enjoyable, and she knows it would be a burden to her partner. Measured in terms of strict time, this division of labor may be unequal. But if we had a way to measure satisfaction, maybe it could be considered "fair and equal." Measurements are relative and subjective.

Socially and politically speaking, equality remains an important struggle. Some of the inequities between men and women are still appalling. And the equality that has been achieved between men and women has made a difference within individual marriages. In Spiritual Partnership, however, we do not focus on strict definitions of equality and fairness, but rather on a spirit of good will. What we want to measure is not, "Are we giving in exactly equal proportions?" but rather, "Do we feel good? Is this marriage nurturing each of us as individuals?"

What you want to ask yourself is, "Do I feel good about what I am giving and what I am receiving in this relationship? If not, how can I modify what I am doing so that I will feel happy?"

As we've said, the giving-taking balance scale requires that you hone two skills: standing up for your partner, even if it is at your own expense, and standing up for yourself, even if it is at your partner's expense. Let's look at another example of each.

Taking Care of Your Partner

In this story, Diane made a decision to adapt to her partner's need. Richard wanted desperately to go to graduate school in philosophy, and Diane was dead set against it. They had two small children and needed both incomes. Besides, Diane worried that his degree would be useless in terms of increased income for them. I invited the two of them to look carefully at the proposed plan, to lay it out in detail. As they talked, I could see a shift in Diane. She saw how clear Richard was about his desire, how animated he became when he talked about it. She began to come up with suggestions for making the plan work. She also talked about how hard it was going to be for her. She was quite afraid. But she had opened the door a crack, and little by little, she was willing to walk through it. Richard was quite demonstrative with his appreciation.

Taking Care of Yourself

Recently a friend of mine, Tammy, was agonizing because she and her husband had decided that they could not afford for her to fly back east for her best friend's wedding. When I saw her in tears, I questioned her more about the "joint" decision and suggested that this might be a time when she needed to take care of herself, even if it was at her partner's expense. We thought through what it would be like for her simply to announce to her husband, Tom, that she had decided to go.

This idea had never occurred to her, and she determined to try it, as an experiment. When she did, Tom was more surprised than anything. He was angry at first, but the next day they both realized it was a better decision. Tammy felt wonderful. She saw that this was spiritual progress for her, too, because it brightened her inner flame. It raised her consciousness about what was possible for her. And because Tom ended up respecting her for her assertiveness and could see that she was being more her real self after this decision—more relaxed, happier, and stronger—the decision ended up bringing the two of them into closer connection.

EXPERIMENT 15

Balance Giving and Taking

1. In your journal, complete these sentences with the appropriate words:

   In our relationship, I am better at taking care of (myself) (my partner).

   I need to pay better attention to taking care of (myself) (my partner).

2. Make two columns. In one, list ways you have taken care of yourself in the past month or so. In the other, list ways you have taken care of your partner.

3. Make a list of ideas for specific ways you can take better care of yourself in your relationship.

4. Make a list of ideas for specific ways you can take better care of your partner in your relationship.

5. From whichever list represents your "weaker suit," choose two items and make a specific plan to do them within the next couple of days.

6. Make a note in your journal about what you tried and how it worked out.

CHAPTER 7

Loving Action 6

Act on Your Own

It may come as a surprise to you that you don't need to obtain your partner's agreement for everything you do. But after working for many years with individuals and couples, I have found that sometimes acting on your own is the greatest gift you can give to both of you.

For example, Rhonda wanted very much to get season tickets to the ballet, but she could never get her husband, Bill, to agree to it. "I don't like ballet that much," he'd say. "Let's just get tickets to one performance." For several years, that's what they did. Rhonda saw it as a reasonable compromise, but she also felt anguish every time she read the reviews of the performances she was missing.

One year, when she was agonizing over which performance to choose, like a bolt of lightning the idea came to her that she could buy a season ticket for herself! "The amount of time between the instant I got this idea and the time I picked up the phone to order myself a season ticket was a nanosecond," she told me. "I couldn't believe the idea had never occurred to me before." She enjoyed every performance immensely, and the next year, she persuaded a good friend to buy tickets with her. Bill was delighted with this solution, as it easily met both of their needs.

Here's another example: Tina and Max bought a much-needed new car. Their second car was quite old and clunky, possessing no new conveniences like power locks or even power steering. Somehow, from the beginning, there was an unwritten assumption that the new car would be Max's. Occasionally, if Tina had a good reason, such as that she was attending a luncheon, she would ask Max if she could have the new car that day.

One day, Tina found herself asking Max for the nice car, and she felt like an idiot. "It's our car," she said to herself. "Why does Max get to call the shots here?"

After thinking it over all day, that evening Tina said to Max, "Ya know, Honey, I got to thinking, we both like driving the new car. I would enjoy taking it to work more often. From now on, let's alternate. You take it one day, I'll take it the next."

At first, Max came up with a few objections. Remembering Loving Actions 2 and 4, give up problem solving and practice restraint, Tina wisely made the comment, "Just think about it," and then dropped the subject.

The next day, Tina said, "So I'll take the new car today, okay?"

"I've been thinking about it," Max said. "What would feel better to me is if we alternate weeks. Then for a whole week, we can feel like, 'This is my car.'"

"That's an even better idea! I like it," said Tina. "I'll start with today, if that's okay." Then she gave him a big kiss, climbed into the new car, and drove off.

Notice: Tina did not start out by making Max wrong, by pointing out that he wasn't being fair or that he wasn't being thoughtful or considerate. She didn't even bring up the "power struggle," that it had somehow quietly evolved that Max got to have the final word on the new car. She just quietly and firmly changed the power dynamics. She didn't ask for the "power" she needed in this situation; she took it.

By instituting a workable solution, Tina used all six of the Loving Actions we have learned so far:

1. She started out with a spirit of good will and did not blame Max.

2. She didn't try to solve the problem by talking about it. When Max wanted to argue, Tina instantly knew that keeping the atmosphere harmonious was more important than the car thing, and she changed the subject.

3. She didn't care who was right or wrong; instead, she asked herself what she could do to make a change. She did not try to change Max or persuade him that he was wrong.

4. She practiced restraint by refraining from making critical, demanding, or negative comments; being defensive; or fighting.

5. She saw that in this matter, her inner scale felt out of balance; she was giving, but not taking care of her own needs. So she found a way to take better care of herself.

6. She found a way to act on her own, without feeling that she needed Max's consent or agreement.

Ways to Act on Your Own

If you have a need that you feel is not getting met in your relationship, chances are very good that you can find a way to meet that need by acting on your own. Many common problems respond to this Loving Action.

- If your husband hasn't gotten around to trimming the hedge, hire someone to do it.

- If your wife doesn't like to critique movies after seeing them, call some friends who do and have a conversation with them about it.

- If your husband is withdrawn and preoccupied when he comes home at the end of the day, use that time to call a friend and share your day with her.

- If your wife spends too much time talking on the phone in the evenings, take her out to dinner occasionally or plan other times when you can have her attention.

- If your partner spends too much time on the Internet, either take an interest in it yourself so you can do some of it together or spend the time on a hobby of your own.

When you can find a humorous way to address the problem, so much the better. One woman told me that her husband kept putting off fixing the leaky bathtub faucet in the spare bathroom, so she put the plug in the bathtub! When he saw the tub filling up, he got the point.

Another man told me that he couldn't get his wife to stop picking lint off his suits. So he put a little thread on his lapel—that was attached to a spool of thread in his pocket. Their children got a huge laugh when she tried to remove that piece of lint!

It is impossible to describe acting on your own in complete detail, because it requires something different in every situation. Sometimes the most significant part of it is just realizing that you have the option of acting on your own; the needed action will be obvious. But sometimes the solution isn't obvious, and you have to free up your creative energy, be brazen, and do the outrageous.

Dallas radio personality Susie Humphreys made us all laugh out loud when she told us that she threw her own surprise party. After fifteen years of hinting, she figured her husband was never going to get the idea. So one night at a gathering of friends, she announced that she was going to surprise herself with a party and told everyone to save the date. They all laughed—until they received their invitations in the mail. Susie included a little map and told people to park around the corner so she wouldn't be suspicious. She filled her house with helium balloons and a big sign that said, "We love you Susie!" Then she assigned two of her best friends to take her out for a drink so people would have time to gather. When she arrived, the house was dark. Then the lights came on and everyone yelled "Surprise!" And Susie cried!

If You Don't Take Care of Yourself, Who Will?

You are the only person who knows what you want, where you feel deprived, and what changes will make you happier. No one else can climb inside you and find out what you truly want, what your fondest hopes and dreams for yourself are. And no one else can make those dreams come true.

No one else is ever going to take a nap for you. No one else can! And what's more, no one else may even notice that this need didn't get met.

If you forget an appointment or forget to make dinner for your children, other people will care! But if you want to take dance lessons and you put this off for months and then for years, only you will miss out. If it is going to happen, you need to make it happen for yourself.

No one else cares about the quality of your life as much as you do.

Where are you neglecting yourself? Is this neglect a trade-off you are willing to make for the sake of some other goal you value even more? Or would you feel better if you acted on your own to fill this void in your life or to correct this imbalance?

Julia's Spiritual Solution

Listen to how Julia "outgrew her problem" by acting on her own rather than trying to "solve the problem" by persuading her partner to change.

Julia was a salesperson for business-related software and made a good income. She was married to a man, Rick, who was having a hard time with his career. He had a low tolerance for bureaucratic regulations and wasn't much of a company man. And the business he had started on his own had run into problems. Rick was proud of his determination to do something meaningful and useful, and had confidence in his abilities. He kept telling Julia he just needed time to figure it all out.

Julia agreed with Rick's values and loved his independent spirit, but they had four children and needed two incomes. She understood that she couldn't "help" Rick figure out what to do. She made a few suggestions, but she knew that this was Rick's problem and that he had to work it out on his own. She was patient and supportive. They did have some savings and would be okay for a while.

As one year stretched into two, Julia became more and more anxious. She and Rick had several fights, which was unusual for them. Julia found that as she lay awake on sleepless nights, what was going through her head were ideas for making more money on her own. One of these ideas began to excite her: she had been a craftsperson years ago, and she thought she could design a bracelet that might appeal to high-end fashion stores. One weekend, she gathered all the materials she would need and went to work. One of her daughters became very interested in working with her. In six weeks, they felt they had a sufficient number of samples to begin showing the work. The first two stores they tried made an order!

After several more months of work, Julia and her daughter took the bracelets to a gift show, where they wrote enough orders to keep them busy for a year and to supplement the family income.

If this family were operating as a Stage Two relationship, it is easy to imagine Julia's becoming angrier and angrier with Rick, blaming him for the problem, pointing out how unfair he was being, trying to convince him that he should just take a job, and focusing more and more attention on "the problem." Julia would have been "right," but that approach would have led to a most unhappy and upset family.

By *acting on her own* in a spirit of good will, Julia instead created a very happy family. She and her daughter became closer. Rick was given the gift of the time he needed to find his passion. And the income problem got handled.

But notice: this solution was not based on what Julia thought was fair or reasonable. She was not asking, "Who is right and who is wrong?" but rather, "What can I do to help out here?" She did not solve the problem by talking it over with Rick, and she was not badgering him to change. She believed that he was doing the best he could and that her support would be far more helpful to him than putting pressure on him. Julia put herself in charge of getting her own needs met, and her spirit of generosity was a gift to both of them.

The Heart of Spiritual Partnership

Shifting from hoping your partner will take care of your needs to being willing to take care of yourself is at the heart of Spiritual Partnership. When you are getting what you want, even if you had to make it happen yourself, you will feel increased inner power and self-love. As you gain respect for yourself and an increased sense of well-being, giving generously to your partner will become a pleasure too. You will be able to give without feeling resentful.

Acting on your own is spiritual because when you act on your own, you are moving toward connection, not separation. You will be helping your authentic self to emerge. You will be expanding your consciousness about your own capabilities. And you will definitely be moving toward happiness and well-being.

Two Important Guidelines for Acting on Your Own

I've found in my work with individuals and couples over the years that the following guidelines are essential when taking the initiative with unilateral action.

Be Careful When You Are Ambivalent

It is best not to act on your own when you are ambivalent, especially if your act will have an impact on someone else or if you are acting over the objection of someone else. Save this Loving Action for situations that feel truly "nonnegotiable" to you. When you aren't sure exactly what you want, that may be the time to go along with your partner's clearer desires. If you act assertively and then later realize you may have made a mistake, it's far too easy for your partner to come back and say, "I told you so." Also, acting on your own has a greater impact for good if you reserve it for things that are truly important to you.

Be Empathic **and** *Decisive*

When you act on your own to do something that you know may make your partner unhappy, the way that you tell your partner what you plan to do is critically important. *You must always use two steps:* first, express understanding of your mate's position; second, be clear that you will not be dissuaded from your own. In other words, be both empathic and decisive. When you are empathic, you take care of your spouse to the best of your ability. When you are decisive, you take care of yourself.

For example, when I once took a trip to New York over the objections of my husband, I said something like this: "I agree this is a strain on our finances. I realize it makes you uncomfortable for me to spend this money. And I'm sorry about that. (empathy) But I'm very clear that I would be just crushed to miss this trip. It feels to me like one of the most important opportunities I have ever had. I've decided I'm going." (decisiveness)

Because expressing empathy does not come naturally to most of us, you may find it useful to memorize a few sentences or to keep a bookmark at this page so that whenever you are going to act on your own and you need to be empathic and decisive, you will have the words ready. Here are some useful empathic-and-decisive statements.

I don't blame you for feeling _____. I'd feel that way too if I were you. But I'm very clear that I need to do this for myself.

I know you don't feel good about this, and I am really sorry about that. That is not why I am doing this. I'm very clear that I need to do this for myself.

I agree with you that _____. And I feel bad that it is making you unhappy. But deep inside, I know I could not live with myself if I didn't do this. It is very important to me for my own spiritual growth.

Remember, *you do not need to persuade your partner that you are right.* If your partner becomes angry or tries to change your mind, do not argue back. Just continue to be empathic and decisive. "I don't blame you for being upset. I can understand why you feel the way you do. But this is very, very important to me, and I am going to do it. I'm genuinely sorry you don't like this, but I have to honor my own strong inner needs."

Your Partner's Response

When you act on your own, your partner will have a response.

Surprisingly often, the response will be positive. Most people want to be married to a capable, independent, fully functioning adult, and they will like the person they see taking charge. Your decisive clarity emanating from your increasingly spiritual essence is likely to be appealing to your partner. Even if what you are doing makes your partner angry for the moment, in the long run your mate is likely to be attracted to the inner calm and happiness that you are exhibiting by being clear about what you want and willing to take care of yourself.

In some cases, your partner may be upset by your emerging independence. Your unilateral action is a seemingly abrupt change that your mate wasn't expecting and doesn't know how to explain or respond to. Especially if your partner is used to having all the power in your relationship or if you have a long-standing habit of acquiescing most of the time, your solo actions may seem threatening. Because you are upsetting a well-established pattern in your relationship, you may both feel confused and uneasy for a while.

Don't let this stop you. Avoid arguing with your partner. Remember what Tina said when Max started arguing about her taking the new car: "Just think about it." Drop the subject rather than "discuss" it. Continue to be both empathic and decisive. Remain firm in your conviction. Your partner will most likely respect you for this as time goes on and you both become more used to the new relationship pattern you are creating. Or your partner may become angry and punishing or may try to control you. You are not responsible for your partner's reaction, and you don't have to fix it or make your partner feel happy about your decision. Just keep being empathic and decisive.

In the vast majority of situations in which you act on your own, you will be eliminating a problem that has been difficult for both of you, and your partner will love you for it. Most of the time, you can meet your own needs without disturbing your partner at all. In fact, you will be supporting your partner as well as yourself.

A man who attended an all-day workshop of mine without his wife spoke with me several months later. I was quite impressed with how much of the general message of Spiritual Partnership he had absorbed. He told me this story:

> My wife and I were experiencing a lot of tension about church. She wanted me to go with her every Sunday, and I had made a clear decision within me that I did not want to attend church at all. We were deeply enmeshed in the belief that if we could just talk this through enough, we could somehow arrive at a solution. And we were exhausted trying.
>
> When I heard you say that you can't solve problems by talking them through and that you don't have to solve all your problems to be happy, I can still remember the huge relief that swept over me. There was a rightness about this idea that made me feel incredibly relaxed.
>
> I decided to act on my own and to be very decisive about my choice. So instead of just hanging around on Sunday morning, so there was always this implication that this time maybe I'd go with her, I planned every Sunday morning for myself. I'd go hiking, go to an art museum, or plan some other definite activity.

I knew I would feel better. But what amazed me is the impact that my actions had on her. We stopped arguing. She never brought it up again. The issue disappeared. Suddenly, it was not a problem anymore, it was a fact of life, and we both adapted to it.

I never told my wife I had a "strategy." I never told her anything about what I learned in the workshop. It makes it a lot of fun for me to experiment. Of course, it is obvious that we are much happier together now, but we don't talk much about why.

Acting on Your Own Solves Two Common Marital Problems

Two of the most common problems for couples are (1) "My partner is not affectionate and loving enough. We don't have enough gentle touching," and (2) "My partner takes me for granted. I just don't get complimented or praised or thanked nearly enough. Sometimes I feel as though my partner doesn't even notice the things I do."

Both of these problems will disappear when you act on your own.

The Desire for More Affection

Let's say you don't get enough affection from your partner. You can solve this problem by initiating affection on your own. One workshop participant told me this, more than a year after our work together:

> For years I felt sad that we weren't a more physically close couple. Our sex life was okay, but I was married before, and I loved the way my former husband was always grabbing me up to hug me or plant a big kiss on my lips. We'd hold hands when

we walked, or cuddle up while we watched TV. Unfortunately, he was alcoholic, and it didn't work out. But I missed that so much in my present marriage.

At your suggestion, I started initiating affectionate touching on my own. Bob responded just fine. Now, I would call us a pretty lovey-dovey couple, but I initiate virtually all of it. That's totally fine with me! Once I gave up the useless idea that it didn't mean anything unless he initiated it, I started getting everything I wanted. Now, we are so used to kissing before we leave in the morning and just before we go to sleep at night that he'll seek me out for a kiss if I forget!

A key idea here was that this woman "gave up the idea that it didn't mean anything unless he initiated it." When she touched her husband or gave him a hug or kiss, there was no judgment in her action whatsoever, no resentment, no irony. And that is always important when you offer affection. You need to do it graciously, generously, as a free gift with no strings attached, no blame, and no expectations that your partner will change.

An extremely effective and much underused form of affection is the freely offered, nondemanding smile. Anytime you are together, just glance over at your mate and smile, then look away. You are not asking for anything; you don't have to wait for a reason to smile. Just catch your partner's eye and smile. It can be a little knowing smile, an "I feel happy" smile, a big smile, raised eyebrows, or just the tiniest little bit of a smile. It might include a little wink or not. Right now, as you are reading this, practice a few different types of smiles.

You can toss your partner a little gift smile anytime. Maybe you are in the middle of a conversation, puttering around in the kitchen, about to get into the car, playing with the children, standing on the subway train together. You can smile when you are feeling good just to convey that. Or you can smile when you are feeling blue or stressed out, as a mini-act-as-if smile. It is a gift to your partner, and it will make you feel good. It's free, legal, nonfattening, and nonpolluting, and doesn't take extra time.

A spontaneous, no-special-reason, warm smile is a little spiritual move toward connection. It is one of the easiest and most powerful ways to create harmony by acting on your own, no matter what else is going on around you.

Don't take my word for it, try it. Experiment.

It may be that when you initiate affection toward your partner, he or she will not respond warmly in return. Try to refrain from any judgments about this. Though it may be a challenge for you, don't take your mate's lack of response personally. Your partner is just being himself or herself. Keep gently offering affection, but keep it at a level that seems comfortable for your partner. Your job as a spiritual leader is to take care of your own needs *and* your mate's needs at the same time, as much as possible. As you experiment over time, you will be able to achieve a level that works for both of you. It could be that you are with someone who is never going to be the warm, cuddly teddy bear you fantasize. But this person has other wonderful qualities that you love. Think about those and allow the level of affection you have when you take as much initiative as you can to be just fine. You can't change it, so go with it. But keep initiating affection if that is what you like.

The Desire for Affirmation, Compliments, and Praise

Acting on your own also works for eliciting the verbal affirmations you crave. Workshop participants are always skeptical about this one and spend a lot of time role playing it as if it were absurd. But all you need to do is take the idea seriously and try it once, and you'll be hooked. I use this particular strategy in my own relationship all the time.

Suppose your partner never comments on your appearance, your cooking, your parenting, your generosity, or whatever else you know you are good at. Your partner takes all your good qualities for granted and just never thinks to mention them.

The solution to this problem is amazingly simple: wait until the two of you are alone and then offer a self-affirming statement, something like this:

I changed the oil in both of the cars this weekend. It always feels good to me to keep up with that.

I feel so good about the way this party went. I loved the candles, and I thought the table looked so beautiful.

I just love this dress on me. The color is so good, and it's slenderizing. Don't you think?

You don't even need to end your comment with a question. Your partner is likely to say something like, "Yeah, you're right. The table did look nice," or "That is a lovely dress. You're gorgeous in it," or even the standard "Honey, you always look beautiful." But even if he or she doesn't respond at all, you have accomplished your purpose: you have brought about your partner's participation in acknowledging something you feel good about.

Another strategy is to tell your mate about compliments you have received from others. "You know, several people actually mentioned how pretty they thought the table looked tonight. It made me feel good because I spent so much time on it. I'm really good at this sort of thing." "It's true, Honey, you really are," your mate may reply.

We sometimes think of scant or nonexistent verbal affirmations as a male propensity. Gender difference specialists tell us that the part of a man's brain that feels emotions doesn't talk. I have found that when I ask my husband, Mayer, whether he appreciates something I did, he says he does, and he will be amazed that I didn't know this. He was actually thinking it, but his thought didn't make it over to the verbal part of his brain.

But in my experience, women fall short on offering verbal appreciations too. When our sweetheart does something that was his job anyway, we don't think to say anything. After all, that's what he was supposed to do.

Men often rely on their competence, dependability, and thoughtfulness as a way to express their love, and they want these qualities to be recognized. They enjoy being appreciated for just going about their daily routine, especially when their daily routine contributes to the family.

So it is important for you, both men and women, to learn to *acknowledge your own accomplishments in the presence of your loved one.* You can receive all the verbal affirmation you crave by acting on your own in this important way.

One man told me this:

> Donna's mother was coming for a visit, and I went to some trouble to rearrange my work schedule so the visit would go well. Donna never said anything about this. Before, I would have felt resentful and unappreciated. But I tried "acting on my own." I just casually told her what I had done, and she was in fact very appreciative. But I don't think she ever would have mentioned it on her own. She was too preoccupied with other details of the visit.

It feels wonderful when someone compliments you spontaneously. But when that doesn't happen, would you rather sulk and be sad, complain to a friend, and continue to feel deprived? Or would you rather act on your own and find a way to meet the need yourself, thus brightening your life and everyone else's too?

Feeling deprived of affection or verbal affirmations will melt away when you act on your own to meet these needs. Try it and you'll see.

Don't Neglect Your Passionate Desires

I have a friend whose business is creating large displays for store windows and trade shows. She's extremely creative and loves working on a large scale. A monumental hero figure in her life is the artist Christo, who creates works of art the size of buildings or even entire countrysides or islands.

One day she heard that Christo was looking for volunteers to help him wrap the Bundestag building in Berlin. She became riveted on this opportunity. It was a fantasy almost beyond her imagining, something she thought was too outrageous even to contemplate, and she passionately, with all her heart, wanted to volunteer.

Her husband was against it.

She sold some family jewelry to pay for the trip, arranged for her aunt to watch her children, and made it happen for herself. She came home elated, a changed person. She had fulfilled a dream.

In the end, her husband saw that this was the right thing for her to do and rejoiced with her.

In contrast, I know a woman, now ninety-one, who started a jewelry business in her home when she was twenty years old. She learned about gems and went to New York on buying trips. When she married at age twenty-seven, her husband took over the business and decided to sell cheaper costume jewelry. My friend never worked in the business again; her job was to stay home and raise the children. She went through her whole life angry that she was never allowed to pursue her own dream. "Why didn't she go off and start her own jewelry business?" we all wonder now. "Why didn't she insist on taking over a part of the 'family' business, starting a branch with fine jewelry?" Of course in the years all this was happening, there was no support for women who wanted to act on their own, and probably, at some level, she never truly realized that any of these choices was an option for her. She poisoned her marriage all those years with her resentment and never figured out a way to act on her own, to make her own dreams come true.

In an interview, psychiatric nurse Roseanne Packard told me, "There is no cancer like regret." She called deep, passionate desires "life agenda items." "Marriage should never stop you from fulfilling a life dream," she said. "Just because you marry, you do not relinquish your most primitive longings."

If you have a "life agenda item" that truly matters to you, act on your own. Don't wait for support; create your own. It is truly a blessing to know what you want to do in your heart of hearts. Never to do it is a tragedy.

Both your smaller, everyday desires and your life agenda items are equally important. Practice acting on your own with smaller desires and be willing to act on your own for the dreams in your life that truly matter.

Acting on your own is a powerful Loving Action.

Acting on Your Own Creates Balance in Your Relationship

The minute you take charge of a situation and are no longer dependent on your partner to obtain the results you seek, whether they are smaller desires or life agenda items, you have more control over your own life.

And you will be giving a gift to your partner also, by freeing up an area of your lives together that may have been stuck. Usually your partner will be heartened to see you happier, more independent, maybe even fulfilling a life dream.

Think of a way you can act decisively about something you deeply want, some way in which you can take initiative, be proactive, and meet your own needs without depending on your partner.

As Goethe said, "Begin it now."

Taking a Stand When Your Limits Have Been Violated

As we've seen, you can't solve a problem by trying to persuade your partner to change. This strategy doesn't honor your partner, and it never works.

However, there are times when you need to let your mate know that you have reached your limit with his or her behavior. When your partner is doing something that violates your own boundary, you need to take a stand. Your partner cannot yell at you, manipulate you, ignore you, be rude to you, be too hard on your children, or, certainly, abuse you, *without your compliance*. You may not be able to change your partner, but you can take care of yourself. Indeed, if you want to grow spiritually, you *must* take care of yourself.

Dealing with Temper, Anger, and Violence

Krysta's husband, Frank, was an intelligent man who ran his own nautical equipment shop. He read voraciously, and once single-handedly defeated a team of five other people at Trivial Pursuit. Krysta loved these qualities about him. But—Frank had a violent

EXPERIMENT 16

Act on Your Own

1. Review the list of problems you drew up in Experiment 1. With regard to each one, think, "Is there a way I could make an impact on this problem by acting on my own?" If there is, try it.

2. If you don't already do this, experiment with initiating affection with your partner. Later, make notes in your journal about how this is going.

3. Think of something you would like your partner to notice and appreciate. The next time you see him or her, acknowledge yourself for this thing as suggested earlier. Later, make notes in your journal about what happened and how it made you feel.

4. Sometime today or tomorrow, smile at your partner and then look away, a nondemand, no-special-reason smile. If you like this, don't forget about it. Do it again every now and then.

5. In your journal, make a wish list for yourself of desires and goals. They can be tiny little goals or great big life agenda items. Star the life agenda items or put them in a separate list.

   For each item on the list(s), ask yourself what would be required to achieve this desire or goal. If you discover something you are not willing to wait for, is there an action you can take to start the ball in motion?

   Remember: if you don't take care of yourself, who will?

temper and sometimes became critical and self-righteous toward both Krysta and their two daughters, who were nine and twelve when I met them. Sometimes he even grabbed the children and shook and frightened them. Frank's outbursts upset Krysta terribly. She would fight back, but never felt on an equal footing with him. Frank always "won." Sometimes after an outburst, the two of them wouldn't speak for three or four days. Then eventually Krysta would make a peace gesture, and life would be okay for a while, until the next episode.

Krysta was desperate when she came to one of my groups. "I want to do something about this, but I have no idea what to do."

At some level, Krysta was allowing these outbursts to continue because she couldn't find a way to communicate to Frank that she would not tolerate them. As a result, not only did there continue to be upset in the family, but the situation took a toll on Krysta's self-esteem, too. She began to believe that she was powerless. It is hard to feel good about yourself when, day after day, you feel like the victim of an intolerable situation.

So how might Krysta take a stand in this situation?

Here is a set of guidelines for taking a stand, for communicating to your partner that your limits of tolerance have been reached and that you will not allow yourself to be treated this way any longer.

The First Steps: Preparing to Take Your Stand

1. If you feel afraid or reluctant to act, enlist the help of a friend or support person. Do not try to do this alone. Stay in close touch with your friend throughout all these steps.

2. Admit that what you are about to do is difficult. You may feel afraid: afraid of how your mate will react, afraid that you won't be able to pull it off, afraid of what the consequences might be. That's

natural. Just be clear that you don't have to wait until your fears go away before you take these steps. Feel your fear and take a stand anyway. Courage is not the absence of fear; courage is the ability to act in the presence of fear.

3. Decide exactly what you want to declare to your mate. When you take a stand, you are not asking your partner to change. You are also not willing to negotiate. So you need to have your plan crystal clear in your own mind.

If what you are declaring is a change in your own behavior, your task is easier. For example, one man in our group simply told his wife that he would no longer attend choir practice with her on Thursday evenings. He realized that he had felt manipulated into going and that he did not want to continue. Acting on his own, he was both empathic and decisive.

What's more difficult is taking a stand about something your partner is doing. In this case, your "stand" will consist of two parts: stating (1) exactly what you are no longer willing to tolerate, and (2) exactly what you will do if the behavior occurs again.

Creating Consequences

The hardest part of taking a stand is always figuring out what consequences you will carry out if the behavior occurs again.

Here's where you have to be creative. Brainstorm with some of your friends for ideas. If you are not ready to separate from this person, thinking up your consequence can be a challenge.

Krysta's limit was Frank's anger and violence toward their girls. For a consequence, she told him that if he ever became violent with them again, she would ask a protective services worker to come and talk with them both. (I'll tell you how this strategy turned out in a moment.)

Another couple I spoke with, Sue and Rick, were feuding because she refused to get a job. They both agreed they needed her income. But she had been working for two years to start a mail-order business, and even though it was actually draining their resources, she didn't want to give up and go back to a more regular job. Rick told Sue that if she didn't get a job within three months, he would take a second job that would keep him away from home every evening. Sue enjoyed their evenings at home and desperately needed his help with the children. She knew her guilt would be unbearable if Rick were working two jobs. His consequence worked with her.

Here are some other consequences couples have established:

- For leaving newspapers strewn all over the house: I will stop our subscription to the daily paper.

- For not throwing dirty laundry in the hamper: I will stop doing your laundry.

- For talking on the phone for more than forty-five minutes after dinner: I will disconnect our phone. (This had been mutually agreed on.)

- For making critical remarks: I will go out with friends every evening for ten weekdays in a row.

- For failing to get the screens put up for six weeks after warm weather began: I will hire someone to put them up.

- For yelling at me: I will start seeing a therapist (even though they both felt they could not afford this).

Taking Your Stand

4. Decide whether you want to write a letter to your partner, with the understanding that he or she will read it in your presence

and you will then discuss it, or whether you want to speak directly to your mate. The advantage of writing your limits in a letter is that you will be giving a clear signal that this concern is different and special and that you really mean business. You also avoid the possibility of losing your nerve or becoming fuzzy-headed in the middle of your conversation. But either way can be effective.

5. Whether you write a letter or pick a time to make a verbal announcement, *begin with something positive.* Even if it is just, "Honey, you know I love you. And there is something I need to tell you," this makes a difference. It's even better to be specific: "Honey, the garden looks gorgeous. I get so much pleasure from it. You are really good," or "Thank you so much for taking the kids to a movie yesterday. That was thoughtful, and I appreciate it." Positive comments like these do not need to be part of the same conversation. Just be sure that sometime in the recent past, you have behaved lovingly or said something warm and kind to your partner. Difficult conversations will go more smoothly if you have deliberately created a loving atmosphere first.

People can always accept bad news more easily if they hear good news first. Don't skip this step. Make it genuine.

6. Speak or write only with "I" statements; avoid "you" statements altogether. Never say, "You are too hard on the children. You lose your temper too often." Instead say, "I am not willing to stand by when you hit the children anymore. I feel horrible when it happens. I have reached my limit."

7. State your position very simply. Do not give elaborate explanations or illustrations. Do not drag up past incidents. Do not give reasons for your position. Your partner might start arguing with the reasons or explanations and get the whole thing off track. For example, if Krysta were to say, "Your outbursts are hard on the children," Frank could say, "No, they aren't. Discipline is good for

them." This is beside the point. What Frank needs to get is that Krysta is not willing to tolerate the outbursts anymore—for whatever reasons. You don't owe your spouse any reasons; you have a right to your position. *The more simply you can state your position, the stronger it will be.* Usually, your letter or statement will be very short, just a few sentences or even one.

8. When you take a stand, your mate will react in some way—possibly with anger, defensiveness, pleading, or silence.

Remember, you are not responsible for your partner's response, and you do not need to make your mate feel better. You are not causing your mate to feel bad; you are doing what is right for you. Focus on that. Here again be both empathic and decisive. You can express genuine concern and understanding: "I'm really sorry if this makes you angry," or "I don't blame you for feeling bad about his. I know this is a very hard problem for you." But you should never try either to "fix" your partner's pain or to blame yourself for it. You cannot be both the disease and the doctor. The most loving thing you can do for your partner is to be decisive and firm about your position, and understanding about your partner's feelings.

9. If you need to take a stand with your partner about something that is seriously dangerous or threatening, consider asking for professional support. If there has been physical abuse or destruction of property, you can ask a police officer to "stand by" as you let your mate know that you will no longer tolerate abusive, destructive behavior. If you are a woman and are afraid your husband might become violent when you take a stand, call a shelter for battered women. An experienced person will be able to guide and assist you.

Revisiting Krysta and Frank

Let's return to Krysta and Frank to see what happened when she announced that she would call a protective services worker if Frank became abusive with the children ever again. Because Krysta had never before taken a stand with Frank on this matter—she had only cried and distanced herself and made it obvious she was unhappy—her consequence startled Frank and made him realize she was serious. For a time, her declaration seemed to have the desired effect. But inevitably Frank lost his temper again, and Krysta, without hesitating, actually called a protective services worker. It helped that she was in a weekly support group and was being coached and reminded every week about what she needed to do.

The protective services worker made an appointment to visit Frank and Krysta at their home. Frank made an excuse and didn't show up for the appointment, but Krysta learned a great deal from the social worker about alternatives for protecting her children from Frank's outbursts. Then the worker sought out Frank at his place of employment. After some time, he agreed to attend an anger abatement workshop run by the county.

Once you decide on a plan, your consequences must be immediate and inevitable the very next time the behavior occurs. If you hesitate for a moment or your partner agrees to try harder and you give in, you have not taken your stand. That's okay. Because taking a stand is something new for you, it may take you a while to get the hang of it. Remember that in spiritual work, we are always more interested in the journey than the destination. If you "chicken out" on your consequences, for any reason, remember that this whole exercise is an experiment. Look back at your behavior. Don't judge yourself. You did the best you could! But do see what you can learn about yourself from this incident. You will learn, not just by having an experience but by having an experience *and then reflecting on it*. Write about it in your journal; talk with a friend. Then start over and take your stand again.

EXPERIMENT 17

Take a Stand

Is your partner doing something that you can no longer tolerate? Carefully follow the steps we've discussed, and take a stand.

Remember, your partner cannot "get away with" any behavior without your compliance. Figure out a way to interrupt the destructive cycle and take action.

Acting on your own and taking a stand are primary tools for taking care of yourself in your relationship. If you aren't willing to take care of your own needs, the whole system of Spiritual Partnership will collapse, because you can't give endlessly without filling up your own cup as well. Acting on your own is the most direct way to identify what you are missing in your relationship and to find a way to fill in that hole by yourself. The stronger and more self-sufficient a partner you become, the more you will contribute to the health of your relationship.

If you have never been a strong, assertive person, or if you come from a family in which one of your parents was timid and unassertive, acting on your own will have a steep learning curve for you. It may not come naturally or easily for you.

That's okay. What is important in spirituality is moving in the right direction, not being there already. Standing up for yourself is what you need to work on. Take baby steps. Figure out one small way in which you are not standing up for yourself and one small action you can take to act on your own. This is the cutting edge of your own spiritual growth. You won't believe how wonderful you will feel when you stop blaming your partner and take positive action for yourself. You will want more of that feeling of inner strength, and you will be on your way.

CHAPTER 8

Loving Action 7

Practice Acceptance

When you encounter something you don't like in your partner, you have two options: (1) feel upset about it and work on getting your partner to change, or (2) accept it and discover welcome changes in yourself and your partner that may surprise you.

Option two is the spiritual choice.

It is also the more effective choice if you seek to bring about change in your relationship, because people change, not in an atmosphere of criticism, complaining, or demanding, but in an atmosphere of love and support.

Acceptance Is the Starting Point for Change

Amanda tried for years to get her husband to do certain things differently when they made love. If she talked about the changes she wanted, her husband would change maybe once or twice and then revert to his old ways. Amanda had the illusion that if she could only explain what she wanted in the right language or at the right time, she could get him to understand how much better her way would be. She kept working with it, gently and with patience, but relentlessly.

One day a friend said to her, "Well, you married a great story-teller and a fabulous dancer, a gorgeous, generous guy with an awesome business, but I guess you didn't get Casanova along with the deal."

The casual remark set off a light bulb in Amanda. It was like a stunning insight. She suddenly realized that maybe she could let go of wanting something different in sex. Maybe she could just accept her husband exactly the way he really was. Maybe she could let go of wanting a different outcome and take what she had. She realized she felt a little sad about this, but the relief she felt at not having to "work at it" anymore more than made up for the feeling of loss.

She didn't have a problem. She had a fact of life.

What happened to Amanda's sex life was remarkable. By letting herself experience what was actually happening instead of superimposing on her real experience that it somehow wasn't enough, she found a whole new freedom and pleasure. She was amazed to see that it was she who was casting a pall over their sex life—just by failing to accept what she had and by instead judging and trying to "improve" it.

Accepting something doesn't mean you have to like it; it means you stop fighting it. It means you let go of wanting a different outcome. Your own ability to behave in a loving and accepting way toward your partner, no matter what, is more likely to bring about positive change than any amount of strategizing or communication.

Think of an ongoing conflict in your relationship. For example, Marcia feels that Todd is overly negative and pessimistic. (Substitute your own real issue.)

Marcia has two basic options for making this problem disappear: (1) she can work on Todd to help him become a less negative person, or (2) she can accept Todd the way he is and find a way to work with his negativity.

"Working on" Your Partner

We have already discussed option one at some length. If Marcia tries, however gently, to negotiate with Todd to become less negative,

- She will be setting herself up as right and Todd as wrong.
- She will be creating conflict and upset, not harmony.
- She will be giving Todd the underlying message that he is not okay, that she would love him more if he changed.
- She will be making it hard for Todd to feel close to her.
- She will unwittingly evoke defensiveness from Todd rather than cooperation. In other words, Todd's negativity is more likely to persist *precisely because* she is criticizing it.
- She is not likely to solve the problem.

Of course, in spite of its drawbacks, option one is still the more widely attempted problem-solving method in the world. It is the Stage Two relationship strategy.

Accepting Your Partner

Option two is to accept your partner just exactly the way he or she really is, to accept the behavior you don't like or the personality trait you would change if you had a magic wand. You recognize that when you fell in love with this person, you fell in love with a whole package, and you don't get to choose little parts of it to send back and exchange.

Accepting your partner has many advantages over trying to change him or her. When you work on accepting your partner,

- You will be focusing on your own spiritual growth, viewing the "problem" as an opportunity to develop your inner peace, your ability to love and tolerate.

- You will be creating peace within yourself (whereas annoyance toward your spouse will cause *you* ongoing suffering).

- You will be supporting your partner by offering the most important gift anyone can give: the message, "You are accepted. You don't have to change to be a good person."

- You will be actively creating harmony in your relationship and avoiding upset.

- You will be "outgrowing" this problem by developing a new level of consciousness rather than assuming you can "solve" the problem through your own clever ways.

- Perhaps most important, you will be creating an atmosphere in which true transformation (for example, in Todd's negativity) is likely to occur.

Again, accepting something does not mean you like it. It doesn't mean you approve of it or that you respect it. It simply means that you stop fighting it. You stop wasting your precious energy railing against something that you can't change by an act of your own will. You graciously let go and allow the universe to be the way it is. Your partner is not likely to change deeply entrenched characteristics. But if you accept them, gradually over time the qualities you dislike will cease to be a problem. Your partner will evolve. Your acceptance will make an impact.

Let's look at another example where acceptance created the change that years of badgering had failed to effect. Meredith and Sam had been married five years and were generally very happy together. But Meredith was quite distressed when she came to see me. Whenever they got together with friends, which was quite often, Sam would interrupt other people with what Meredith considered to be corny humor. She would talk with Sam about it, and he would agree to cut back, but he never did. Meredith clearly was laboring under the illusion that if only she could choose the right words, if only she could find an effective way to convey to Sam how annoying his habit was, he would see her point and stop. She wanted me to help her find a way to communicate with Sam.

Instead, I said to her, "What if Sam never gets your point about this? What if he forever goes on interrupting people with his corny humor? Maybe he is never going to become the gracious social person you hope for."

The idea came as a shock to Meredith. We discussed it for a while, and I could see that this was a genuinely new idea to her. Before my very eyes, I could see a shift take place in her. She relaxed. She even laughed at herself. "Gee," she said. "Maybe that wouldn't be so awful." What a concept!

When I spoke with her several weeks later, she told me that a great weight had lifted from her shoulders. On several social occasions, she noticed that other people apparently did not find Sam so annoying. Or even if they did, so what? She realized it was not her problem. "I'm having a lot more fun at these gatherings," she told me. "By superimposing this standard on Sam, I was torturing myself. Now, all that is gone, and I just let Sam be the way he is. I even laugh at his jokes myself sometimes, and he loves that. He even mentioned it. And he makes me laugh at home more. I was actually standing in the way of our having more fun! In a million years, I would never have guessed that I was the problem here."

What most people do not realize is that *only when you accept what is will change ever occur*. What you resist will persist because it is invested in its own survival. When you accept something, only then do you set into motion the circumstances that will allow either you or it to change. Let us look in more detail at this little-understood fact of life. Then we will talk more about exactly how you can practice acceptance within your relationship.

How Change Happens in Spiritual Partnership

Accepting the way a person is does *not* mean that that person will never change. Quite the contrary; as paradoxical as it may sound, *accepting that which is unchangeable is the starting point for deep and genuine change.*

   To understand how acceptance is the starting point for change, let's begin by looking at the opposite.

The Impact of Criticism

As we've seen, when you try to persuade someone to change, the person will probably resist your efforts and is unlikely to transform. We will look in more detail now at why this is true.

   Let's return to one of the examples that opened this chapter, in which Marcia kept trying to persuade Todd to be less negative.

   Todd is negative by nature. Negativity and pessimism are a "mask" or defense he adopted early in his life to give himself a feeling of control. Negativity is his way of staying safe. At some deep, unconscious level, Todd believes that his negative worldview is necessary for his survival. To threaten his negativity is to threaten his very existence. This may not seem true to the rest of us, but it is true inside Todd.

   It therefore makes perfect sense for Todd to fight to keep his negativity alive. When Marcia assaults his negativity, his reaction is to strengthen it all the more! He believes his very survival depends on it.

I had a personal experience of this early in my own spiritual growth. I must have been reinforced as a child for my big smile and cheerful demeanor. So I somehow got the message that smiling equaled survival. When in doubt, smile. When in trouble, smile. When feeling fragile, smile. When I became an adult, people told me they found my persistent smile to be inauthentic. I was stunned and upset! I now see that at some level, trying to live without my smile terrified me. The level of fear was irrational. I felt as though I would disappear. I recall trying to give a presentation without smiling, as an experiment, and finding myself so panicked that I could not continue. *So I returned to smiling with even more conviction.*

My pasted-on smile was fighting with great passion for its own survival. At some level I believed that my smiling habit was the key to my survival, that without my ability to smile my way through fear, I would die.

This may sound melodramatic, but I assure you, it's true.

Psychologist Harville Hendrix explains deep survival instincts physiologically. The brain, he says in *Getting the Love You Want*, is divided into two basic parts, which he calls the "old brain" and the "new brain." The old brain links us with all other living things on the planet, because "all vertebrates from reptiles to mammals share this portion of the anatomy," and with the history of the development of life on the planet.

> [Y]ou are unaware of most of the function of your old brain. . . . Scientists . . . tell us that its main concern is self-preservation. Ever on the alert, the old brain constantly asks the primeval question: "Is it safe?" . . . As it goes about its job of ensuring your safety, your old brain operates in a fundamentally different manner from your new brain. One of the crucial differences

is that the old brain appears to have only a hazy awareness of the external world.

So here's what happened inside me: I felt vulnerable or attacked or unsure of myself. My old brain, not logically attached to events in the real world, said, "This is not safe! Go directly to old-brain survival drill: smile!"

In the same way, Todd's survival instinct kicked in when Marcia criticized his negativity, and the negativity, in its old-brain attempt to protect Todd, became all the stronger.

That's what happens when instead of accepting the traits that you don't love in your partner, you criticize them.

Now let's look at what happens when you practice acceptance.

The Impact of Acceptance

Suppose that Todd makes one of his negative predictions. Before, Marcia would have said, "There you go, being so negative again. Think of the positive side. You are so doom-and-gloom." Or whatever.

But because now she accepts that negative comments are a part of the package that is Todd, she says something like, "Yeah, it probably won't turn out well" or "You may be right." And that's it. It's over. There's no upset, no bickering. Somewhere, Todd's subconscious picks up that he has been validated. As Todd feels increasingly validated, loved, and accepted by Marcia, maybe his old brain will feel less need for its protective negative behavior.

Todd will never transform into Pollyanna. But as he experiences unmitigated love and support within his marriage, his negativity may lose its urgency and may become less predominant. Marcia may never come to love this quality in Todd, but by accepting it, she is eliminating one entire area of potential conflict.

Changing the "System"

Notice that when Marcia accepted Todd's negativity, she also changed her own response to it. This changed the dynamics between the two of them right away. And because Marcia changed, Todd may eventually change also.

Here's why: every relationship is a system, a unit. Every part within the system has an impact on every other part of the system. So if one of you makes a change, it will have an impact on the other.

This is why the spiritual approach to relationships requires less effort than the Stage Two model in which both partners had to "work." If you change the way you respond to your partner, you will be setting in motion a change in the system.

The system theory of family therapy was a revolutionary breakthrough when it became widespread in the 1950s and 1960s. Before that, the only strategy available to us was psychotherapy in which pathology was assumed to be psychological. Treatment would consist of figuring out who in the family was the problem person and "fixing" that person. Family therapy recognized that the pathology was not within one troublemaker, but lay instead in the interaction among the family members. Maybe the son was angry and withdrawn, not because he had a psychological problem, but because his mother was invasive and controlling. What family therapists discovered was that one small change in the system would change the entire system and all the people in it.

This theory explains why practicing acceptance will bring about change in your relationship.

Let's say your problem is that your partner is critical of you. I grant you, that is very hard to accept in a spirit of good will. But if you can be the "big" person, practice restraint, and refrain from making an issue out of the criticism, it will just become part of the landscape. If your partner never derives any satisfaction from criticizing you, he or she may eventually take this criticism habit elsewhere and do less of it in your marriage. The system won't keep operating the same way if you don't react in your old habitual manner.

I saw this exact phenomenon happen recently with a friend I'll call Chris. She and Warren had been living together for six months and were compatible and happy together. There was a problem, however. Warren was having trouble letting go of a previous relationship with a woman named Marne who lived two thousand miles away in Cleveland. Warren had the illusion that if he talked enough about her, at the same time affirming Chris and saying how much he loved her, he could make his obsession go away. At first, Chris tolerated these conversations. But quickly she realized that she was a biased listener because she had a stake in the outcome, and she felt it was inappropriate for her to serve as Warren's therapist. So, acting on her own, being both empathic and decisive, she nicely told him that she would not be a part of any more Marne conversations.

This decision created some tension. Every time Marne's name came up, Chris would begin to bristle. "I'd rather not hear this," she would say. She resisted. But she also saw that this was creating tension that had not been present before and that what she was resisting was persisting. So she changed tactics again.

> I just tell him, "Go to Cleveland. Go see her. Work it out with her," not sarcastically, but sincerely. He gets clear he doesn't want to do that, and the whole thing goes away. I use the martial arts approach. I just continue in the direction he is already going. I don't resist it. I accept that that's where he is. I can't change it. It's just what is.

Chris's comments remind me of this poem by Lao Tsu:

As the soft yield of water cleaves obstinate stone,
So to yield with life solves the insoluble.

What happened with me and my inappropriate smile was that I
began, not to judge it or force it away by an act of will, but to pay
attention to it. One day, I was talking in a small group about something unpleasant, and I noticed that I was smiling! It felt weird. As
I continued, I let myself *not* smile, and I could feel a big difference
inside myself. I felt more relaxed, more connected to what I was
saying, and more connected to the people in the group. After that
experience, I paid attention more often, and gradually, the inappropriate smiling disappeared, not because I forced it away by an
act of will, but because I *accepted* it. When I allowed it to be there
and began paying much closer attention to it, I noticed how toxic
inappropriate smiling felt to me, and the habit began to disappear all
by itself. I was allowing myself to be more authentic. Change happened by itself, not because I engineered it. All I did was pay attention to what was happening within me.

Change Happens When You Surrender Control

Of course, most of us want certain changes in our partners. The way
to create these changes is to begin with what is actually the case and to
accept it. Change happens when you stop trying to control everything
yourself. When you allow things to be the way they are and resist
intervention, natural processes generally work toward what's best.
Even competent therapeutic intervention starts with total acceptance of what is. That is where change has to start.

The English novelist G. K. Chesterton said, "Faith means believing the unbelievable, or it is no virtue at all." Having faith that acceptance will lead to change is just this sort of virtue. It means believing
the unbelievable. Right now you cannot even imagine that some

unpleasant quality in your partner will ever transform. But I hope that by now you do understand that badgering him or her to change will never have the desired effect. So your alternative is to accept the unpleasant quality and find creative ways to live with it.

Genuine acceptance is a way of gaining a larger perspective and a new level of consciousness so that you will be able to "outgrow" your problems.

Guidelines for Moving Toward Acceptance

Here are some specific strategies that will support you as you work on letting go of control, accepting what is, and learning how change really works.

Decide Whether This Trait Is a "Dealbreaker"

You may decide that some quality or behavior in your mate is something you choose not to live with.

- Your partner is physically or verbally abusive or is addicted to drugs or alcohol.
- Your partner is not sexually faithful to you.
- You want a baby, and your partner doesn't.
- Your partner can't control his or her temper.
- You see that staying with your partner will not contribute to his or her or your own spiritual growth.

Everyone draws the line at a different place, and you have a right to draw it wherever you want. Especially if you are not yet married to this person, keep your eyes wide open. Pay attention. Accept the real person you are with, not a fantasy of who you hope the person will become.

If the trait is something you chose not to live with, then you need to make a decision. Do you want to leave the relationship? Or do you want to practice acceptance within the relationship? For example, if your partner is an alcoholic, if you accept this and decide you want to stay with him or her, then you will join an Al-Anon group and adopt a clear strategy about what to do when your partner upsets the family by drinking.

In *Seat of the Soul*, spiritual writer Gary Zukav is very clear that spiritual growth is a higher priority than any vows one once made:

> All of the vows that a human being can take cannot prevent the
> spiritual path from exploding through and breaking those vows
> if the spirit must move on. It is appropriate for Spiritual Partners
> to remain together only as long as they grow together.

Of course, you must also consider the welfare of any children who will be affected.

If you are having trouble deciding whether or not a certain trait is a dealbreaker for you, regardless of whether or not you are married, you may find it helpful to read Chapter 10 of my book *How One of You Can Bring the Two of You Together*; in that chapter I explain exactly how to go about deciding whether to stay or walk away from a relationship.

Most of the changes you wish you could create in your partner are not dealbreakers at all, but fall within the vast realm of little and big qualities that you wish were different but that you can, in the end, accept.

Look for Your Partner's Natural Tendencies

One of the great benefits of the personality systems that have now become popular, such as the Enneagram or the Myers-Briggs Personality Inventory, is that all this information has helped us become more accepting of each other.

The Enneagram, for example, is an ancient system that divides everyone into nine basic personality types. Type 1 people have a tendency to be perfectionist; type 2, to be supportive of others; type 6, to worry and be anxious. Such personality traits arise from deep in our psyches and are fundamentally unchangeable, says this theory.

The effect on most people of studying the Enneagram is an almost instant greater acceptance of people in their lives. "Oh, now I totally understand my boss," one Enneagram workshop graduate told me. "It is deep in his very nature to worry and to be anxious about everything. Now I see that all his checking up on me and advising me has nothing to do with me. He has a need to do this because of his own irrational fears. He's a 6. He is just behaving the way 6s behave."

Enneagram students also learn how to respond most effectively to the various personality types. "The way to get through to perfectionists is to validate them for their thoroughness," one Enneagram teacher told me. She went on,

> For example, a friend was helping me to get ready for a party, but because she was spending way too much time perfecting our minimal decorations, we were not going to be ready on time. At first I said to her, "Just let that go. Forget the balloons. Just scribble those little signs; they don't have to be so neat." That was completely ineffective. Then I realized, she's a 1! Perfectionism runs very deep with her. So I validated her perfectionism. I climbed right in there with her. I said something like, "Those signs look beautiful. You've done a gorgeous job with them. Would you mind getting back to the rest of them later and helping me with the table right now?"

The Enneagram is a useful system, and becoming familiar with it can help you understand and accept difficult personality traits in other people (and in yourself).

However, you don't have to learn the Enneagram to take advantage of the lesson it and other personality systems teach. The lesson is this: people's fundamental personality characteristics will never truly change. So both to support other people in a spirit of love and good will and to get along better with them, we can (1) pay attention to what a person's basic traits are and (2) accept and adapt to these traits.

Take a moment now to think about this. List a few adjectives that describe your partner's basic personality.

Now think about a recent incident that upset you. Was your partner just being his or her natural self? Can you feel more accepting and tolerant knowing that your partner was expressing a deep innate quality?

After an Enneagram class, Jerry realized that his wife, Sylvia, has a natural, deep-seated tendency to be helpful and caring, to reach out and support others. She feels safe and happy only when she has some ways to express this intrinsic need. Jerry viewed her need to help as excessive. When a neighbor's mother died and Sylvia spent two days over there, managing phone calls, cooking, and generally running the crisis while his own household was neglected, he became irate. Looking back on the situation now, he sees that helping out in a crisis is an intrinsic part of who Sylvia is. It would truly be going against her fundamental nature for her to come home and take care of her (or her family's) own needs when someone else was in a crisis.

My husband, Mayer, and I are at opposite ends of the "be spontaneous–plan ahead" continuum. On the one hand, when I try to schedule something two weeks ahead, he becomes anxious. "I don't know whether I'll want to do that then," he'll say. On the other hand, if we don't plan way ahead, I become anxious because I'm afraid we will never do anything.

One time, we each took the same personality test. One of the charts we received after the test was scored illustrated how we measured in this very quality. We couldn't have been farther apart on the scale. We had a good laugh over it. Now that that quality has been labeled and measured in us, we have a much easier time accepting it in each other. Our difference has been the source of a lot of humor, and we are quite clear that we have to find ways to accommodate each other's needs while not betraying our own.

Like the various personality charts, information about gender differences has also helped couples become more accepting of each other. Although the popular press has perhaps diminished the value of important studies by oversimplifying them, general ideas can nevertheless sometimes be useful: women want affection and closeness; men want security. Men tend to withdraw under stress; women want to connect, to talk things through. Men use conversation to make decisions and solve problems; women use conversation to express feelings and establish connection.

Just being aware of these tendencies helps us accept them when we see them. Instead of trying in vain to change the opposite sex, we adapt. For example, if I am trying to talk something through just to express my feelings and see if I can achieve greater clarity, but Mayer is busily trying to solve my problem, I can say to him, "Thanks for your ideas, but I just want to talk this through for now." He understands what I mean and is not offended. Accepting and labeling our differing propensities ahead of time helps us manage them.

In short, then, look for your partner's natural tendencies. This will help you accept that these are part of the package you love.

Pretend That the Quality You Dislike Is a Scar

Suppose the person you love has an accident that results in an unfortunate visible scar. You wouldn't like this, but you also wouldn't reject your mate for it. You would be supportive and would help your mate accept the unacceptable. Imagine it were a physical disability or illness. Would you be critical and demand change?

Our deep personality characteristics are somewhat like scars. They are difficult and maybe even impossible to change. What is the "scar" in your partner that you can learn to accept, as you progress in your spiritual journey toward connection, love, and surrender?

Act as If

It may be hard to imagine accepting something that annoys you terribly about your partner. His libido is way too high. She interrupts all the time. He'll never go with you to your beloved horse shows. She's a workaholic and never around. He's an Internet junky, married to his computer. She flies off the handle and becomes angry way too often. He always puts his own needs first.

You want change. It's hard to accept living with these qualities.

So begin by using our always-helpful strategy, Loving Action 3: act as if. Behave as if you are accepting of your partner's annoying trait. In the end, it is your behavior that is going to make a difference. If you act accepting, even when you don't feel accepting, you will get to see what this feels like. Your behavior may actually have an impact on your feelings; you may become more accepting. Further, you will be changing the dynamic between you and your partner, so something different is likely to happen.

Jim was very unhappy with his wife, Diane, for becoming so active in her professional association that met on Saturdays. He wanted so much to have the whole day with her so they could plan excursions or just relax together. Every Saturday, he made an issue out of it, always trying to persuade her that this organization was part of her old life, not her current one, that she received little benefit from it, that their relationship was much more important. On and on he would go, so that Diane always had to go off to her meetings feeling annoyed and hurt and angry.

After I talked with Jim about the idea of acceptance, he shifted. Although he was not at all in the mood to accept Diane's behavior, he decided to behave as though he did. His first move was to plan a beautiful hike for himself, so that as Diane left for her meeting, he left for the woods. The next Saturday, he did the same thing. Suddenly, they stopped fighting. Jim still wished Diane would come with him, but he found he was actually accepting that this probably wouldn't happen. By acting *as if* he accepted her decision, he found he *was* accepting it.

"I made an important discovery," Jim told me excitedly. "I was the one causing the problem, just because I wouldn't accept Diane for who she was."

Jim's discovery is so important, it is worth repeating: when there is a problem, it is not caused by the one who won't change but by the one who won't accept what is!

So start by acting as if you accept something that upsets you, and see what happens.

Say to Yourself, "This Is Not a Problem; It Is a Fact of Life"

As we discussed earlier, when you view something as a problem, you assume there must be a solution. When you view something as a fact of life, you realize that your task is simply to begin to work with it, to adapt to it—in a word, to accept it.

This is exactly the shift that Jim made when he began to accept Diane's Saturday meetings. Jim told me this:

> I realized I had been working really hard to solve this problem. In my fantasy, the solution was that Diane would see the light and let go of her whole organization thing. The more that didn't

happen, the more out of control I felt. I kept imagining the perfect conversation with her in which, if I just said the right thing in the right way, she would be willing to compromise. When I realized that I had no problem to solve, the whole thing shifted for me. When I started thinking about adapting to this fact of life, I came up with different ideas. For one thing, I asked Diane more about the organization, why it was so important to her and what she liked most about it. I was surprised to learn, when I really listened to her, that the social contacts there were as important to her as the business aspects of it. And then of course, I took initiative and started planning my own activities so that I wouldn't feel I was wasting Saturdays.

Diane told me that the hardest part of my unhappiness with her was not that I complained about the time on Saturdays, but that I was actually putting her down for something she loved. I was belittling her and her favorite pursuit. I now see that she has a right to an interest that doesn't interest me, and that part of loving someone is loving the parts you aren't so happy about.

When you try to solve a problem by persuading your partner to change, you will often carry around the belief, as Jim did, and as Meredith did when she was unhappy with Sam's joking, that if only you could state your request in the right way, somehow find the right words, you would succeed. You think the problem is that you have not communicated well enough with your partner. It may come as a great relief to learn that you can give up on this quest for the perfect words or the perfect timing. Maybe the answer is that you will never achieve the change in your partner that you so long for.

This may make you feel sad, and even resentful or deprived. That's okay. Those feelings are appropriate when you let go of a cherished dream and realize you may not ever get what you want. But you should also feel relief. You can give up trying to move this mountain and get on with your life.

Say to Yourself, "This Has Nothing to Do with Me"

The phrase we learned in Loving Action 4, "This has nothing to do with me," is useful here too. Let's review it briefly.

It is difficult to be graciously accepting when your mate's annoying habit is aimed directly at you. For example, if your partner tries to control you or often nags at you, criticizes you, advises you, ignores you, is impatient with you, or even yells at you, it may feel to you as though you are living with a fly buzzing around your head, and it may be very difficult to "accept."

This is a challenge. But remember, your partner would be this way with anyone. The behavior isn't aimed specifically at you; you just happen to be the one who is in the way when the behavior is happening.

When you say to yourself, "This has nothing to do with me," it will help you remember, "This unpleasant behavior on the part of my partner is like a scar; I don't like it, but I can learn to live with it, graciously and quietly, without reacting."

Self-Acceptance

As you work on accepting parts of your partner that you don't like, take the opportunity to do the same for yourself.

Self-acceptance is the ultimate aphrodisiac. When you know and love your authentic self and feel comfortable with all your best and worst qualities, you become more approachable and easy to love.

Self-esteem can be said to be the ultimate goal of all spiritual practice. In his book *A Path with Heart*, spiritual teacher and author

EXPERIMENT 18

Acceptance

1. If you had a magic wand, what would you change about your mate? Make a list in your journal.

2. Now look at each quality you have written down and say to yourself, "What if this never changes? What if my partner will always be this way?"

3. Review the strategies in this chapter, pick one, and apply it to one "fact of life" that you would like to begin to accept. As you try this, make notes in your journal or talk with a friend.

Jack Kornfield writes, "Much of spiritual life is self-acceptance, maybe all of it."

Though they talk about it in different language, all the great religious traditions teach self-acceptance. "Love your neighbor as yourself," said Jesus. God loves you just the way you are. No matter what your shortcomings, you are okay. Buddhism teaches that we create our own suffering through attachment, anger, and hatred. Anger or hatred toward your partner will cause you limitless suffering. When you accept what is and let go of needing to be or to have something else, you truly find inner peace, self-love, and self-acceptance.

You're Fine Just the Way You Are

You are fine, exactly the way you are right now. Even if you don't exercise enough. Even if you don't have the possessions or status or job you wish you had. Even if you have doubts about your marriage.

Even if you hurt or failed someone. You can't change reality; you can only either fight it or accept it. Accepting it, however unpleasant, is the only route to inner peace. When you refuse to accept any part of what is true for you, you are making life harder for yourself. What you refuse to accept will persist.

Accepting yourself is not about getting yourself into a perfect state so that it is easy to accept yourself. First you lose weight, win the lottery, establish your dream home, fall in love with a perfect person, rise to the top of your profession—and then you accept yourself. No, accepting yourself means that right now, exactly as things really are in this moment, you accept them. "This is my existence, this is my life." It's not about getting better; it's about accepting who you are right now. If you decide you have to be someone else in order to love yourself, you will never find self-love.

Does accepting yourself mean you can't have goals and dreams? Not at all. It means that you don't have to achieve those goals or dreams in order to be a good person. Having goals and dreams is part of what you accept about yourself. It's part of what is real for you right now. Maybe you are even experiencing envy right now or anger or failure. That's what is going on for you right now. It's okay. It doesn't need to be any other way.

The continuing search for improvement—in yourself, in your relationships—keeps you in a state of discontent. In spiritual work, the discontent is the problem. If at each moment you can accept, "This is what is happening right now; this is reality; this is my existence," that in itself will remove the discontent and move you closer to the objectives you desire. Having accepted yourself, you may still be feeling upset, but you are not also putting yourself down for feeling upset. Even if what is happening right now is that you are depressed, or your partner is angry with you, or you are anxious or under stress, you will get through it faster and be calmer as you go through it if you can accept, "This is what is happening right now. It isn't pleasant, but I accept it, and I know it will pass. This is not a problem; it is a fact of life."

When you feel you are doing the best you can at any given moment, given your particular circumstances, that is all you can ask of yourself. Doing the best you can is total and complete success. You may be aware that you could do better in some ways. Good! You haven't arrived at perfection yet. Accept that too.

Accepting Parts of Yourself You Don't Like

The opposite of self-acceptance is self put-downs or self-hate. This is the part of you that rails against some aspect of who you are and what your life is right now. It is like trying to swim upstream or to ride a horse in the opposite way from the way it is going. Self-judgment uses up lots of your good energy, in a way that does not serve you at all.

Remember, accepting something does not mean that you necessarily like it. In fact, self-acceptance is precisely about accepting those parts of yourself that you don't like. Accepting the parts of yourself that you like is no challenge.

Self-acceptance gives you inner power and strength. If you accept, rather than fight against, the whole imperfect package that is you, you are freed from ever having to prove to anyone that you are a good person. You know deep within that although in some ways you can always do better, you don't have to do better before you can totally love yourself. When you get this feeling, you will experience yourself as powerful in the world. And you will be able to give up struggling. Self-acceptance is freedom.

It is possible to "work on" becoming more self-accepting. Most of this work is about getting to know yourself better, because you can't love or accept parts of yourself that you don't even know about yet. Spiritual work is about uncovering aspects of yourself that have been hidden to you, usually because they are too painful or frightening to experience, with the ultimate goal of learning to accept and even love those difficult parts of yourself. These old hurts or little pockets of low self-esteem are what is. Ignoring, denying, or resisting them is delaying self-acceptance.

For example, when I became aware of my inappropriate smiling, I had to look beneath the behavior to figure out why I was doing that. I asked experienced guides (therapists and spiritual teachers) to help me, and it took time. But I began to see that I smiled because I feared that the real me—that is, that little ember that glowed beneath the persistent smile—wouldn't be lovable, or even likable. I began to discover parts of myself that I didn't like at all and was eager to hide from the world. I had to become acquainted with those parts—painful regrets, insecurities, fears. Only when I found out what was in the dark snake pit of my psyche could I possibly begin to accept those parts of myself. Gradually I began to see that all those awful things weren't so awful after all. I could live with them. Denying that they were there took way too much energy and made me feel like a half-person. I wasn't only the good parts of me, I began to see. I was all of me. And all of me was perfectly okay.

So you can work toward self-acceptance.

However, it is also true that you cannot earn self-acceptance the way you work through school and earn a degree. Self-acceptance is a gift that comes at unexpected moments. It settles over you, in a gently ecstatic moment, unbeckoned, like grace.

A Most Moving Story of Self-Acceptance

When I worked as a hospital chaplain, I spent many hours in conversations with David, an athletic young man who had broken his neck in a diving accident and was almost completely paralyzed. His rage and cynicism were boundless. He felt he should have known better than to dive where he did and blamed himself for the accident. He told me over and over that he wished the accident had killed him and that he hated the stranger who had rescued him. He also talked a great deal about his grandfather whom he adored, who had died just three months before the accident.

One day, he couldn't wait to talk with me. He had had a dream in which the stranger who saved him came back and offered to help him take his own life. They were just about to do it. But then his grandfather came into the room and just looked at him, so heartbroken and disappointed. So he stopped.

David could talk about nothing else but that dream. We started writing letters to his grandfather. One morning, he told me his grandfather visited him again during the night and told him to get involved with helping other patients in the hospital. So David started helping in the rehab room, talking people through their routines. One day he met a man who was injured in a car accident on the way to his own wedding. The story touched David so much that when he came back to his room, he couldn't stop sobbing. He cried for about two weeks, every time I saw him.

Then his mood began to soften. He talked about his family. He even began to talk, ever so tentatively, about his plans for the future.

One day I entered his room and was actually startled by what I saw. David looked gorgeous. There was a new energy in his face, a relaxed quality I had never seen. I'll never forget his next words:

"I'm a quadriplegic," he said to me. "I have a new life."

His revelation came to him in a telephone conversation with his mother. She was trying to arrange a way for him to be a part of the neighborhood football game when he came home for Thanksgiving. "My mother is still wishing this accident didn't happen. She doesn't accept it," David told me. "But I do."

EXPERIMENT 19

Self-Acceptance

1. If you had a magic wand, what would you change about yourself—in the present and also in your past? Make a list in your journal.

2. Now look at each quality you have written down and say to yourself, "What if this never changes? What if I will always be this way? This is who I truly am."

3. Write a love letter to yourself in which you talk freely about the aspects of yourself you don't like. See if you can move from dislike to loving acceptance, even if just as an exercise in this letter.

David was experiencing the grace of self-acceptance. Never before or since have I seen such a clear example of it.

All the work you do on the Eight Loving Actions will also lead you in the direction of greater self-acceptance. It is a lifelong journey. Sometimes we feel more self-accepting, sometimes less. But the more we engage in spiritual practice, the more we can accept ourselves—even when we are not being self-accepting!

CHAPTER 9

Loving Action 8

Practice Compassion

If you want to be happy, be compassionate.
If you want others to be happy, be compassionate.
—THE DALAI LAMA

Compassion is the ability to imagine yourself in someone else's shoes and to behave accordingly. It means you deeply understand what someone else is going through *and* are moved to help. The literal meaning from the Latin is "to suffer" (*passion*) "with" (*com*) or "to feel with." The Dalai Lama calls compassion "a mental attitude based on the wish for others to be free of their suffering, associated with a sense of commitment, responsibility, and respect towards the other."

So what does it mean to say that to practice compassion is a Loving Action in your relationship?

It means that when your husband is yelling at you because you spent too much money on clothes, you take a deep breath and say to yourself, "The poor guy grew up in such a poor family and his father was so terrified about money all the time, this must be so hard for him to see all that money I spent. Underneath the anger, he's scared. I can respect his point of view. I need to find a way to meet my own needs and his too. I can do this."

Maybe you don't do this instantly, but as time passes, that is the direction in which you move. Put yourself in your partner's shoes. Try to understand *why* your partner behaves in this way that bugs you. Remember that your partner has a right to behave this way and has reasons for behaving this way, reasons that go way back in history. It is not the case that you are right and he or she is wrong; you see things differently. You both have a right to your opinions.

That's compassion. That's providing spiritual leadership in your relationship and being the "big" person.

Or when your wife is nagging at you for the millionth time that you should be better organized, you say to yourself, "She has a right to want me to be better organized. She's doing her control thing again. She had to be controlling to survive in her family. But she is making progress, and I can support that progress by gently affirming her and then finding a way to be disorganized that won't upset her. Not only that, she's right; a little more organization would be good for me."

This may seem like a tall order, but it's what compassion means. When you see your partner upset, even if it is at you, this pains you too, and you feel moved to help.

We'll return to these examples later in the chapter to see exactly *what you can do* when you feel compassion in these situations. But first, let's look more closely at what compassion is.

Compassion in Daily Life

It is easier to experience and express compassion for someone when you are not seen as the cause of the person's upset. For example, your partner announces she did not receive the promotion she had so hoped for. Or he learns that his mother has cancer. Hearing this, you feel sad; you can imagine how you would feel if you were in this situation, and you feel moved to do whatever you can to help. You may hold your partner while he or she cries. You might offer to fix dinner that night or to make flight arrangements, or you might take over extra household chores. You truly wish you could take the pain away. That's compassion.

Compassion Versus Blame

The opposite of compassion is blame.

Many people go through life blaming their parents for their personal problems, blaming their partner for the difficulties in their relationship, blaming their boss for their unhappiness at work, and blaming the universe for being unfair in general.

"My parents favored my brother; they abandoned me." "My partner is too . . . [controlling, demanding, self-oriented]." My mate . . . [talks too much, talks too little, doesn't listen to me, works all the time, is inconsiderate]." "My boss is unreasonable."

You may be right about what your parents did wrong, how your spouse could improve, or how your boss could be more effective. But staying stuck at the level of blaming them will never move you forward.

When you blame someone else for whatever is going on in your life, two things happen:

1. You have to carry around toxic, negative, angry thoughts and feelings.

2. You prevent yourself from looking at your own role in the problems, which is the only area you can do anything about.

Let's say your partner is being his usual thoughtless self. He fixed himself a sandwich and didn't even think to ask whether you might want one.

If you blame him, you will be carrying the "blame poison" inside you: "Look at how thoughtless that was! It makes me so angry! I can't believe someone can be that self-absorbed and selfish!" Meanwhile, your partner is enjoying his sandwich. He did something that triggered it, but you are creating your own upset.

If you take a compassionate approach instead, you might say to yourself something like, "My poor, sweet husband. He grew up in such a selfish family, where they didn't do favors for each other. He still hasn't been able to overcome that. It probably never even occurred to him to make me a sandwich. Imagine!"

Now, you act on your own, make yourself a sandwich, and join him for a pleasant lunch. There is no toxic anger inside you, and you have found a way to fix the situation for yourself by using a Loving Action (acting on your own). You know inside yourself that he will probably never completely change this self-involved aspect of his personality. So you don't even need to bring it up. You just be the "big" person by understanding that he is limited in this area by the childhood he had, and you let it go.

Compassion and Forgiving

Compassion is not about who is right and who is wrong; it is about where you choose to put your energy in any situation. Can you forgive someone for making a mistake? For doing something that hurt you? For being less than what you hoped for?

Intuitive writer and teacher Caroline Myss once said in a lecture that not forgiving someone is like taking rat poison and hoping the other person will die. If you remain angry and self-righteous about your partner's forgetting to make you a sandwich, he will be enjoying his sandwich while you are poisoning yourself with anger. Anger, blame, and self-righteousness diminish the quality of *your own* life and do nothing to change the situation that is causing your anger.

Gordon's father was abusive and unpleasant. His mother divorced him when Gordon was nine. For the next three years, Gordon's mother paid a great deal of attention to him; they were a pair and went everywhere together. Gordon felt loved and affirmed at last. Then Gordon's mother fell in love and married again, a man who liked Gordon and did all he could to establish a relationship with him. But Gordon would have none of it. He resented this stepfather for coming between him and his mother.

Now Gordon is thirty-two and has a son of his own. He is still cool toward his stepfather and angry with his mother. He feels his mother should have done more to protect him from his real father in the early years and that she should not have "abandoned" him when she remarried. His parents do all they can to build bridges with Gordon now, but Gordon is not receptive. He wants them to see what they did to him and admit they were wrong. Now that he sees how much he loves his own son, he is incredulous that they could have treated him as they did when he was a small child. Why didn't they love and adore and protect him the way he now loves his own son?

Gordon is right. But he is drinking the rat poison and hoping his parents will die—or at least feel punished. It is Gordon who is unhappy and confused, angry and unforgiving. His parents now feel bad about what happened in the past, but realize they are helpless to change that. They watch Gordon suffer and struggle, but they are helpless to do anything about it.

The choice is Gordon's: he can continue to blame his parents for years to come, or he can have compassion for them, realize they did the best they could at the time, given who they were and what resources they had available to them, and let go of the hurt he is choosing to carry around.

Recall what we said about blame: by blaming his parents, Gordon is (1) carrying around toxic, negative, angry thoughts and feelings, and (2) preventing himself from looking at his own role in the problems. Only Gordon can free himself from this toxic energy of blame and anger that he is still carrying around. His parents remain patient and are accepting of Gordon, just the way he is. They hope that someday he will experience compassion for them and forgive them, but apart from their ongoing acceptance of him, they can do nothing to help bring this about.

Moving from blame to compassion is not easy. When the pain is very deep, compassion doesn't happen overnight, and it won't happen just because you read about it. It takes work, and it takes time.

Doris had an affair, lasting about two months. She finally told her husband, Fred, about it, full of remorse and regret. She begged for forgiveness and assured Fred over and over that what she really wanted was him and their wonderful former relationship back. Fred told her that he wanted to forgive her, that he believed her remorse. But he was deeply hurt, and found that, as much as he wanted to move toward her, he couldn't. His heart was closed. Doris had to be patient. She kept behaving in a loving way toward him, and she waited and waited. They talked. They both wanted to be in love again. Fred tried.

After almost a year, Doris thought up an unusual surprise for Fred. She arranged for a very favorite old high school buddy of Fred's to make an unexpected visit. Fred was very moved when he realized all Doris had to go through to arrange this, and something inside him shifted. His heart began opening again.

Both Fred and Doris had compassion for each other throughout their whole year of struggle, but the healing took time.

Compassion will ultimately lead to forgiveness. When you genuinely and wholeheartedly forgive someone, you will become a freer, happier person. Hanging on to hurt and failing to forgive keep the rat poison inside you, not the person who hurt you. Forgiving is a difficult journey, but it will set you free. The reward is commensurate with the pain.

The journey to genuine forgiveness can begin with acting as if you forgive, which is essentially what Fred did. Intellectually he forgave Doris; he wanted to forgive her; he tried to behave as if he forgave her. But the deep wound took time to heal. Like the process of grief, forgiving someone goes through stages and takes time, especially if the hurt is profound.

While Fred was going through his healing, Doris had compassion for him. She understood that he needed time, and she was able to be patient and give it to him. The year was terribly painful for both of them. But their patience and compassion were rewarded.

Time alone is not sufficient to heal a wound and to bring about forgiveness. Both Doris and Fred wanted to be in love again. Their will was strong. So they didn't just wait. While they were letting time go by, they were both working to exhibit compassion for each other. They were envisioning their hearts being open to each other again. And, above all, they were paying attention.

Learning Compassion

You can begin to cultivate compassion by being aware of your own instinctive feelings of compassion toward others. For example, when you hear a tragic story in the news and your heart goes out on a kind of internal autopilot to the people involved, pay attention to that. It is a good, healthy, spiritual feeling. Begin to practice feeling compassion for people in the news. Whether you are hearing of victims of a famine or the horrible atrocities of war, or a family who lost a child in a freak accident, let yourself feel the sadness along with the desire to help. You may feel you would do anything if you could take their pain away. That's compassion.

You don't have to act on all the compassion you feel. Unless you are Mother Teresa, you can't. But do act on your compassion when you can, when you are especially suited to help in some way, or if the situation falls right into your lap.

Melodie Chavis, author of the remarkable book *Altars in the Street*, lived in a violent, drug- and gang-infested neighborhood, and was committed to staying there to be a part of turning the neighborhood around against, as it turned out, staggering odds. One day, after several years of this, she read a story in the paper about a woman who had called the police to report drug activity right in front of her house. The very next day, the woman's house was set on fire and burned to the ground. Melodie didn't hesitate a moment when she read this: she got in her car and drove right over to see this woman, to express her compassion and see what she could do to help.

Cultivate Compassion for Yourself

Developing compassion for yourself will help you feel it for others, and the opposite is also true. Sometimes you can feel it more easily for others than you can for yourself, but start paying attention to both. If you are filled with self-loathing, insecurities, or low self-esteem, if you don't like yourself very much, then your first job is to deeply understand what you yourself are going through *and* be moved to help. It may even be easier to minister to someone else's pain when you are—or have been—in pain yourself.

Life is hard. Pain and loss are inevitable. Envy, low self-esteem, fear, betrayal, jealousy, heartbreak—it is all bound to arise within you at some time or another. The mistake is to run from the pain, to try to escape it, to deny it, to cover it up. Pain is a direct channel to your authentic self, your soul, and being in alignment with your soul is the source of joy. Accept the pain and then do the work to heal it, and that starts with compassion.

If you can stay with your pain, even for a few minutes, you can learn from it and begin to heal it.

Rachel was a senior in college when she joined one of my support groups. She had been a star in high school. She earned all A's, had the lead in the class play, and was president of the French Club. But her high school was small and rural, and when she came to a big, tough university, she had had to struggle the whole time. She was graduating somewhere in the middle of her class and, in spite of several earnest attempts, had never found a place to fit in during her whole four years. She tried to keep up a bright front, but we could sense despair lingering just beneath her pleasant demeanor.

We encouraged her to explore the despair. Little by little over several weeks, she discussed it, until one week, she began to sob, saying, "I feel so lost. I don't know who I am anymore. I feel I have nothing to offer in a relationship." When her strong emotions began to subside, she told us how good it felt to express this despair and to feel our compassion pour out to her.

Then we encouraged Rachel to *be* the friend she wished she had and to talk to Rachel. We asked her to start by saying, "Rachel, I deeply understand what you are going through, and I am here to help."

Rachel was a paragon of compassion. She said something like this:

> Poor thing. You have had such a hard time in school! You had so many rough breaks and near misses. It just feels like the universe is in a conspiracy against you, doesn't it? It's no wonder at all that you feel so alone and that you don't feel good about yourself the way you used to in high school. You were a brave soul to come to this huge university and to stick it out here. I promise you, things are going to get better. You still are that same Rachel you were in high school, only now you are a lot wiser. You are going to be fine. Soon you will get a lucky break.

Putting yourself in this group was a wonderful thing for you
to do. Just stay with yourself, keep believing in yourself. I'm
here with you. I'm not going anywhere.

Rachel is a model for all of us.

It is hard to reach out with compassion to someone else if you
have never experienced it for yourself. Yet it is also true that experiencing genuine compassion for someone else will help you develop
the capacity to feel it for yourself.

If you are feeling low, try the same experiment Rachel did. Be
your best friend and write a letter to yourself.

The more compassion you experience for yourself, the more you
can feel for others. You won't have to imagine yourself in someone
else's shoes, because you have actually been in those shoes yourself.
Then you become a "wounded healer," by far the most effective kind.

The Wounded Healer

In the old medical model of healing, one person is wounded or ill,
and the other person is the healthy, all-knowing healer. In contrast,
the "wounded healer" model of healing assumes that both persons
are wounded. The healer heals, not by handing down superior knowl-
edge, but by eliciting the "wounded" person's own internal healer.
We are all in this boat together. We are all wounded and in pain.
And it is that commonality that enables us all to heal each other.

My role as "healer" is simply to remind you that you can heal
yourself, and vice versa. The twelve-step programs are filled with
healers who have deep compassion for others in the program, because
they learned how to have compassion for themselves. Compassion
for yourself will enable you to experience it for others, including
your partner.

Developing Compassion for Your Partner

To convert resentment or blame into compassion, you need to look beyond the immediate situation to the person behind it.

What is the source of your partner's behavior? What led up to this personality trait that you don't like? Maybe, given the circumstances, your partner is doing the best he or she can be expected to do. If, for example, your mate grew up in a family where everyone was cool and undemonstrative, where no one ever hugged or said, "I love you," that may be a big part of the reason that your partner is not romantic with you.

Here are four suggestions that will help you develop compassion toward your partner. If you can set aside some time to think through or, even better, write through these ideas, they will help you build your capacity for compassion in your day-to-day routines with your partner.

Look Behind the Person

Look at your partner's background and ask yourself how it might have contributed to who he or she is today.

In our workshops, we use the following questions as a guide. I suggest you take some time to (1) write out your answers, (2) discuss these questions with a friend, or (3) use these as a guide for discussion in your support group if you are in one. If you and your mate are building your spiritual lives and Spiritual Partnership together, by all means sit down and interview each other. Such a conversation might be very enjoyable for you, possibly moving, and certainly educational. But in phrasing the questions, I will assume you are doing the exercise by yourself.

Family Background

1. What was it like for your partner to grow up in his or her family?

2. How is your partner like his or her mother in attitudes, behavior, and beliefs?

3. How is your partner like his or her father in attitudes, behavior, and beliefs?

4. Is your partner heavily influenced by any siblings or by his or her relationship with any siblings?

5. How does your partner feel now about his or her family?

Previous Experiences

1. What do you know about your mate's previous experiences that might have had an impact on the situation or behavior that troubles you now?

2. How might these previous experiences be influencing him or her?

General Personality Type

1. What are the two or three most dominant qualities in your partner's personality?

2. Complete this sentence with as many different adjectives as seem appropriate: My partner has a strong tendency to be _____. For example, your partner might tend to be perfectionist, helpful, achievement oriented, melancholy, overinvolved, optimistic, quick to anger, good natured, well organized, left-brained, and so on.

3. What is your partner's astrological sign? How does he or she match or fail to match the characteristics that are traditionally assigned to that sign? If you think astrology is silly, just think of

it as a metaphor, a useful way to describe personality types with which you can agree or disagree.

4. In general, men have a tendency to invalidate or ignore feelings and move directly to solutions, to cope with stress by becoming silent and withdrawn, and to show their love by being good at what they do or by doing big, impressive favors. Women have a tendency to value and express feelings, to cope with stress by asking for support and talking things through, and to show their love with small favors and affectionate gestures.

   In what ways does your mate's behavior correspond or fail to correspond to these generalities?

What did you discover by asking these questions? Maybe your mate isn't being malicious, thoughtless, ungrateful, or deliberately neglectful of you. Maybe you are just seeing your partner being the very best at who he or she really is.

Look for Significant Stories

Think back over the stories you have heard about your mate's childhood. Is there a story that exactly characterizes him or her?

For example, one workshop participant, Matt, was upset with his wife because he felt she took gift giving to a ridiculous extreme. She was always bringing little gifts to her friends for even the slightest excuse. She gave lavish presents to her nieces and nephews on their birthdays, and Christmas shopping always started about February for her. When we came to this exercise, Matt told us this story that had been repeated many times about his wife:

> On my mother-in-law's sideboard sits a little porcelain sculpture of a small family around a table. The story is that when

my wife was about nine, she had a job helping neighbors rake up their leaves in the fall. When her parents' anniversary arrived, she took all the money she had saved up for a couple of years, went to her favorite store all by herself, spent a long time picking out the perfect little sculpture (according to the store owner, who was a friend), and proudly presented it to her parents.

As Matt told us the story, several of us even felt a tear on our cheek, imagining this sweet nine-year-old selecting her gift and happily, proudly spending all her money on it. We helped Matt realize that giving and generosity are part of Nicole's true essence, part of what makes her feel happy and fulfilled.

Many of the stories we hear are not so touching; they are painful. Stories of children being neglected or beaten or even abused. Stories of parents being too busy, missing important events, or forgetting to pick up a child at the right time.

Whatever story you pick that helps you understand your loved one, remember that that little child stills lives inside your grown-up mate. When you see that behavior coming out, relate directly to the little child. Does it help put you in touch with your compassion?

Say the "Mantra"

Part of compassion is holding your partner up to his or her own standard, not some arbitrary standard or fantasy that you have in your head.

Memorize this "mantra": "She is doing the best she can" or "He is doing the best he can," and when you are having trouble feeling compassion for your partner, say it over and over to yourself.

People bring different resources to a marriage. For example, with regard to thoughtfulness, when you are giving 100 percent, you may be wrapping up clever gifts, leaving notes in funny places, doing the dishes for your partner, and bringing home a book or new jacket for your mate, just as a surprise. But when your partner is giving 100 percent, maybe all that means is opening the garage door for you, as usual. Maybe thoughtfulness was not part of your partner's family growing up, and his or her experience with it is limited. You can make a deliberate choice to feel compassion for your partner instead of disappointment for yourself.

When you feel anger toward your partner and are unable to be in touch with any compassion, you will probably think this is because your partner's behavior is so unreasonable. *But in fact, you are coming up against your own limitations, not your partner's.* Your spiritual challenge is to make a shift. Work hard, even for a moment, to put yourself in your partner's shoes and think about compassion. Say to yourself, "He's doing the best he can" or "She's doing the best she can." Whatever the wounds are that cause your mate to behave in certain ways, your compassionate attitude may begin to heal them. As we've said over and over, in order to heal we all need compassion and love, not criticism and blame.

Cultivate Your Partner's Dreams

Make a deliberate effort to find out what your partner's dreams are. Then put yourself in his or her shoes and see if you feel moved to support these dreams. When you catch yourself focusing on what you consider to be your mate's deficits or drawbacks, consciously think instead about the person he or she is striving to become. When you look at your mate, don't be thinking, "What can you do for me?" but rather, "How can I support you? What is the deep desire in you that I might nurture? What is the hurt in you that I might help heal?"

It's easy to love people when they are happy and doing well and are generous and loving back. But when they most need your love is when they aren't doing well, when they feel low and can't believe in themselves, when they are having setbacks in their lives.

Finally, remember that the real benefit of compassion, like all spiritual ideals, is to make you into a happier, more peaceful and fulfilled person. It sounds as though compassion is about helping the other person. But the more compassion you can find in your heart, the more loving kindness you can offer to those around you, the more joy you will experience for yourself.

Putting Compassion to Work in Your Relationship

Let us return now to the example in which your husband is having a fit at the amount of money you spent on clothes. As we see how a Spiritual Partner might play this out, we will also review some of the other spiritual principles we have learned so far.

You start proudly and excitedly showing your husband the clothes you have just bought for a special occasion. He becomes upset and anxious and starts trying to convince you to take the clothes back. Of course the knee-jerk, unconscious response would be to hurl back a defensive retort. "This was not a lot of money. You have no idea what clothes cost. And *you* just spent all that money on running shoes! That was okay. Stop and look at how these look on me! You're so anxious about money, it's going to shrivel you up with worry. Life is too short." Whatever.

A Different Way of Reacting

But as a Spiritual Partner, instead of delivering this return tirade, you would first employ several skills we have already learned. You would use restraint by saying, perhaps, "I feel defensive." That would give you time to breathe and think. Next, you could be both empathic and decisive. You might say something like, "I know you feel like this is a lot to spend on clothes. It is a lot of money. I don't disagree with that. And I'm so sorry it upsets you when I spend money on clothes. Believe me, that is not my intention." That's the empathic part, and it may be enough for the time being. Let your partner talk, and continue to be understanding.

Now, where does the compassion come in? Compassion means you are truly unhappy that your partner feels so upset, and you are moved to do whatever you can to help. Now you are in a difficult place. Here is where you must draw on your own commitment to *balance* taking care of yourself and taking care of your partner, Loving Action 5. To give yourself some time, you might say, "Honey, let me look this over. I did spend a lot today. Maybe there is something I can take back. Give me a little while to think about this."

Good! You have stopped trying to get anywhere through more communication. You have refrained from blaming your husband and making him wrong, and you have asked yourself, "What can I do?" With your spirit of good will, by agreeing to review your purchases, you have created harmony in place of upset. You have not asked your partner to change. And you have taken upon yourself both the burden and the power of maintaining the balance of giving and taking.

No formula can tell you what to decide now. Only you know whether there is in fact something you could take back that would please your husband and not make you feel resentful. Or whether you believe the amount you spent is truly reasonable and that you need to convey your opinion to him, decisively, but without making him wrong, as we learned to do in Loving Action 6, act on your own. Your job is not to persuade him to agree with you. Your job is to be understanding and affirming of his feelings and opinions and at the same time clear that this time, you are going to go ahead with what you believe is right for you.

This example is very close to home. When I went shopping with an image consultant for my very first book tour, this was our scene. I was *not* a model of compassion and good will. In fact, I became defensive, and Mayer and I had quite a fight. We both felt unsupported and betrayed. When we stopped fighting, neither of us felt good, and we just went off to our separate corners.

After a couple of hours, I looked back over all the clothes and decided there was one very expensive suit I could return, and that I would actually feel better about that too. It was a lot of money. But before I could go downstairs to tell Mayer this, he came up and said, "Sweetheart, go ahead and keep everything. I want you to feel absolutely wonderful on this book tour. We can spend the money. It's not that big a deal."

We were both exhibiting a spirit of good will arising out of compassion. We were both very sad that the other person was upset, and we were motivated to do something about it.

If you think it is difficult, even unrealistic, to be feeling compassion for your partner when *you* are the one who is feeling wronged, deprived, or unsupported, think about Jesus. While he was in the act of being wrongfully murdered, he was able to say, "Forgive them Father, for they know not what that do." Their evil, Jesus knew, was a result only of their ignorance, their low level of consciousness. He felt compassion for them.

And I love what Vietnamese Buddhist monk Thich Nhat Hanh said about Buddha:

> When I was a novice, I could not understand why, if the world
> is filled with suffering, the Buddha has such a beautiful smile.
> Why isn't he disturbed by all the suffering? Later I discovered

that the Buddha has enough understanding, calm, and strength; that is why the suffering does not overwhelm him. He is able to smile to suffering because he knows how to take care of it and to help transform it.

A World Without Compassion

We live in a culture that laughs at the idea of compassion. Most spiritual teachers call it a fundamental component of spiritual life, yet we have virtually no familiarity with compassion in our public or private lives.

The model that permeates our lives is retribution. Someone is to blame, and someone must pay. Our prison system is the most blatant example of a complete and utter lack of compassion. Within the last several years, even the term *correctional institution*, which hinted at some attention to rehabilitation, has been officially dropped. Now our prison system doesn't even pretend the least interest in helping or supporting inmates. They did something wrong; they pay the price. It's only fair. Each individual alone is to blame (as if he or she didn't emerge out of a dysfunctional subculture or family, created by overwhelming social and economic inequities), and when you screw up, these are the consequences: an even worse, appallingly dysfunctional society (prison), fully supported by our tax dollars. "In God We Trust"? Not in our prison system. In our ability to be as cruel and vindictive as possible we trust.

The demand for retribution arises out of righteousness and hatred and beliefs like this: "I'm right and you're wrong. I'm the good person; you're the bad person. I would never do anything that horrible. You must be punished." And in some cases even, "I'm so good and you're so bad, I get to say that you must die!"

This sounds extreme, yet I have heard politicians say almost these very words, with a completely self-righteous tone in their voices. This is the model our country sets for us. It is most unspiritual.

Avoiding the Impact of a Blaming World on Our Personal Lives

This general attitude easily filters into our personal lives. A therapist told me that during the third session with a couple she was seeing, the wife became very angry and shouted out, "Why don't you tell him he is wrong!" The very idea that her husband might be doing the best he could or that she herself might have some role in the problems they were having or that she might even be able to exhibit some degree of compassion was foreign to her. To fix the problem, punish the person who is wrong!

Is it any wonder Mother Teresa once commented that the United States was the most loveless country she ever visited? And of course, with the rapid advance of the global economy, we are now exporting our values all over the world. As spiritual people, we have a huge job to do, and we need to work fast.

But, you may ask, doesn't it make sense to be angry and self-righteous in the presence of obvious malice and ill will? How will we bring about change if we don't get up a good head of steam when we see destructive behavior? What about genocide? What about the destruction of the planet for short-term profit?

Anger is a natural human emotion (when it has not been softened through spiritual practice). But judgment and blame are the antithesis of compassion and are not spiritual—that is, they are not behavior that brings you into closer and closer alignment with your highest self.

When someone does something mean spirited or cruel, that person is experiencing a lack within himself or herself. A nonspiritual person will see only the cruel or thoughtless act. A compassionate person will feel the underlying pain of the mean-spirited person and want to reach out and help.

Evil, thoughtlessness, and cruelty are simply ignorance. That's all. Evil people would not be evil if they were spiritually aware, if they were guided by their soul's longing for inner peace, if they were moved by love. They are evil because their spiritual consciousness has not been raised. They are not motivated by deep inner convictions; they are able to respond to the world around them only on a moment-by-moment basis. They live out of habit, with a limited view of the world. This is ignorance, deprivation. It is to be pitied, not judged.

If you respond with more hate to someone who is cruel, you will be compounding the darkness, moving both of you further from the light, further from consciousness. When you hate and feel self-righteous about evil, you do not diminish the evil; you increase it! Now there are two people moving away from light and toward darkness!

Blaming and hating do nothing to reduce the problem at hand. All they do is diminish the one who is doing the hating and blaming. The spiritual response to anything negative is compassion.

Compassion does not preclude constructive action to limit the damage of the selfish, greedy, or mean-spirited aggressors. Gandhi was compassionate toward his British oppressors. But out of his compassion, he acted on his own to gain independence for his people. Compassion increases consciousness, love, and connection, in both the one who experiences the compassion and the object of the compassion. Anger, judgment, and blame decrease these spiritual qualities for everyone involved.

From Judgment to Compassion

I had a personal experience recently that taught me this lesson. It was a mild incident, to be sure, but it showed me the dramatic difference, within myself, between judgment and compassion.

I called a single friend of mine, very excited because I wanted to introduce her to a man I thought she would genuinely like. I had an intuition that there might be a real match there. I left an animated message on her voice mail. The next day, I received a response on my voice mail that was unexpectedly negative. "I don't know," my friend said. "You and I have very different tastes in men. From your description, I'm pretty sure it wouldn't work. I mean, I'd meet him if you insisted, but I have my doubts."

I was stunned by this response, and as the moments passed, I realized I was angry. I felt I had presented her with a beautiful package, all wrapped up with a big bow, and she had thrown it in the trash—without even opening it. I had the good sense not to call her back for a few days, as all that was running through my head were sarcastic and nasty retorts.

I thought she was being unappreciative and rude. But I was increasing the "darkness" by blaming and being angry with her. I was right, and she was wrong. I felt insulted, belittled. That was all I could see.

I mentioned the incident to another friend, who promptly said to me, "She must just be scared about meeting anybody who might really work for her." In an instant, my anger softened. Suddenly I felt sad for my friend. *My focus shifted from me to her.* Whatever was keeping her from meeting this lovely man was narrowing her life, limiting her options. Maybe it was fear, maybe it was her need to be in control. Or maybe her intuition was more on target than mine! "She has a right to be who she is," I realized. "I don't know what is going on inside her. I want to support her, not force my agenda on her."

When I shifted from focusing on how this incident affected me to looking at what might be motivating her, I felt compassion and let go of my own hurt.

The Christian mystic Thomas Merton says,

> [T]rue love and prayer are learned in the moment when prayer
> has become impossible and the heart has turned to stone.

When you are angry and full of blame, when your heart has turned to stone, when compassion is difficult even to imagine—that is when feeling compassion will be a challenge and will truly lead to spiritual growth.

We do not live in a world overflowing with compassion; quite the opposite. All the more reason that those of us who are on a spiritual path, who are striving to become more in alignment with our highest potential, need to cultivate compassion. Begin with your partner.

The power of compassion is unlimited. All the great models of spiritual leadership in history—people like Jesus, Gandhi, and Martin Luther King Jr.—have had true compassion for their enemies.

And compassion starts with each of us, within ourselves and toward all those around us. The more we each exhibit compassion at home and at work, the more it will spread until, conceivably, compassion could begin to have an impact on corporate greed, world poverty and hunger, the destruction of our planet, and even war. I will let Vietnamese spiritual teacher Thich Nhat Hanh have the last word on this subject. As you read this, think not only about our planet but about your own relationship:

EXPERIMENT 20

Compassion

1. In your journal, write answers to these questions:

   In what ways am I not being compassionate toward my partner?

   How would I behave if I were feeling compassion?

2. Gradually work on the questions listed in the "Developing Compassion for Your Partner" section. As you have time, write out the answers in your journal or discuss them with a friend.

3. In what ways are you increasing the darkness rather than moving toward the light? That is, what are you feeling angry or self-righteous or even hateful about? What would it be like for you to convert these feelings of anger into compassion, as I did with my friend, when I began focusing on her instead of on myself?

One compassionate word, action, or thought can reduce another person's suffering and bring him joy. One word can give comfort and confidence, destroy doubt, help someone avoid a mistake, reconcile a conflict, or open the door to liberation. One action can save a person's life or help him take advantage of a rare opportunity. One thought can do the same, because thoughts always lead to words and actions. With compassion in our heart, every thought, word, and deed can bring about a miracle.

PART TWO

Putting Spiritual Partnership to Work in Your Relationship

CHAPTER 10

Exactly How to Use the Eight Loving Actions

For some readers, reading about the concept of Spiritual Partnership and Loving Actions may create a sufficient inner shift, and reading this book may be all it takes to make a difference in your relationship. I'm sure that by reading this far, you have a solid understanding that you have options available to you besides "sitting down and talking"—such options as adopting a spirit of good will, giving up problem solving, forgetting about who is right and who is wrong, acting as if instead of reacting automatically, practicing restraint, balancing your own giving and taking, acting on your own, and practicing acceptance and compassion. You have seen that there is some overlap in the Eight Loving Actions and that they all might be summed up under the general concept of good will and a generosity of spirit toward your partner. You now know that you can always ask yourself, "What is my role in this conflict? No matter who is right or wrong, what shift can I make that will ease this situation? If I were to act in accord with my highest spiritual values right now, what would I do?"

Old habits die hard, however, and practicing the Loving Actions in a systematic way will help you learn them well so that they become deeply entrenched. Deliberate experiments will help you replace old counterproductive Stage Two relationship habits more quickly.

If you would like to practice the Loving Actions in a focused and systematic way, the simple structure I suggest here will help you do that. This "program" may be the easiest couples work you have ever attempted. There's no preparation (except for the chapters you just read). There are no long questionnaires to fill out. You don't have to set aside big blocks of time or persuade your partner to sit down and do a structured exercise with you. Spiritual Partnership is just a new way to be, a new way to think, a new way of doing what you already do in your relationship.

The only thing you need to bring with you as you get started is a little willingness. Even an ounce will do. It doesn't matter if you are skeptical or pessimistic. It doesn't matter if you don't feel like doing an act. Just do it, for a set amount of time. That's all. Remember, only a change in your *behavior* will bring you to new feelings and welcome changes in your relationship.

What follows is a suggestion for using the Loving Actions as a simple program for improving your relationship. The program consists of five steps:

Get Ready

1. Assess your relationship.

2. Make a commitment to your relationship.

3. Make a commitment to the program.

Get Set

   4. Set up support appointments.

Go

   5. Begin experimenting with the Eight Loving Actions.

Step One: Assess Your Relationship

On a scale of 1 to 10, 1 being just this side of calling a divorce lawyer and 10 being completely fabulous, how would you rate your level of satisfaction and happiness in your relationship right now? Go ahead, choose a number.

Be assured, as we observed in the Introduction to this book, the Eight Loving Actions will improve your relationship *no matter where you are on the scale*. I have literally seen 2s and 3s move to 10, and I have seen 10s make discoveries that moved them into even closer intimacy—more than they had ever known or imagined.

Now, if you haven't done so earlier in this book, take a moment to list what you see as the biggest problems in your relationship, the main obstacles to happiness. Then list what you see as the greatest strengths in your relationship. What do you adore about your partner? What do the two of you do well together?

I suggest you write these lists in your journal. Take time with them and be completely honest with yourself.

Step Two: Make a Commitment to Your Relationship

This program using the Eight Loving Actions assumes that you want to improve your relationship, that you love your partner and are committed to making the relationship work really well for both of you. If you feel that commitment, skip to step three.

If you are not certain that you feel that commitment, this program will be extremely useful for you. Here is how it will help:

If your relationship is so bad that you are thinking about leaving your partner, but you have not done so yet, either you are genuinely ambivalent or you so far haven't mustered up the courage to do what you know you need to do: walk away. In either case, this program will give you great help.

If you are ambivalent, then what you need is more information. That's exactly what doing the Eight Loving Actions will give you: more information. Do a Loving Action and take careful notes about what happens. Notice how it makes you feel. Even angrier? Softer and more understanding? Every subtle feeling counts. How does your partner respond? Notice and write down everything.

It's a known axiom that if you keep doing the same things, you will keep getting the same results. That's probably what has been happening in your relationship for years. The Eight Loving Actions give you *something new to try*, and you are absolutely certain to get different results. You have no idea what those new results will be until you try the experiments. By the end of this program, you will either know for certain that you want to leave or be clear that your own new attitude has created positive changes that you like.

For the purposes of this program, then, if you can't make a genuine commitment to your relationship, make a commitment to finding out exactly what your level of commitment is.

Exception

If your partner is abusing you, either physically or emotionally, do not use this program. If your partner is addicted to drugs or alcohol, do not use this program. Instead, call someone and ask for help. Find a minister, priest, or rabbi in your area, even if you don't know the person. Look in your phone book for psychotherapists or for domestic abuse programs or substance abuse programs. If you can't find anyone else, call your local police department and ask for a referral to a domestic abuse program or a counselor. You must take care of yourself. If you don't, no one else will. Don't let fear stop you from asking for the help you need. *You cannot manage this problem by yourself.* No one else ever has. You must call someone and be totally honest about what is happening.

Special Warning to Singles

Do not use this program to stay in a relationship when you know you are settling for less than what you truly want or deserve. While you still have the opportunity to choose the person who will be your lifelong partner, *choose carefully!* Don't make the mistake of staying in a relationship you are less than enthusiastic about or that has significant problems just because you aren't paying attention!

One of the most common mistakes singles make is to spend months or years in what I call BTN relationships: better than nothing. BTNs keep you out of circulation for finding the true love of your life, and they lower your self-esteem. I have written extensively about BTNs in my book *If I'm So Wonderful, Why Am I Still Single?* and about exactly how to keep your standards—and your spirits— high as you search for your soul mate. Here, suffice it to say that if you truly desire a committed relationship and are not yet in one, that in itself might be a reason for you to end your relationship. Move on and hold out for what you truly want; only then do you have even a chance of getting it. Save your skills as a spiritual leader for a relationship you are certain you very much want to be a part of.

As Benjamin Franklin so wisely said, "Keep your eyes wide open before marriage and half shut afterwards." (By "half shut afterwards," I'm sure he meant "be accepting," not "be unconscious." There is a world of difference.)

Step Three: Make a Commitment to the Program

I suggest you give this program at least eight weeks. Make a commitment to yourself right now that you will, to the very best of your ability, try the Eight Loving Actions for eight weeks.

If you rated your relationship 7 to 10, maybe just reading this book is all you need to do. A shift in attitude and a few Loving Actions when they are appropriate here and there will enhance your already thriving relationship. You may not need this program.

If your relationship is from 1 to 6 on the scale, I encourage you to be extremely deliberate: set up an exact program and follow it precisely. Make this program a major priority for yourself for the next eight weeks. *It is impossible to do this program seriously and not see changes!*

If you are going to set up a precise and deliberate program for the next eight weeks, you will need three allies: a journal, a calendar, and a support person or support group.

If you haven't already done so, find a notebook or an attractive bound blank book that you can use as a journal. And find a calendar to keep with your journal.

Set Aside Your Problems

For the eight weeks of this program, do not discuss your problems with your partner. The point of this program, remember, is not to solve your problems but to create, as Jung put it, a "new level of consciousness," a "higher or wider interest" so that "through this broadening of outlook, the insoluble problem loses its urgency."

If you catch yourself discussing your problem with your partner; having an old, familiar argument; or even *experiencing* your problem (your partner is criticizing you, you are doing all the housework, your partner falls asleep in the middle of your conversation, your partner doesn't listen to you, and the like), *immediately do something positive yourself.* Either take care of yourself in some way or do something thoughtful and generous for your partner. Deliberately create a positive atmosphere. Remember that your relationship is far more important than this annoying incident.

Keep Your Expectations Open

Avoid fantasizing or hoping for any particular results from your experiments. Do not become attached to any particular outcome.

This is not easy to accomplish, but it is an important value for anyone on a spiritual path. (We will discuss it in more depth in Chapter Fourteen when we talk about spirituality.) The Eight Loving Actions will give you a fine opportunity to practice this value.

There are two reasons it's important to keep your expectations open: the first is that it will help you avoid pain and disappointment if what you hope for doesn't occur; the second is that if you are riveted to one outcome, you may miss quite wonderful serendipitous results that you never even imagined might occur.

Winifred was an avid Balkan folk dancer. More than anything, she wanted her husband, Jonathan, to take up the hobby too. He sort of liked it, but in order to enjoy it fully, he would have had to dance every week so he could learn a number of dances well. This he was never willing to do.

Winifred tried Loving Action 6. Acting on her own, she hired a folk dance teacher to come to their home every Thursday evening for a lesson. She told Jonathan she was doing it for herself, but invited him to join her. Jonathan did the lessons, but he still would not go out dancing with her except occasionally.

They both enjoyed the teacher and found themselves involved in long conversations with her after the lessons. Jonathan suggested that she bring her husband with her the next time and that they all go out for dinner after the lesson. Over dinner, the other couple talked about how much they miss playing bridge because none of their friends play. Because Jonathan and Winifred both play, they set up a bridge evening and had a wonderful time. Now they all play bridge regularly. Winifred still goes dancing without Jonathan, but she doesn't care because they have now found a different hobby they enjoy together.

That's serendipity. Acting on her own worked for Winifred, but not at all in the way she had anticipated or hoped for.

Step Four: Set Up Your Support Appointments or Group

The more external support you can set up for yourself, the more successful your program will be. The minimum you need is a support partner. Even if you and your intimate partner are doing the program together, find someone else. A second person is necessary to help you pay attention and to keep you focused. When you talk through an experiment you did, you will learn more from it. And because you will be accountable to this person, you are more likely to stay on track.

The ideal support person is a friend who is using this program at the same time you are. Do it together.

When you find your support person, make an appointment to talk with him or her *every week at the same time*. You will report exactly what experiment or experiments you did that week, the results, and exactly what experiment or experiments you will do in the following week.

Even better than one support person is a support group. If you can locate two to five other people who want to practice Spiritual Partnership and you form a support group that meets at the same time every week, you will all gain tremendous help. Hearing about other people's successes will boost your own motivation. Other people will have ideas for you that you might never think up on your own.

The structure for the group can be very simple. Be sure to use a timer and divide the time equally among all members. Each person should report what occurred during the week and then, with the help of the group, decide exactly what experiment to undertake for the next week.

For information about a therapist in your area who is trained and certified to conduct a Spiritual Partnership support group, visit our Web site at www.susanpage.com.

Step Five: Begin!

Chances are that, having read this far, you have already begun to use the Spiritual Partnership philosophy. If even once you have avoided an argument by unobtrusively changing the subject; if you have felt annoyed but chosen not to express this but instead to behave in an upbeat way; if you have figured out a solution to a conflict by acting on your own and being both decisive and empathic; if you have deliberately refrained from making a critical comment; if you have consciously agreed to something you didn't truly prefer, in a spirit of good will; if you have dropped all discussion about some ongoing conflict because you now realize that discussing it more won't solve it; if you have shifted to accepting, with compassion, a difficult trait in your partner, rather than still trying to change it— then you have already begun to feel the personal power and new possibilities of Spiritual Partnership.

Let your first priority be to move directly toward a harmonious atmosphere in your relationship. You can bring about remarkable, rapid transformation by dropping problem-solving, behaving in a loving way no matter how you feel, and curbing critical comments. Know that by focusing on generosity and a spirit of good will and on finding your own creative solutions to the problems that disturb you, you will be maturing spiritually and psychologically at the same time you will be renewing the sparkle in your relationship.

However, even though you are getting the feel of Spiritual Partnership, you may achieve more depth and more enduring change by setting up deliberate experiments on a firm schedule. Especially if you are working with a support partner or in a support group, a systematic approach will strengthen your learning.

Choose one Loving Action that strikes you as useful in your situation and focus on just that one for a specific period of time. It is often effective to start with practicing restraint, but you may prefer to begin with a different one. Make a pact with yourself that you will not make any negative, critical, or demanding comments to your mate for one whole week (or that you will act as if, or whichever Loving Action you choose first). You probably won't achieve perfection the first week, but you will learn a great deal about yourself. The experiment will raise your awareness and offer you new insights.

Even if you have never kept a journal, start one now. The few minutes it takes you to jot down your commitment to an experiment for a specific time frame, and then noting what you learned by doing it, will make your experiments vastly more productive. Include the exact experiment you plan to do and for how long, exactly what occurred with each incident, how you felt, and how your partner responded. For example, you might start by writing something like this:

July 3, 2006

Experiment: Monday morning, 8 AM through Wednesday evening, 11 PM I will refrain from making any negative, critical, or demanding comments to Ed.

Monday, 11 PM: A little victory: I was going to remind Ed to take out the trash, and I just let him read, and before he went to bed, he just now took it out! I thanked him. He kissed me. It's working! I feel proud of myself and happy.

Tuesday, 9 AM: Oops, I told Ed I didn't think he was dressed right for his big meeting today. He didn't change clothes, so my remark did nothing except make neither of us feel very good. I sent him off with a little fight instead of excitement. Too bad! I see how this could have been different! I feel sad about the incident, but happy I am getting this insight!

And so on. Talk over each entry with your support person or support group. Highlight your best insights.

Each time you try out a new Loving Action, take time to write out the associated boxed experiments I have suggested.

When you have experimented with one Loving Action, try out another one, always *as an experiment*, and always for an exact set time with a beginning time and an end time. The amount of time can be anything from five minutes to the entire week. It's perfectly fine to repeat your first experiment over and over. Or you may want to try a new one. Just keep experimenting, paying attention, and recording your experiences. Use each of the Eight Loving Actions at least once.

One of the things that may happen is that you will find a way not to do an experiment you have set up. This is very common. You may have a reason, such as that someone came over or your partner went out for the evening. Or you may just have been unable or unwilling to do it. Period.

This is a result! Remember, with an experiment, there is no such thing as failure. No matter what happens or doesn't happen, you learned something, and that is all we ever ask of an experiment. Record what you learned in your journal.

I worked with a woman who stayed in a support group for eight weeks, but did not actually carry out a single experiment until the last day of the last week, and even that was halfhearted: she attended a business dinner with her husband, but left early. After eight weeks, by paying attention to her unwillingness to experiment at all, this woman began to see how debilitating her own anger was and that she was the only one who could change it. That was a big lesson for her.

Another possibility is that you will do an experiment and see no response whatsoever from your partner. This is also common. No noticeable response is a response. Write it down. Or all you may notice is a tiny glance or gesture or a single remark. Everything counts. Pay attention. Notice everything and write it all down.

That's it. That's all you have to do. The rest will happen by itself.

Don't make the mistake of saying to yourself, "I'll do all this sometime, after _____." Don't put this program off another minute. It does not have to take any extra time. Start right now, in as structured or unstructured a way as feels right for you. Have a good time with your experiments. I wish for you refreshing personal insights that bring you a new inner strength, the experience of old problems fading away, and above all, new harmony and passion in your relationship!

CHAPTER 11

Frequently Asked Questions

Most people are skeptical when they first hear about such a "magical" solution to deeply rooted, extremely difficult relationship problems. You may be too, as you have read through this book. Let me address some of the most common hesitations people have when they first hear about Spiritual Partnership.

Q: *Can these Eight Loving Actions create changes that will last over a long period of time?*

A: A profound inner shift to a new way of seeing is something that never goes away. Of course people revert to old, habitual behaviors. But once you have seen that a new possibility exists, you can never again be completely in the dark or pretend that you didn't once see the light.

Spiritual Partnership is not glib or simplistic. It is a way of putting into practice centuries of wisdom from the great spiritual traditions on this planet. We all have demons that separate us from love; what differs is only the nature of those demons. Your soul knows how to conquer all of yours.

Like other aspects of our spiritual journey, the growing and learning in relationships never end. Backsliding is to be expected, but Spiritual Partnership helps you slip and slide up the *spiritual* path instead of some other well-meant path of relationship techniques that will never get you to where you truly want to be. *Whereas most strategies suggest that you make small changes within the old systems of communication and fairness, Spiritual Partnership invites you to shift to a completely new system.*

Spiritual Partnership is not a destination, but a path, a journey. Just getting onto the correct path is what feels so good to so many people right at the beginning. It feels "magical" because, for most people, it is something they have never tried before. It usually makes a difference quickly, and yes, the results from the changes you make will endure.

Q: *Spiritual Partnership can't possibly work miracles for everyone. Aren't some partners just plain incompatible?*

A: Yes. It is true that some partners will never be truly happy together. Practicing Spiritual Partnership may help you decide not to remain together. It may give you the information you have been looking for in order to decide what to do.

Relationships don't have to be "good" to be spiritual. We often learn important spiritual lessons from relationships that are difficult and that don't last. If you are on a spiritual path, everything that happens presents you with an opportunity to practice and grow. It isn't what happens that makes something spiritual or not spiritual; it's what you learn from what happens that makes the difference.

Spiritual Partnership helps you discover whether you are likely to do well together and offers you guidelines for deciding what to do about your relationship.

When you experiment with Loving Actions, you will fairly quickly see whether your new behavior will bring about any changes, either in you or in your partner. Most likely, changes you never anticipated *will occur.* They have never happened before because *you have never tried this new behavior before*—largely because you simply never thought of it.

If, after ten or twelve weeks of earnest experiments, no changes at all have come about, you have valuable *new* information. For example, you may discover that you don't feel good acting with loving compassion toward your partner. Or your partner may not respond at all to your loving and compassionate acts. If either or both of these occur, your spiritual response might be to separate.

(A word of caution here: you may think that you know ahead of time exactly what will happen when you try a Loving Action. But you don't know whether your hypothesis is right until you actually try the experiment. *You will learn, grow, and change, not from* thinking about *doing a spiritual act, but by* actually doing *the spiritual act.* Many, many couples who expected nothing to change when they tried Spiritual Partnership have been amazed at the positive changes that did occur.)

In the game of bridge, there is a play known as a finesse that is called for in a certain situation. Depending on which player is holding the king, the finesse may succeed or fail. Even if it fails, the finesse was the right thing to do in that situation. In the same way, if you focus on being the most spiritually evolved partner you can be, in accord with the guidelines in this book, your efforts may preserve your relationship or help you conclude it. Either way, you were doing the right thing, behaving in accord with your spiritual values.

Q: *Why do you sometimes work with only one member of a couple? Spiritual Partnership can't possibly work unless both partners practice it, can it?*

A: Most strategies for couples require the active cooperation of both partners. Together you learn to listen, to support, to reach compromises, to resolve conflicts.

Spiritual Partnership invites you to *act on your own* by bringing your personal spiritual practice right smack into the center of your relationship. It invites you to ask, "If I were going to behave in a spiritual way right now, what would I do?"

So in fact Spiritual Partnership *is* something that you do by yourself. Nothing I have suggested in this entire book requires the cooperation of your partner. That is precisely why Spiritual Partnership is both easier and more effective than traditional approaches based on communication.

Consider Maria and Doug. Doug had a second job as a landscape designer that kept him away from the family on weekends and evenings. He loved this work, but Maria felt they did not need the extra income and that the family did need Doug at home much more. Two years of pleading and negotiating on Maria's part had effected no change.

When Maria was introduced to Spiritual Partnership, she began by proactively and deliberately accepting what she knew she could not change, not with a feeling of resignation, but in a spirit of love and good will, a fundamental spiritual principle. That one shift transformed the atmosphere in the relationship. Then she began finding ways to involve Doug more when he was available, and persuaded Doug to let his teenagers "apprentice" with him on the job. Doug loved this. Maria was now happier and more relaxed so that the time she spent together with him was much more pleasant. In a short time, Doug decided to cut back and save Saturday afternoons for

Maria. They came to adore their Saturday afternoons and used them for special outings or time with friends.

As long as your partner is responding positively to your spirit of good will and compassion, you don't *both* have to "learn" it. Don't worry; your spirit of good will and love will rub off! (If it doesn't rub off *at all*, you may want to reevaluate staying in the relationship.) In fact, by moving far beyond the conventional categories of right, fair, and equal, Spiritual Partnership reaps results that go far beyond those that are *merely* right, fair, and equal.

The idea of "working on your relationship" by yourself is quite radical, I realize, and may not seem appealing or even possible to you. It's perfectly okay to feel some fear or anxiety about undertaking any of the experiments in this book—all by yourself. After all, you may be trying something that runs counter to a lifetime of conditioning. All I hope is that you don't let your fears stop you from experimenting. Gently allow yourself to try something new, even though you feel afraid. All we are suggesting in Spiritual Partnership is that you take initiative, that you provide some quiet leadership. If you find you are hesitating to experiment—because it feels strange or you are afraid of what might happen—talk about this with your support person. Find one small experiment that you feel willing to do, and start with that. Don't feel you have to change everything all at once.

For some people, being able to work alone is a singular advantage of Spiritual Partnership over other approaches, because they have never been able to move beyond the very first step of convincing their partner to cooperate. If you would state your problem as "My partner won't go to a counselor" or "My partner will never talk about the problem," then the suggestions in this book are perfectly suited for you; your need for that elusive "talk" is over.

If both you and your partner want to embark on Spiritual Partnership together, you'll have an exciting time; it works well when you journey together. But if your partner isn't up for it, don't worry. Your partner has a right to be uninterested or unwilling; whatever the reason, that reason is valid for him or her. Respect it. You can achieve progress in your own spiritual journey using Spiritual Partnership by yourself, and your relationship will reap extraordinary benefits.

Q: *I'm worried that Spiritual Partnership is just a dressed-up way of telling women to back down and give in to men. Will Spiritual Partnership take women backwards?*

A: Let's look again at Maria and Doug. When Maria finally began to accept Doug's passion about landscaping, it may have looked to an outsider as though Maria finally just gave up and let Doug have his way. She lost. Once again as always, the woman wimped out, and the man got his way.

But look closer. Actually, giving up is what Maria had been doing for two years, under the old "negotiation" system. Negotiation never got her anywhere except resentful. And, in the face of her resentment, Doug never changed. Maria quite literally had no choice but to give in. And she felt resentful and angry.

When Maria, in a conscious spiritual act and on her own initiative, gave up her fight and became gracious about the landscaping, everything shifted. And notice that Doug did make some changes! He made them in an atmosphere of love from Maria, not in the atmosphere of negativity and making him wrong that she was creating before.

Maria did not become accepting and compassionate as a technique to get Doug to change; she did it to experiment with putting Spiritual Partnership into practice. But it was only when she began to provide spiritual leadership in her relationship that genuine changes began to happen.

Did Maria lose? Did Doug get his way? In Spiritual Partnership, we don't even ask these questions that betray the old way of looking at things. Maria succeeded in behaving in accord with her spiritual values; she became accepting of Doug, just the way he really is, and gave up trying to change him; she acted out of love, both self-love and love for Doug. Then whatever happened, happened.

Recall the little flame that each of us has glowing deep within us. All of life is an effort to keep that flame burning brightly. By endlessly "negotiating" with Doug to stop his landscaping, Maria was inadvertently giving him the message, "You are a bad person; you are being unfair and inconsiderate." Doug's little flame was begging for love and support but was receiving only criticism. It was actually *appropriate* for him to respond to Maria's assaults by defending his behavior, by standing up for his own little flame instead of allowing Maria to squelch it. Stage Two communication skills can set up adversarial positions like this, and we can become trapped in them for years.

As we have seen, your partner is much more likely to make the changes you would like if you take the initiative to create an atmosphere of love and support, if you deliberately find ways to stoke your partner's inner flame and help it burn brightly.

At first glance, Spiritual Partnership may sometimes look as though someone is being asked to give in, to lose, to "sacrifice." But in fact, those categories don't exist in Spiritual Partnership— where your task is to find ways to balance self-love and love for your partner.

You are always in control of that balance.

In Spiritual Partnership we learn specific ways to focus more on loving than on being loved, more on understanding than on being understood. Thousands of couples have now learned that it is when they learn to love more freely and openly, while still taking good care of themselves, that love comes flooding back to them, often in greater abundance than they had ever dreamed.

Q: *What is the relationship between Spiritual Partnership and psychology?*

A: We have just come through several decades in which a psychological model dominated our understanding of relationships. We heard about how hard it is to escape early childhood programming, how we project our own unresolved issues onto our partners, how we subconsciously choose partners who will help us resolve issues with our parents, how our personality type affects our behavior, and how to understand and manage gender differences. We learned how to listen to each other and ask for what we want. We discovered the importance of viewing our families as a system in which each person plays an unwitting role in keeping dysfunctional patterns in place.

An important aspect of Spiritual Partnership is the move toward increasing awareness. Becoming aware of how all of these psychological dynamics affect your own relationships is an important part of Spiritual Partnership. Understanding your own or your partner's personality type, early childhood programming, habitual behaviors, and "dysfunctional patterns" may be an enormous help to you in experiencing acceptance and compassion, in practicing restraint, and in acting on your own.

Spiritual Partnership incorporates and builds on hard-won psychological wisdom. Indeed, we wouldn't be ready now for the move to Spiritual Partnership without all this important work that has gone before.

A relationship with a competent therapist, couples counselor, or therapeutic group can be a great aid in spiritual work. When you engage fully in psychological work, you will definitely increase your self-awareness. You will receive help in distinguishing between your "conditioned" self and your authentic self. And, because therapeutic relationships and therapy groups are intimate, you will experience connection, perhaps even a brand-new level or type of connection, an important aspect of spirituality.

Traditionally, psychoanalysis was seen as different from spiritual work. "Psychology helps you build a stronger ego," the belief went, "whereas the goal of spiritual work is to transcend the ego." It's true that the final goal of some spiritual practices is a loss of the experience of self as self. But I believe that at the less "advanced" levels of spiritual practice where most of us live, the goals of psychology and of spiritual work are similar: to become more self-aware, more authentic, more loving, more capable of positive connections with those around us, and happier in our lives.

In his book *A Path with Heart*, Buddhist teacher Jack Kornfield sees psychological and spiritual work as mutually supportive:

> Many serious students and teachers of the spiritual path in the West have found it necessary or useful to turn to psychotherapy for help in their spiritual life. Many others who have not done so would probably benefit by it. . . . What American [spiritual] practice has come to acknowledge is that many of the deep issues we uncover in spiritual life cannot be healed by meditation alone. . . . The best of modern therapy is much like a process of shared meditation, where therapist and client sit together, learning to pay close attention to those aspects and dimensions of the self that the client may be unable to touch on his or her own.

Alan Lew spent ten years in an intense practice of Zen Buddhism and then became a rabbi. In his autobiography, *One God Clapping*, he tells of the time when he was wracked with indecision about whether or not to leave his first wife and found that meditation was not helping him. Finally he decided to seek support from a therapist. In just a few sessions, he was able to gain insights about early family imprinting that brought him great clarity and peace of mind.

In my own life, during an important phase of my spiritual journey, my guides were psychotherapists. The breakup of my first marriage plunged me into the dark night of despair. I was confused, without direction, and filled with self-loathing and shame. I soon found for myself a therapy group that became so safe for me that I could share my deepest vulnerabilities.

Even more important, the therapist and group members kept pointing out to me, ever so lovingly, patterns that did not serve me, lies I told myself, behavior that distanced me from others just when I was trying to become closer. They were able to see through my defenses, and each time they saw glimpses of my genuine inner strength, they nurtured it. Over and over they watched me cover up deep feelings with a smiling facade, and over and over they pointed it out, until I thought their patience would surely be wearing thin.

Gradually, sustained by their love, I began to talk about painful regrets. Ever so gradually, honesty began to replace the habits I had developed over the years to protect myself. Though it was occurring in a "psychological" setting, this was most certainly spiritual work. It was moving me in the direction of connection and authenticity.

In short, we are making two observations: (1) psychological and spiritual goals are often closely related, and (2) psychological tools can be very helpful in the journey of spiritual growth.

CHAPTER 12

Communication Within Spiritual Partnership

As we have established throughout this book, communication is not necessarily the best tool for achieving a healthy relationship. If your relationship is troubled in some ways, Loving Actions will lead you back to love and mutual enjoyment faster and more effectively than trying to talk your way into a happy marriage.

Loving Actions will carry you far beyond a "functional" relationship to one of pleasurable companionship and deep mutual joy, love, and respect, and you'll never discontinue them once you have discovered their magic.

After Loving Actions have helped you establish a solid base of intimacy and love, however, verbal communication can play its appropriate role: deepening the connection between you. Talking may not be the best path *to* a great relationship, but excellent verbal communication *is* one of love's great rewards—a sign of a great relationship, not a means of getting to one. Love gives rise to many expressions of affection, and talking is one of them.

Communication as the Heart of Intimacy

To understand the proper role of verbal communication in love, we must first review the meaning of *intimacy*, a much misunderstood term. Intimacy is not romantic walks on the beach, sexy evenings in front of a warm fireplace, or elegant dinners. Intimacy is not sex.

These activities might take place between two people who are intimate, but they are not themselves "intimate." In fact, when they take place between two people who are not genuinely intimate, they are what I call pseudo-intimacy, or intimate-type behavior.

Intimacy is, quite simply, stripping away your outer, more public ways of being and sharing your inner life with another person. It is radical, honest self-disclosure, trusting another person enough to share your deepest fears and your greatest vulnerabilities. Intimacy is all about discovering and telling your truth.

There are two steps involved in telling the truth. First, you have to discover what your truth is; second, you have to trust another person enough to share it. Verbal communication is a part of both of these steps.

Discovering Your Truth as an Individual

Jessica could feel herself becoming anxious. After eating well for months, suddenly she found herself snacking on junk foods. She wasn't sleeping well either. When a friend asked her how she was, she discovered that she felt uncomfortable saying, "Things are great," but didn't know why. Everything she looked at in her life seemed to be going well.

Her friend wisely took her out for a glass of wine one evening and started to ask her a few questions, such as "Tell me how your new job is going."

"Oh, I just love it," Jessica started out. "I feel so lucky. The people I work with are really good."

It took Jessica thirty or forty minutes of telling stories about work and describing the people there for her to discover, to her own surprise, that she was actually feeling undermined and unsupported at work and that she was insecure about one aspect of her job. She realized she was quite angry—with herself mostly—for not standing up to two people who, she now saw, were sabotaging her workplace situation.

Communication helped Jessica *discover* her own truth. This is step one.

Jessica was grateful to her friend for picking up on her anxiety and offering to help her explore it. It frightened her to realize that without that opportunity to think out loud about what was going on at work, she might have gone on for months without understanding the source of her anxiety and without recognizing that she needed to stop being so "nice" at work and instead be more assertive.

It's a sad fact of life in these times that for many people, opportunities to discover what is truly going on inside them are few. Such opportunities usually don't arise spontaneously; we have to create them, and we usually don't take the time to do it.

What is required is leisurely, open-ended time in which you deliberately talk with another person about your life, your feelings, your aspirations, your disappointments, your worries. The other person can be a friend or relative, an intimate group, a paid professional such as a therapist or counselor, or your intimate partner.

Personal growth retreats or workshops can also be excellent catalysts for discovering hidden truths about yourself. Or many people have gained valuable insights in women's groups and men's groups. You have to meet long enough to establish trust with each other.

Then, typically, each person is allotted at least a half hour to talk about one worrisome issue. Alert group members can listen for clues about what might need to be explored in more depth.

For example, at a recent meeting of my own women's group, one member I'll call Brenda said, "I think I'm feeling okay about my father's death. I seem not to have any more unfinished business about that."

Another woman, listening below the surface of these words, said, "Tell us a little more about that." Brenda spent the next forty minutes talking about her father and ultimately told us one remaining regret that was terribly hard for her to speak about. Her tears came from a very deep place.

Both Jessica and Brenda used communication to discover what was true for them. All of us need to do this. Truths that are difficult to talk about *want* to stay hidden. But when they stay undercover, they will certainly betray you. The parts of yourself that you don't know about have disproportionate power over you. They take control. Talking about your feelings is one of the few ways to discover more about your hidden truths.

Another way is to communicate with yourself by writing. Whatever method you choose, usually you have to find some proactive method of digging around inside yourself in order to discover what is true for you right now. Many people go through their whole lives without doing this work. People who have done little to discover their buried truths are often quite transparent to other people. Think about the boss who subtly belittles his employees all the time as a way to make himself feel superior and powerful. To those around him, his insecurities are obvious, but he may never discover them himself. He may never create an opportunity for himself to examine his own behavior, to sort through his feelings, to say out loud to someone else the thing that makes him feel most vulnerable, most afraid. There is obviously a great deal about himself that he doesn't know, and unless he deliberately begins to explore his feelings, he will never find these things out.

Discovering Your Truth as a Couple

Couples sometimes avoid talking about painful truths for years. They realize that they are feeling more distant and may crave a return to their former feelings of closeness and love. But if no incident or person helps them find a way to talk about what is happening between them, they may take many years to uncover painful topics or may never talk about them at all. What a tragic waste!

Mitch and Opal loved being together and had much in common. After the birth of their second child, Opal's interest in sex fell off dramatically. As their formerly pleasurable sex life became almost nonexistent, they were both afraid to talk about it. Each became resentful of the other. They longed for their old closeness, but the less they talked about the forbidden topic, the more frightening it became. They were both afraid that if they brought it up, they would destroy their relationship altogether.

After ten years of virtually no sex, Opal read an article in a magazine about women like herself. She felt the article must be talking about her, it was so accurate. Although she was afraid to do it, she found the courage to show the article to Mitch. They stayed up an entire night and into the next day (they both called in sick—well, they surely were healing) talking, talking, talking, crying, holding each other, talking some more, and finally making love. The problem didn't reverse itself instantly, but the difference was that now it was a problem they would work on together, lovingly and patiently, to solve; they no longer blamed Opal for it. They sought professional help, and, largely because they restored their spiritual connection, they once again became sexually desirable to each other.

"If only we had had that conversation ten years ago," Opal told me. "I guess we didn't know enough. We weren't ready. But I am so grateful that we didn't wait another ten years."

If There Is a "Charge" on It, Talk About It

In my women's group, we have a saying: "If there is a charge on it, talk about it." We mean that if you feel any kind of energy surrounding a certain topic, and especially if you feel resistance to talking about it, *talk about it*. The harder it is to bring it up or to get going on it, the more important it is to discuss.

We have an understanding that it is perfectly okay, in fact encouraged, to start by declaring, "I don't know exactly what I want to discuss today," or "I think I want to talk about my relationship, but I don't know what to say." Often these are the most productive sessions. While the person talking explores complicated feelings, we listen. We support her fully. We witness her giving birth to some new understanding about herself.

Note that resistance to talking about something often comes in the form of excuses like, "This isn't very important," or "I keep thinking I should talk about this, but I don't have anything to say about it." Consider using those statements to start a conversation with your partner or with a friend. You may have to preface your statement by saying something like, "Would you mind just listening for a while so I can try to figure out what is going on with me?"

I believe "If there is a charge on it, talk about it" is one of the most important guidelines in life. Sometimes it takes a while to realize that there is a charge (emotional energy) on a certain topic. But whenever you realize that there's something important that you are not talking about, find someone, somewhere, with whom you can discuss it in an open-ended fashion. This is one of the most direct routes to your authentic self, to consciousness, and to connection—in short, to your spiritual growth.

Sharing Your Truth

Having a "discovery" conversation with your intimate partner can be a beautiful experience and can build closeness between you. But, as we've seen, these conversations often take place in other contexts, with other people. What is essential for intimacy, however, is that you share with your intimate partner what you have discovered, even if you discovered it elsewhere.

This is step two. When you share your deepest truth with someone who receives it lovingly and without judgment, this is real intimacy.

Planning for Communication

It is easy for couples to get caught up in life and to forget to share and talk in an intimate way. Some informal structures or deliberate planning can make a big difference. In fact, one of the best "structures" for intimacy-building communication is no structure at all. But for most of us with our busy lives, we need to structure unstructured time!

I believe every couple needs to create "no-agenda" time with each other. When you are driving somewhere together, lingering over Sunday breakfast with nothing special to do later (but talking, not reading the paper), soaking in a hot tub before bed, taking a walk—these are times when topics that need to be discussed have a way of surfacing.

Mayer and I feel grateful to our dogs for compelling us to take walks every evening. No matter how late it is, no matter how tired we are, we *have* to walk the dogs. We always enjoy it. Many evenings, we know we would never have decided spontaneously to go outside and take a walk. But every evening, there we are, enjoying the evening air, the quiet of our neighborhood, the bright sky; watching the progress of the moon and the planets; and talking. We brainstorm together about each other's businesses. We talk about what is going on in our families. We speculate and dream about the future. We share feelings about movies or current events. I often think after something gets said that it probably never would have been spoken if we hadn't been engaging in idle conversation. Most of these things aren't life changing. But there have been times when we generated ideas or shared feelings that did turn out to be important.

Soaking in a hot tub, lingering after dinner with friends, going on weekend outings, enjoying lazy Sunday afternoons, taking long drives in the country—you know how best to build these unstructured times in your own family to allow for spontaneous conversation—as well as relaxed times of sharing each other's company with no conversation at all. This is the kind of "communication" that is critically important in Spiritual Partnership.

Verbal Communication in Spiritual Partnership

Now we have a complete picture of the role of communication in Spiritual Partnership. When you are working to live out your spiritual values in your relationship—trying to become more connected, more in alignment with your essential nature, more conscious, and more motivated by love—you will not use "communication skills" to try to change your partner to better meet your own needs or to persuade your partner that you are right and he or she is wrong. Rather than trying to solve problems by endlessly discussing and arguing about them, you will lovingly act to bring about change. You will use restraint, act in loving and generous ways even when

EXPERIMENT 21

No-Agenda Time

1. If you don't already do this, in the next several weeks plan some relaxing time with your Spiritual Partner, time when you will be together with no particular agenda. Take a drive or walk, take the children to Grandma's for a day and just hang out together—whatever works for you.

2. Sit down with yourself for a minute and think, is there any topic that has a charge on it, something you've been avoiding talking about? Where in your life is your emotional energy right now? Does anything feel unresolved? If so, find a relaxed time to bring up this subject with your partner or with a trusted friend. Remember, you can start by saying, "I'm not sure what I want to say."

you don't feel like it, take creative initiatives to find ways of working with incompatibilities and conflicts, and be as accepting and compassionate as you can be.

What you *will* use verbal communication for is to enjoy each other, to share your interests and your daily lives, to tell stories, and to further your own and your partner's spiritual growth through deeply intimate sharing. Because feelings are the avenue to expanded consciousness, you will use communication to discover and explore feelings that lie deep within you, feelings that may be difficult, surprising, loathsome. In the safe and loving bosom of your Spiritual Partnership you will continue your journey of self-discovery and of bringing yourself into greater alignment with your highest self.

CHAPTER 13

Making Mature Judgments

Loving Actions, guidelines, and rules—and even rules for breaking the rules—will always eventually reach their limit. They are useful learning tools, but of course the world doesn't conform to the tidy categories we establish for the sake of pedagogical simplicity.

As we gain spiritual maturity, we will confront situations in which the Loving Actions and other guidelines we have discussed are insufficient.

Asking the Right Questions

Marianne and Bert had been married for forty-one years when Bert had a stroke that left him severely impaired, both mentally and physically. He lived in a nursing home, and Marianne visited him every day for the first year he was there, but he didn't know her and didn't seem to respond to her presence. Gradually, Marianne visited less frequently, but always two or three times a week. She loved Bert, and she knew that at some level, her visits were important to him.

Then she met a man whose company she enjoyed. His wife had died five years before. The two of them provided wonderful companionship for each other. They wanted to live together. Would this be dishonest at some level? Would it be an act of betrayal against Bert? Would it be "adulterous" and therefore a "sin"?

Although some religions would superimpose inflexible rules on this situation, the spiritual approach is to ask, "What course of action is the most authentic for each of us? What would lead toward connection and away from separation? What does love require? Where does our consciousness lead us? How can we surrender to the natural rhythms of the universe?"

The answers to these questions will be different for different individuals. No preestablished guidelines or Loving Actions cover this situation. We have now moved into the vast realm where spirituality doesn't prescribe a course of action but instead prescribes a set of questions. Now, as a spiritual seeker, you have to rely on the effort you have put into your spiritual practice and on the answers you receive when you go deep within to your most authentic self.

What does love require? What course of action will cause the least harm and hurt? What will bring about the most love and happiness? Whatever we decide, will our action be kind? Will it be consistent with our compassion? Will it bring about good?

Difficult Choices

Marsha was twenty-five and about to enter law school when she learned she was pregnant. She was stunned, for she had been careful to use contraception. Though she was fond of the boyfriend who was the father of this child, she knew he was not the person she wanted to marry. She now wished she had not rushed into being sexual with this man, and felt she had learned a spiritual lesson, that she needed to make decisions like that with her deeper, more authentic self, rather than her eager-to-be-liked "public" self.

Marsha's clear feeling, coming from her most authentic self, was that she did not want to continue her pregnancy. She did not want her child to have only one parent. She did not want to interrupt her plans for her life or her commitment to use her skills and education to help other people. Nor did she want to parent an infant while trying to do well in law school. Yet she was deeply affected by knowing that she had created a new life within her.

"What does love require?" she asked herself. "What course of action will cause the least harm and hurt? What will bring about the most love and happiness? Whatever I decide, will my action be kind? Will it be consistent with compassion? Will it bring about good? What action will bring me into closer alignment with my higher self?"

Though Marianne, Bert, and Marsha are real people, I'm not going to tell you what they each decided. Because what matters here is how *you* would decide if you were in these situations.

Maybe your decision is completely obvious to you; maybe it would be a terrible struggle for you. But what will make your decision spiritual is not *what* you decide, but *how* you decide. Is your decision moving you toward connection, authenticity, and love? Spirituality is not the easy route; it is the "road less traveled."

The Ambiguity of Truth

Let's look at the sometimes ambiguous area of telling the truth.

Common wisdom is that when you are close with someone, you will be fully honest with that person at all times. When you are angry, withholding your anger will eat away at your insides and show up indirectly somewhere else. When you feel cheated, you are responsible to speak up and ask for what you want. When you have done something you regret, you must confess it right away. Withholding is unhealthy for yourself and your relationship.

In some situations, these statements will be valid. But the spiritual approach is not always so clean and straightforward. The pressure to be fully honest at all times robs you of the right to make discriminating judgments in different situations. Sometimes the wiser and more spiritually enlightened choice is to withhold painful information or to manage your feelings on your own and not inflict them on your partner. Judgments like these must always be made in consultation with your higher self after asking yourself not only what is truthful but also what is useful and loving.

Your spiritual task is to be fully honest *with yourself* at all times. This is a major undertaking. Then, when you are with your partner, use judgment about what you say and when you say it.

Love or Deception

I have a friend who sometimes splits the cost of a purchase between her credit card and her checkbook. "My husband sees the credit card bill," she explained to me, "but my checkbook is my own business. He doesn't understand what clothes cost, but I feel clear that we can afford what I buy. I'm not going to negotiate every purchase with him or justify my purchases to him. So why not spare him the pain?"

Is my friend being deceptive? If she had promised her husband that she would not exceed a certain dollar amount or that she would not buy a certain item and then did so anyway, concealing the purchase by paying cash for it, that would most likely be considered deceptive. But if she had made no such promises, was she simply acting on her own to reduce the conflict in her relationship and take care of herself? Or was her most loving action to be fully open with her spouse about all her purchases?

What did love require in this situation? What course of action caused the least harm and hurt? What brought about the most love and happiness? Was my friend's action consistent with compassion? Did it bring her into closer alignment with her higher self?

You decide.

Sparing Pain or Telling All

The tricky part of withholding something from your partner to "spare him or her pain," is to figure out whether you are deceiving yourself for your own convenience. Are you denying the true impact of your actions on the two of you?

A woman in one of my groups used the same thinking to justify an affair she once had. She and her husband had an excellent relationship with no major problems and were very involved with each other's lives. They both felt secure and knew that nothing and no one could destroy what they had together. Barbara (which is not her real name) was twenty-five hundred miles from home at a convention. She ended up going to the convention dance with Roy, a friend and colleague, and by the end of the evening, one thing led to another.

> This was someone I knew well and trusted thoroughly. I knew our secret would be safe. And I just couldn't see how anyone would be harmed by my letting myself go into this pleasurable experience. I will say, though, that I never wanted to do it again. I didn't feel it would be the same if it were premeditated. And now, I don't like having this deep dark secret that I will never tell my husband. But I still definitely feel that it was the right

thing to do at the time. For what reason should I have denied myself this deeply pleasurable moment? Who would have been served?

I have told Barbara's story in many of my groups and never seen consensus. Some feel that Barbara's deception clearly does hurt her husband and tarnishes forever the closeness between them. Some feel that spirituality calls on her to tell him the whole, unvarnished truth. Others disagree, saying that truth telling in this situation would cause unnecessary pain and would be self-indulgent of Barbara.

What do you think?

Spirituality calls on you to ask the right questions. But it doesn't dictate what the right answers will be—for you. What will help you make mature spiritual decisions is your spiritual practice. The more you commit yourself to the Loving Actions of Spiritual Partnership, the more you will experience the power of love, compassion, and acceptance, and the better equipped you will be to make difficult decisions based on spiritual principles. When you are aligned with your soul and at peace with yourself, you will trust the messages that flow from your authentic self. This state is the ultimate goal of any spiritual practice, including Spiritual Partnership.

PART THREE

Seeing Spiritual Partnership in a Broader Context

CHAPTER 14

Defining the "Spiritual" in Spiritual Partnership

Throughout this book, we have been relying on the concise definition of *spiritual* that I offered in the first chapter. It is now time to explore this term in much greater detail.

What do you mean when you use the term *spiritual*?

I have long been interested in the variety of responses this question elicits and have spent years formulating my own definition. I offer it here to encourage dialogue and also to highlight the ways in which the spiritual journey and the relationship journey weave together.

To review what we said in Chapter One, to be spiritual is to recognize your connection to the universe and to everyone and everything in it, and to strive each moment for the thoughts and actions that will increase and not decrease this connection. Spirituality is bringing yourself into closer and closer alignment with your highest self.

Your spiritual journey is your own personal journey

- From isolation to connection
- From your conditioned personality to your authentic self
- From fear to love
- From sleep to consciousness or awareness
- From control to surrender
- From restlessness to inner peace

We will explore each of these aspects of the spiritual journey in depth. First, however, let's look at the idea of spirituality in communities.

Spiritual Communities

The components of spirituality I've just mentioned are at the heart of many specific religions, or spiritual *communities*, such as Methodists, Zen Buddhists, Baha'i Faith circles, Jews—any religious group large or small. Each has a long history, sacred stories, rituals, practices, and scriptures that are embedded in a particular history and culture. The community is bound together by traditions that connect the community to its mission, and its members to each other.

An inherent danger of religious communities is their tendency to ossify certain "beliefs" in order to safeguard the continuing existence of the community. It is natural and important to have beliefs. But a belief that you buy into without first questioning it might have the effect of limiting rather than expanding your spirituality.

Knowing is different from believing. Figuring out for yourself what you know to be true is exactly what the spiritual quest is. Your authentic self doesn't need to "believe" anything; it knows the truth. Great spiritual teachers guide us, not to inform but to transform us, to help us discover what we know is true. Each of us must do this for ourselves.

When you *believe* something, you have to work at it. Your body may be tense, your personality rigid. You must be vigilant to keep out anything that doesn't conform with what you believe. At some level you will be worried that some new piece of information could shatter your belief.

Knowing has a power that comes from deep within. When you are operating from your authentic self, your body, mind, and spirit will relax. You will never feel you have to defend yourself. Truth has the gentle strength of a giant sequoia tree that has quietly lived on this planet for many centuries.

If you are part of a religious community, it is important to respect the integrity of your spiritual tradition and to participate in it fully and with devotion, *as long as it is moving you in the direction of freeing you up, and not in the direction of limiting you or closing you down.* Remember that both Jesus and Buddha railed against the religious communities of their time.

Spiritual Practice

A spiritual *practice* is a ritual, discipline, or routine that in some way connects the person doing it to his or her own spiritual path and to the great spiritual truths.

To help seekers achieve the states of connection, authenticity, love, consciousness, receptivity, and inner peace, spiritual communities employ a great variety of *practices.* Jews study the sacred word. Sufis dance. Buddhists meditate. Christians pray. It is widely taught that the cultivation of a quiet mind, an inner stillness, is a great aid in the gradual acquisition of spiritual qualities, and that "attachment," "coveting," or preoccupation with desire is a deterrent to spirituality.

Most traditions teach us that pain is a natural part of life and especially of spiritual growth, but that suffering comes only when we treat pain as something that is unwelcome. Many teachings are quite specific about the barriers to spiritual growth: ignorance, craving, apathy, fear, and greed. And of course, most traditions teach ethical behavior: the Ten Commandments; the Eightfold Path of Buddhism; the Golden Rule; the laws of Judaism. All of these teachings, rituals, practices, and stories help move us along the path toward the great spiritual truths and toward a greater alignment with our highest selves.

Of course, affiliation with a particular religious community is not essential to being spiritual. It is the rare person who can achieve spiritual growth without support from some kinds of teachers or guides. But there are as many spiritual paths as spiritual seekers. Each one of us is on a highly individualized spiritual journey and has our very own support systems and timelines for pursuing it.

Let us now explore in more detail each of the six aspects of spirituality.

Connection

We are not separate from each other or from the universe or from anything in it. We are each simply one form or another of being.

At one time, there were no separate beings; there was only being itself. Then, eons later, there was life. Then life began to manifest in different forms. Then a time came, ever so gradually, when we became conscious that we had life; we began to experience our experience. And somewhere in that time, we began to experience ourselves as different from each other.

We experience ourselves as separate now. But deep, deep in our psyches or in our collective psyche, we know that it was not always that way. Each of us is a part of being, just as each drop is a part of the ocean.

Spirituality invites us to remember the time when there was nothing but being itself, when being was bliss because there was no separation, no division, only one unified, glorious oneness.

Spiritual practice is an attempt to remember and even to feel or sense this lost awareness of unity, of being itself, of the one essential nature that we all share. Mystical unity with the universe is the ultimate goal of spiritual seekers. Any attempt to put the experience into words is futile, because it will be attempting to describe something that can only be experienced. Yet all spiritual writers use words and metaphors in an attempt to describe the indescribable.

> We do not "come into" this world; we come *out* of it, as leaves from a tree. As the ocean "waves," the universe "peoples." Every individual is an expression of the whole realm of nature, a unique action of the total universe.
>
> —Alan Watts

There are definitely stages to the dawning awareness of yourself as a part of all that you see. As you practice Spiritual Partnership, you may have fleeting glimpses of the essential nature that you share with your partner, or even experiences of mystical unity.

The Spirit That Connects Us with Each Other

Sobonfu Somé, an African woman from the Dagara tribe, left the close community of her people to share with the West the spiritual message of the Dagara people. In *The Spirit of Intimacy*, she writes,

> When indigenous people talk about spirit, they are basically referring to the life force in everything. For instance, you might refer to the spirit in an animal, that is the life force in that animal, which can help us accomplish our life purpose and maintain our connection to the spirit world.

The spirit of the human being is the same way. In our tradition, each of us is seen as a spirit who has taken the form of a human in order to carry out a purpose. Spirit is the energy that helps us connect, that helps us see beyond our racially limited parameters, and also helps us in ritual and in connecting with the ancestors.

Along with spiritual seekers from many traditions, Sobonfu views the problems in our society as a direct result of our lost connection with spirit, with community, and with each other. She is appalled at the way we live our lives separated from our families and from any connection to spirit.

So the first thing we mean by spirituality is anything that moves us toward connection: connection with each other, with the spiritual dimension of our lives, and, ultimately, with everyone and everything in the universe. Spiritual practice helps us discover that in our purest essence, we are all part of the same human experience. We take on different external forms, but we all share in life itself. Separation and difference are illusions that spiritual practice seeks to transcend. When you experience empathy with your partner, when you are filled with feelings of compassion, when you experience love for a newborn baby or an animal or certainly toward your Spiritual Partner, or when you are filled with awe at the beauty of nature, you are experiencing manifestations of your deep connection with the rest of life and with all of being.

Authenticity

The human race is a tribe of mask builders.

Take Joe as an example. When he was six years old, Joe was playing with a little kitten, and someone came along and called him a sissy. Joe felt bad, unloved, rejected. He wanted that terrible feeling to go away. So he built himself a little mask: tough guy.

Joe found that if he wore his mask, he could fit in better with the guys. His mask covered up both the pain of rejection and the sweet, pure little boy who enjoyed the kitten.

Think of Joe as having three layers: on the outside is his tough-guy protective defense, which we might also call his conditioned personality or the mask he puts on to present himself to the world. Psychologists call it a defense. Under that is the shame he felt at being called a sissy, the fear that he is unlovable, the reason he needs his mask. And buried deep beneath that fear is a perfect little Joe, just as he really is, adoring of kittens, playful, confident, loving, and lovable.

When Annie was growing up, her father traveled all the time, and her mother also had a career and was almost never home. Annie took over lots of household responsibilities from a young age. Her parents often criticized her but rarely praised her and almost never hugged and kissed her.

Annie longed for expressions of love from her parents. Her pain over their indifference to her was almost unbearable. Her heart ached; her body cried out to be hugged.

So Annie built a mask: self-sufficiency. Rather than having to feel the terrible pain of her parents' lack of love, she subconsciously tricked herself into believing that she did not want or need their love; she learned never to ask for or to expect it.

The mask worked. Annie never had to feel the pain of longing for love and receiving nothing. Her mask covered up both her unrequited longing *and* the pure, genuine Annie inside who truly wanted love. Both her pain and her true self were hidden behind her defense, the personality she developed to protect herself from pain.

Masks Are Like Prisons

Mask building is a normal, sometimes even healthy response. Masks, or defenses, are the human organism's way of protecting itself from hostile elements in its environment. Your mask is your public self, the personality you show to the world.

In the beginning, our masks protect us. But after a while, they diminish us. Long after our defenses have outgrown their usefulness, we allow them to become mindless habits. Joe is now completely identified with tough guy; he can't cry. Annie has never been in a close relationship. Neither Joe nor Annie has any awareness of their self-built prisons.

Defenses distort our view of the world. Everything we see or hear is filtered through our habitual behavior, so that what we see is biased. Joe thinks that all he has achieved is a result of his ability to be tough. Annie sees everyone through her loner disguise and so becomes convinced that no one is warm and loving.

Your spiritual journey is your journey through the protective outer shell and the pain it was constructed to hide—both from yourself and from others—to the pure, authentic you, free of fear and so comfortable with yourself that you don't need to hide.

There is much conversation these days about soul, which I believe is another way of talking about authentic self. When you are identified with your public self and have lost touch with your true desires and passions, you are out of alignment with your soul. Your soul knows what is best for you and longs to bring you back to your true self. Your soul is your authentic self calling out to you, guiding you back home to the fullest expression of your true self.

The true you is unique in the universe and therefore vitally important. When you stay behind your mask, you look and behave like a lot of other people who have donned similar masks, instead of the fresh, shining presence that is your genuine self. Most of the world consists of masked people busily relating to other masked people, taking their masks ever so seriously, fervently caught up in doing work that is someone else's work, participating in relationships that are cluttered with defenses, and unwittingly teaching their children to build the same masks they have worn all their lives. They never embark on a spiritual quest, and they go through this entire life without ever discovering who they truly are. That is the difference between spiritual and nonspiritual people.

Your Own Journey to Authenticity

What is your primary personality characteristic? Are there times when you use it to cover up powerful feelings, either powerfully happy or powerfully sad?

Those two questions are enough to start a spiritual journey, one that can create a rewarding opening up of your life. It doesn't matter how you pursue the answers; you could begin by having a conversation with a friend, by meditating, keeping a journal, or attending a personal growth class or retreat. If you have never asked these questions, expect the search to take time—and to lead to other questions and other answers. They aren't the only entry, but those two questions are one gateway to a lifetime of spiritual discovery.

> The basis of insincerity is the idealized image we hold of ourselves and which we impose on others.
>
> —Pablo Picasso

Your Self and Your Love Life

As we have seen, one of the keys to happiness in life is a passionate, loving connection with another person. But sometimes when you feel the longing to connect deeply with another person, whether or not you are in a relationship, that deep longing might really be for yourself. A connection with someone else is impossible if you don't first have a connection with yourself.

When you connect with your true self, you will feel deep emotions; your longing will be satisfied. Moreover, until you do this, you won't feel satisfied connecting with another person. Your public self is incapable of true intimacy; it can engage only in a charade. Only your true self can make a real connection.

What you may be longing for is both: a person who can support you in reaching behind your public self to the feelings that lie hidden there. In a workshop, one participant stated this quite directly: "I long for someone who can crack open my shell. I feel like Humpty Dumpty, and I want someone to love me enough to shove me off the wall."

How Authenticity Deepens Connection

Your personal journey to authenticity and deep self-knowledge and self-acceptance is the direct path to a deeply satisfying love relationship. *Your soul has the power to love far, far beyond what your personality is capable of.* The more attention you pay to your soul—that is, the more you are motivated by your deepest inner stirrings, and the more you become your most authentic self—the more you will be able to connect with your partner at a deep level.

A woman who was a part of my women's group for several years presented us with a dramatic example of the difference between personality and authentic self and the impact the move to authenticity can have on relationships. She had an unusually warm demeanor, smiling and encouraging people all the time. We began to call her Florence Nightingale, in the most loving way, to help her become aware of how often she rushed in to help and even rescue others in the group. Sometimes her soothing comments were inappropriate because they prevented the person talking from going more deeply into her problem, where she would have a chance to discover something new about herself.

One week, "Florence" came to the group in a great deal of pain herself; her mother had been diagnosed with cancer. As we helped her express her deepest fears, we all noticed a huge transformation in her. Tears came from the deepest part of her. Her face softened incredibly. After she had cried and talked for a time, this face that had been so tightly "happy" began to shine with a radiant beauty we had never seen. Because she had become "real" with us by sharing her own deep vulnerability, an act that required enormous courage and trust on her part, we all felt connected to her and deeply touched. I can recall being overcome with love for her, whereas before, I had found her mildly annoying. Her own experience was similar; she felt much closer to us!

After that group session, this woman spent more and more of her time with us as her real self, still warm and compassionate, but not so afraid, not so tightly wound, not reverting to her habitual behavior out of fear. We all remarked about how much closer we felt to her, how much more trusting we felt. Our connection with her deepened because she had learned how to be authentic with us.

Often it is a relationship itself that brings you in touch with your authentic self. When you invest yourself in a person and pin hopes and dreams on a certain relationship, you are automatically making yourself vulnerable. It is in the nature of love that you become dependent on your lover in some ways. Even though a certain amount of dependency is completely healthy and normal, it can be frightening. This fear is part of the authentic you. Don't run from it because it feels strange and unpleasant; welcome it. Vulnerability always presents you with an opportunity for spiritual growth.

The you that is more real and less "conditioned" almost always feels vulnerable when it first comes out after being buried for a long time. First you feel the vulnerability, the fear, the shame, the sadness. But if you are part of any relationship in which you can experience being fully accepted and loved for the person you truly are, vulnerability and all, you will get to experience the profound pleasure of relaxing into your real, unadorned self, just as my friend "Florence" did. In that state, you are totally lovable. Others are likely to be drawn to you, to feel love for you, and to feel deeply connected.

Now, imagine having an experience like that with someone you already love.

Shedding Your Mask

In much of our lives, a public self is appropriate. But each of us must find at least one person with whom we feel safe enough to be real. That is a primary spiritual task. The person can be a lover, a friend, a family member, or a helping professional. Then we grow by finding more and more places in our lives where we can shed the public facade and be real, thereby inspiring others to do the same. That is why the spiritual quest sometimes leads people to leave high-powered jobs where they are laughed at or ridiculed for being authentic, or to exit relationships in which their newfound genuine self turns out to be threatening or distasteful to the other person.

So your spiritual journey to authenticity is intertwined with your journey to find true happiness with another person; they are both aspects of the same search. Spiritual Partnership is a commitment to support the search for authenticity in yourself and your partner.

Love

If spirituality is being authentic and experiencing connection, love is the manifestation of these qualities; it might be called "spiritual behavior." Love is not just the absence of conflict, but a distinctive way of being in the world. Love reaches out; it promotes the well-being of others. It seeks harmony. It creates joy, rapture, passion, and happiness.

The opposite of love is not hate, but fear. The primary fear is, "Deep down inside, I feel weak and fragile, inferior, bad. I don't want anyone to see this." Fear is the energy that contracts and closes down or that lashes out, is manipulative and greedy. Love is the energy that expands, opens up, shares with others, seeks to heal.

Self-Love

Self-love boils down, again, to being real, because to know your authentic self is to love yourself. If you have access only to your public self and don't know your real self, you will find it hard to feel self-love, for you can't love what you don't know; you can only fear it.

There is a difference between genuine self-love, which is the result of self-exploration, and what I call "pseudo self-love." Some people appear to love themselves because they talk about how talented or successful they are. At worst they can be arrogant, self-involved, and more interested in telling their own stories than in listening to anyone else. These people use their "aren't I wonderful" veneer to cover deep insecurities, which are often more apparent to those around them than to the people themselves. People who are genuinely self-loving operate from a still, quiet strength that comes from deep within. They have no need to broadcast it to others.

Most people have a major misconception about self-love. They believe that people who are self-loving are that way because they are good people to start with. They came from reasonably good families; they are smart, good looking, and successful; and in general, everything they touch turns to gold. They no longer have any fears, faults, or insecurities. They are self-loving because the "package" they have is easy to love.

Wrong.

Many self-loving people had a rough time growing up, just like everyone else. They still have painful regrets, low self-esteem, insecurities, envies. But they have learned how to love the bad along with the good. Self-love is not about loving the parts of yourself that are easy to love; that's no challenge. Self-love is about loving all of yourself, including the parts you don't like or don't want to look at. Self-loving people have become well acquainted with their fears and anxieties, their bad moods, their pain, their shame, and their regrets, and they have learned to love the entire package.

You are who you are. You have done what you have done. You had the parents you had. Some things you can change, some you can't. So you have a choice: you either can fight and loathe and remain a victim of your past and the parts of yourself you don't like, or you can lovingly accept them. You can ride the horse in the direction it is going. That's self-love.

Recently I took a friend out to lunch for her fortieth birthday. "So how does it feel to turn forty?" I asked her.

"I really like it," she told me. "I finally feel that I'll take what I've got and be happy with it. If I haven't accomplished all my self-improvement goals by now, I figure I probably never will, and that's just fine. I'm going to quit pestering myself to get better organized and write more letters and bake for the kids more and all that stuff. I'm not perfect. I'm not even where I thought I'd be at forty. But I'm very content. Somehow turning forty seems to give me permission to let go of the struggles and enjoy myself."

That's self-love.

Loving Others

If we put love on a continuum, on the left might be greedy, selfish, abusive behavior toward another—complete lack of love. And on the right might be Mother Teresa, who devoted her life completely to the alleviation of suffering in others. Also over toward the right would be Johnny Appleseed, who put out his campfire because he saw that mosquitoes were flying into it; my friend who gives a dollar to every street panhandler he passes; or a schoolteacher who encourages and supports children every day.

Spirituality calls on us to move farther over to the right, little by little, as we are able—to cultivate our capacity to love.

Moving toward love is a challenge, because our culture values not love, but money, and the two value systems are incompatible. When a company exploits child workers in developing countries to increase its profits, it is using the money value system. So is the person who works twelve hours a day, consistently neglecting his or her family. The money value system is staggeringly powerful in this society. Some would say that a society that trains its members to produce and achieve, to accumulate and consume, is systematically and deliberately destroying their ability to love, that the unfettered drive toward growth and profit precludes love.

But love is the spiritual choice.

What Does Love Require?

Everyone's expression of love is different. We won't all care for the sick or volunteer in homeless shelters. The point is to carry out whatever your life requires of you with as much love as possible.

What if, with regard to every decision we ever had to make, we were always to ask the question, "What does love require?" In our complicated world, the answer might not always be clear. But certainly we could quickly eliminate many nonloving alternatives.

The Loving Actions we have learned in this book offer us some options for answers to the question, "What does love require?" It's not a question we ask very often, but it is what the spiritual life requires of us. What a different world this would be if corporations operated in accord with that question! But for them, it's "What does profit require?"

Love is not just kindness but is actually a manifestation of authenticity. In our pure essence, all of us are loving. Only when we abandon our true selves in favor of selves that fit in better with our money-oriented and fear-based society will we behave in ways that are not loving.

Consciousness

> If most of us remain ignorant of ourselves, it is because self-knowledge is painful and we prefer the pleasure of illusion.
> —Aldous Huxley

Consciousness, or awareness, is the spiritual tool that we use to achieve the first three aspects of spirituality: connection, authenticity, and love. It is not enough just to live your life. As a spiritual person, you make a commitment to yourself to experience your life, to reflect on it, and to become an active agent in your own being.

Becoming conscious is like climbing a mountain with an ever elusive peak. At each level of the mountain, you assume that you are seeing everything there is to see. Then something nudges you into climbing higher, and when you do, you see how limited your previous view was. You can never know what lies above you on the mountain, but you will know everything that is below you. As long as you are only partway up the mountain, you may still be living with illusions or misconceptions. Your view of the world will be limited.

The challenge in becoming more conscious, or expanding your awareness, is that you may not know just where you are limiting your own thinking or your capacity to experience something new. Or, even if you do, you may like your station on the mountain and want to stay there. It is risky to keep climbing. Who knows what comfortable viewpoint may be threatened, what old truth may be shattered?

The higher you climb toward the summit of full consciousness, the more you will learn, not only about the real world but also about yourself. The summit, the ultimate spiritual goal, is an accurate view of yourself and of everything and everyone else. Most of us normal folks never reach the summit, but we learn from spiritual teachers who have.

The experience of becoming increasingly conscious is different for each of us. Roughly, however, it consists of two parts: (1) receiving new information about yourself and (2) paying attention to the new information. New information alone isn't enough.

Acquiring New Information

There are endless ways to acquire new information about yourself. Keeping a journal, talking with friends, recording your dreams, meditating, joining spiritual or personal growth classes or groups, and working with a spiritual teacher or therapist are just a few examples. Sometimes you receive new information or insights through deliberate effort, but often they come through serendipity or chance.

In this book, we are focusing on your relationships as a source of new information. It certainly isn't the only source, but it is a good one because it is already an integral part of your life.

Paying Attention

On Aldous Huxley's utopian island, magpies flew around all the time calling out, "Pay attention. Pay attention. Pay attention." We should all carry those magpies around inside our own heads. For paying attention is the second essential aspect of raising your consciousness about yourself. You can't just acquire new information; you need to reflect on it and integrate it.

Pay attention: Do you have emotions inside you right now that you are not acknowledging? After you just now made that remark to your partner, how are you feeling inside yourself? What might you have said instead? Are you exercising choice about your relationship, or simply repeating routines? Are you doing what you most want to be doing right now? Have you had a new insight about yourself lately?

Paying attention to yourself may give you new information that can be life changing for you. A woman in one of my Spiritual Partnership support groups, Bobbi, was often told that she talked too much and that she interrupted. She was always stunned to receive this feedback and did not agree that she was offensive. Bobbi's response was to curtail her behavior deliberately, but angrily. She would arrive at the next group, determined to keep her mouth shut. Her resolve usually lasted about a half hour, because she would become resentful, and besides, she had valuable contributions to add to the conversation.

I suggested to Bobbi that she make no effort at all to change her behavior, but that she instead start paying attention to herself. At first, nothing changed. But then Bobbi reported to us, "I actually caught myself interrupting this week! I was amazed. And you know what? *It didn't feel very good to me.*" Over a period of time, as Bobbi took more and more notice *of how she felt* in conversations, she saw what others had been trying to tell her.

Even more important, Bobbi began to experience what it felt like to be more quiet, to listen without adding her own comment every time. To her surprise, she would sometimes feel very sad and even become tearful. As we explored what the tears were about, she discovered she was afraid she would be left out, that she had a deep fear of being invisible. This fear evoked a great deal of pain for Bobbi. She sobbed relentlessly. It turns out that she had felt invisible in her family as a child. Revisiting that old pain was very hard for her. But can you see that her willingness to experience that pain enabled her to "update" her fears, to see that her pain was old pain and that she no longer needed to live in fear of it?

Psychologist Carl Jung says that neurosis is a substitute for real pain. Bobbi's interrupting, her neurosis, was a substitute for her real pain of feeling invisible. Only by experiencing your real pain will you stop running from it.

Over time, Bobbi kept paying attention to herself in conversations. Eventually she found that she could be appropriate—letting others speak, adding a comment only occasionally—and that now she felt far more "seen," accepted, and loved than before.

It is easy for us to see that Bobbi's compulsive interrupting was her protective personality trait that she invented so she wouldn't have to feel the pain of being ignored. Interrupting had become so habitual for Bobbi that she quite literally didn't notice it. Ironically, as is often the case, her habitual behavior exacerbated the problem she was hoping it would solve. But it enabled her to hide the terrible pain of feeling invisible to those around her. She hid that pain from herself and others for many years. The deep pleasure she experienced when she chose to shed her annoying habit and then still felt accepted was the pleasure of discovering her authentic self. Bobbi had "raised her consciousness." This is an important aspect of spiritual growth.

Note that Bobbi's spiritual journey toward authenticity also enabled her to move toward connection. This will be true of you in your own relationship also. It is why Spiritual Partnership heals the wounds of love so much more effectively than the Stage Two model of communication and problem solving.

The important point to see here is that this entire chain of discovery, this climb up the mountain of consciousness, started just because Bobbi began paying close attention to herself, in particular to the "information" that others felt she interrupted too much. She (1) received information and (2) paid attention to it.

Perhaps it is not too radical to say that all of spirituality boils down to paying attention. Paying attention is the way you become aware of your isolation. It is the way you discover what is real for you and what is protective, habitual behavior. It is the way you discover old, deeply buried pain. And it is the way you learn that you can, after all, love the real you, not just the dressed-up, public you.

Observer Self

We might call your ability to pay attention your "observer self." It is as if there were a part of you that is always able to pull back from your life drama and watch the drama happening. So now there will

EXPERIMENT 22

Paying Attention

Identify one characteristic about your personality or one habit you have. Do you exaggerate? Are you an advice giver? Do you correct or contradict people? Are you quiet, giving, controlling, passive, shy, loquacious, critical, funny? Do you tease?

Now, don't do anything to change this quality, but start paying close attention to it. Just catch yourself doing it. Notice it. See what happens as you tune in to this one quality over a period of time.

be two parts of you: one part is all caught up in, say, an argument, fighting for your point of view, passionate about the importance of your cause, utterly absorbed in the moment. The other part is able to pull back from the little scene and watch you arguing. "My, I certainly am passionate about this!" your observer self might think.

Or "That last thing I said wasn't quite accurate."

When you activate your observer self—that is, when you become conscious—you can make choices about what you are doing. In contrast, if you are completely immersed in yourself, you will operate on automatic pilot, with no bigger picture, no sense of the consequences of your actions or their impact on other people, no understanding of why you do what you do, no awareness of how your behavior fits into the larger drama of your life.

As you begin to develop your observing self, one of the first obstacles you will encounter is that you can't see what you aren't aware of. This is frustrating, but it doesn't matter. What matters is that you *become aware that* you can't see what you aren't aware of, that you open yourself to possibilities. As spiritual writer John Welwood says, "My awareness of being lost, confused, or stuck *is never itself lost, confused, or stuck.*" In seeing that you are lost, you are already less lost. You are on the path; just stay on it. Keep paying attention.

Beliefs

It is important to pay attention to what you believe, because your beliefs affect everything in your life, and beliefs can change in the wink of an eye.

Annie told me a remarkable story. Her sister, Vicky, was a state senator, very active and visible in the community and extremely bright and successful. Annie herself was a gardener who felt lucky to have a job she loved. Annie loved Vicky and they got along well, but

Annie always felt inferior to her shining, exuberant, successful sister. That was just the way it was.

One day in a casual conversation, a friend said to Annie, "Did it ever occur to you that you may be as smart as your sister?"

The remark stunned Annie. The truth was, this had *never* occurred to her. The whole family had always taken for granted that Vicki was the smart one. But in an instant, Annie realized she could change this belief and adopt a new one: I am as smart as my sister. It was like an earthquake in her life. She began finding a great deal of evidence to support her new belief. Her self-image gained a huge boost.

Nothing had changed but her belief!

Beliefs can be limiting. A belief is a point in life at which you have decided to stop growing, at least for the time being. It is natural and important to have beliefs. But being open to expanding your consciousness means being open to reexamining your beliefs when you hear something that lures you beyond what you believe now.

Beliefs may have momentous impact. In my work with single men and women who are looking for love, I often ask them to identify their self-limiting beliefs. They say things like these:

I believe I can't be the person I want to be and be in a relationship.

I believe that what I would gain by being in a relationship is not worth what I would have to give up.

I believe there is a true shortage of suitable men and that my chances of finding one who suits me are very small.

These singles will have a very different experience from the woman who told me this:

I believe that there is no way in the world that I will end up single. I know absolutely that I will end up with a wonderful man. I believe, in fact I know deep down, that we will have a wonderful marriage.

We always behave in a manner that is consistent with what we believe, so the woman who believes she will find love is actually much more likely to find it than the people who believe that love is beyond their reach. Those people will see all of the world as evidence that what they believe is true. If they could change their belief, they would find plenty of evidence to the contrary. Your beliefs greatly color the way you see the world.

So what are the beliefs that govern your life? Do your beliefs enhance or diminish your life? Are they part of your conditioned personality, or do they come from deep within you, from your authentic self?

As you pay attention, beliefs you take for granted may begin to surface and beg for reexamination.

Resistance

Most of us resist expanding our consciousness. Just as no one wanted to hear from Copernicus that the sun did not circle around the earth, we don't want to hear that our perch on the mountain isn't just fine where it is.

Resistance is a normal and very common part of the spiritual journey. The secret is to view your resistance as one more opportunity to pay attention. Now you pay attention to your feelings of resistance. That's all you need to do. Alan Lew in *One God Clapping* puts this beautifully:

> Real mindfulness comes about not by an act of violence against our consciousness, not by force, not by trying to control our consciousness, but rather, by a kind of directed compassion, a softening of our awareness, a loving embrace of our lives, a soft letting be.

Compassion and Consciousness

If we understand spirituality to be a climb up the mountain of consciousness, every step affording us a more accurate view of our world and allowing us to become more authentic and more connected, then the problem of evil is easy to understand.

Evil is not some independent force, like Satan, who lives a separate life and does battle with the forces of good. Evil is simply ignorance, a lack of consciousness. "Evil people" live at the very bottom of the mountain with limited awareness and a tiny vision. They have not exercised their capacity to pay attention to themselves even a tiny bit. They are completely identified with their protective habits, maintaining a frantic effort to stay far from their inner pain. Their evil behavior is their public self, their neurosis, the behavior they have adopted to fend off pain and cope with their environment.

The spiritual response to evil, therefore, is not hate, but compassion. Hate and anger are moves toward separation, not connection. When you feel hate or anger, you are diminishing yourself, allowing habitual feelings to overwhelm your spiritual values of understanding and compassion. Furthermore, you will have no impact on the person you hate. You cannot help heal someone else's limited vision if you are trapped in your own feelings of anger or hate. If you have no compassion in your heart, you become like the ones you hate, the "evil" ones who have no consciousness, who behave out of habit. You enter their realm, way down at the foot of the mountain.

When you think about the areas of dissatisfaction in your marriage, you may not think of your partner as evil, but you probably feel anger and maybe even hate. If you can instead view your partner with compassion, as a fellow human being who is doing the best he or she can under the circumstances, you will be raising your own consciousness and moving toward connection.

Hate, anger, envy, and hurt are one perch on the mountain. If you pay attention to them, to how they feel and what results they bring, you will gradually begin to rise above them, to find a higher consciousness that replaces them with compassion.

Surrender

> And which of you by being anxious can add one cubit to your span of life?
>
> —Matthew 6:27

The invitation to trust, to relinquish control, to "let go and let God" as they say in the recovery movement, is pervasive in spiritual teachings. Do not try to superimpose your own will on the universe; instead be receptive, for life may not turn out as you plan or expect.

Interestingly, many differing "beliefs" or theologies lead to this same conclusion. Some religions say your fate is already predestined, and nothing you can do will change that. Others say that you come to self-love and authenticity only through grace; "salvation" is a gift, and nothing you do will affect it. Some say that events in the universe are completely random, that they aren't "fair" or just.

Bad things happen to good people, as Rabbi Harold Kushner explains. Don't look for a reason, but look for what these random events can teach you. Others believe in the great cosmic energy of karma, that viewed over eons of time, what you do now will come back to you, or what you did some time ago is coming back to you now. Some see the world as a great spiritual school where everything that happens should be viewed as the particular lesson you needed to learn.

All these worldviews end up at exactly the same place: relax. Let go. Be open to what is really happening, not what you think should happen or wish would happen. Don't try to control the river; flow with it.

Letting Go

Letting go does not mean that you no longer want the things you want or that you no longer have any goals or desires. It means that you are no longer *anxious about* achieving these goals or fulfilling these desires. If they don't happen, your inner peace will not be destroyed. It means that you do everything you can to bring about what you want and still trust that whatever the universe provides is okay.

I was once a finalist for a big, highly visible job at the University of California. When they chose someone else, I was shattered. But now I see that if I had taken that job, I might still be a frazzled bureaucrat and might never have written any of my books. I could have avoided a great deal of suffering at that time if I had been more trusting, more able to surrender, less attached to my fervent desire.

Some of life's happenings are definitely harder to accept than others. Some things are terribly hard to accept. But spirituality is not just for the easy times.

Letting go is a deep trust that even without your intervention, things will work out. It is recognizing that trying to force other people or events into your own mold will cause you stress, that clinging feverishly to a particular outcome will cause you suffering, and that the universe will go ahead anyway. It is seeing that you are helpless by yourself, that only when you surrender to the great cosmic flow, the rhythms of nature, the way life really is, will you be strong. You can work *with* the forces in the universe that make things happen, but you don't have to make everything happen yourself.

Surrender is something you can practice. But it also arises naturally when you are connected with your authentic self. When your self-love is as strong as a giant redwood tree, even the worst storm cannot destroy you. Anxiety and controlling behavior are substitutes for inner strength.

Think of a disappointment, unachieved goal, or loss in your own life. It is natural for you to experience emotion: grief, sadness, and anger. But to develop spiritually is to develop the ability to move on so that your loss does not destroy you, but makes you stronger. Christopher Reeve stands as an extraordinary model of someone who was able to accept the unacceptable and move forward with his life.

Julia Butterfly Hill, the remarkable woman who lived in the top of an ancient redwood tree for two years to save it from the ax, tells in her book, *The Legacy of Luna*, of the time she was in the grip of a violent storm with extremely high winds. "I was trying to hold on to life so hard that my teeth were clenched, my jaws were clenched, my muscles were clenched, my fists were clenched, everything in my body was clenched completely and totally tight."

Then, she said, the tree itself spoke to her. "Julia, think of the trees in the storm."

> And as I started to picture trees in the storm, the answer began to dawn on me. The trees in the storm don't try to stand up straight and tall and erect. They allow themselves to bend and be blown with the wind. They understand that power of letting go.

Gratitude

I once heard a spiritual teacher suggest that every prayer should be a prayer of gratitude. The idea appealed to me.

Later that day, I found myself searching for the very first star I could find in the evening sky. Ever since childhood, I have always used the first star as an opportunity for a little prayer of petition. My brain automatically recites the verse I learned at my mother's knee, and I make a wish, but I do it in the form of a prayer.

On the evening in question, I prayed for the health of a friend who was in treatment for cancer. But then I remembered "Make every prayer a prayer of gratitude," so I changed the prayer. I prayed something like, "Thank you for this wonderful friend and for all she has brought into my life. Thank you for letting her find her cancer so early and for all the treatments available to her. Thank you for all the doctors helping her. Thank you that she has such a positive spirit about all this that I know will help heal her."

Although this whole scene happened inside my head and took only seconds, it made quite an impact on me. After my first prayer, I felt sad and desperate. There was an urgency to the prayer, and a helpless feeling that went with it: "Please, *please* help my friend heal. You *have* to make her better." But after my prayers of gratitude, I felt strong and confident.

Gratitude is a kind of letting go, a surrender, a way of bending with the wind. Remembering to be grateful is a way of remembering that you don't have to control the universe.

Happiness

The result of a spiritual life is happiness.

The more you recognize your oneness with the essential nature of all things, the more you access your authentic self, the more you love, the more you expand your consciousness, and the more you bend with the wind, the more you will experience happiness.

You will move through life from inner strength, with purpose and passion; you will know what you do best, and you will find a way to do it; you will feel enthusiasm and a zest for life, and you will love and be loved by beautiful people. Whatever the universe has in store for you, you will accept gratefully, even if it is not what you had in mind. Because you have compassion and love for yourself, you will feel it for others; you will be filled with a spirit of generosity and good will and will choose to help and support others.

Your relationships will bring you pleasure. Especially as you learn to practice Spiritual Partnership, you will bring a loving, upbeat energy to every relationship and group you are in. You will be accepting of a wide variety of people and their behavior. Because you will know how to manage conflict in a spiritual way, people will welcome your leadership and influence. You will be able to let go of any attempt to control the universe and will operate from a deep trust. You will be filled with gratitude.

Of course you won't feel that way all the time.

To be on a spiritual journey is to be like a well-tuned violin. The strings are taut and vibrant, but they can play a wide variety of songs: sad songs, exuberant songs, songs of passion, songs of grief, fiercely energetic music, or music that is quiet, almost still. You may find yourself in the grip of terrible disappointment, envy, indecision, or grief. You may feel depressed or lonely. But the more you develop your spiritual capacities, the more you will be able to bend and sway with these experiences.

Don't resist them. Rather than thinking, "As a spiritual person, I shouldn't be feeling this," think, "As a spiritual person, I need to accept that this is how I feel now. This is real for me right now. It's painful, and I'm going to let it happen, let it run its course. I will see what I can learn from this experience. I will accept what is, and I will pay attention."

To be spiritual means to do the right thing as often as you can. It's a bit like parenting. You may learn good parenting skills, such as listening to your children instead of contradicting them. But then

EXPERIMENT 23

Your Own Spirituality

Answer these questions in your journal or discuss them with your partner or a friend.

1. Do you agree that the six components of spirituality described in this chapter constitute an adequate definition of spirituality? What would you add, subtract, or change to create your own definition?

2. Which one or two of the six components represent the biggest challenge for you personally? Where do you feel a need to focus your own spiritual work for now?

you will catch yourself contradicting your children! Later you say, "Here's the way I might have handled that better."

Just so with spirituality. You know the right direction to go. You practice the disciplines you need. You view every challenge as an opportunity to learn. But you won't get it perfect every time.

Being perfect isn't what will make you happy; being on the spiritual path is.

CHAPTER 15

The Future of Spiritual Partnership

The idea of viewing your relationship as a spiritual journey, of strengthening both your inner life and your relationship at the same time, and, in particular, of "working" on your relationship by yourself are new, even shocking ideas to most people.

Certainly, the ideas of bypassing communication as a tool for conflict resolution and of moving directly toward the happiness and pleasure you seek are surprising ideas.

I am often asked how I came to this innovative way of working with couples, how it fits in with what else is happening now, and whether it is likely to catch on. This chapter is my response to these questions.

The Development of "Spiritual Partnership"

Over the past twenty years or more, three separate threads in my life have been weaving themselves together into the tapestry I now call Spiritual Partnership: my marriage, my work with couples, and my spiritual journey.

From the very beginning of our relationship in 1981, I felt there was something different about Mayer and me. It wasn't that we had fewer conflicts or incompatibilities than other couples. It wasn't that we loved each other more or that we had better communication skills or more therapy. But because of some elusive factor, we didn't allow our differences to come between us the way, it seemed to me, other couples did. We got over arguments quickly. Our mutual love and affection were virtually always apparent to both of us; they never went underground.

It was my search for the "elusive factor" that led me to write my second book, *The Eight Essential Traits of Couples Who Thrive*. I interviewed other happy couples to see if I could tease out any factors that happy couples universally share. "The factor" was not hard to find: happy couples all approached their relationships with a spirit of good will. They were on each other's side: allies, not adversaries. Their spirits were open to each other. Their good will superseded their differences. It is a quality that is conspicuously absent in couples who are not doing well together.

When I observed this spirit of good will in couples, I found that it was usually consistent with other traits as well: happy couples had very little ambivalence about being together. They *wanted* to be happy together; they *believed* they could be happy together (this was critical; most couples buy into our culture's pervasive negativity about marriage and don't believe true happiness is possible); and they were *committed* to being happy together. Also, they made a deliberate effort to spend time together; they shared optimism and a sense of adventure about life; they maintained a long-term perspective; and they paid attention to physical affection and sexual pleasure.

Teaching the Essential Traits

Next, I made a stunning realization: traditional couples work does not teach these essential traits at all, but instead encourages couples to examine their problems. Strategies for couples are developed by psychologists, who are trained for and interested in, not relationship health, but relationship *pathology*. They spend all their time with couples who are experiencing high levels of dissatisfaction, and they then write books about how they help those couples. Maybe this is a biased approach, I thought. Would we come up with very different strategies if we taught people what we have learned from happy couples instead of from unhappy ones?

So I began to conduct workshops for couples that deliberately bypassed problems and instead taught couples how to be happy together.

The results were extraordinary. Listen to June, a workshop participant who was interviewed on a radio talk show:

> Our problem was money. We fought all the time about it. Our therapy seemed to dig us deeper into our positions about it. Neither of us could change. We both felt in despair.
>
> Susan made us agree not to discuss money at all for three weeks. At the beginning of the three weeks, we were to plan three activities per week that would allow us to spend fun time together. They had to be activities that left us both feeling financially comfortable. We even arranged to swap child care with another couple in the group who were doing something similar. And we thought up plenty of free and low-cost things to do: hikes, renting videos, flying a kite, playing Frisbee, taking walks, hot tubbing at a neighbor's while they were gone, going to a craft fair, driving in the country. We gave these outings

more time than usual, because we made our relationship a priority for this period of time.

We were happier during that three weeks than we'd been for years. And we didn't want to let go of it. Then Susan taught us about good will, which we now invoke often, and about creating time for sex, which has made a big difference.

Money? Well, we've each given up the need to be "right." I spend more money on my own, without checking in with him all the time. He has let go of micromanaging me. And I respect his limits. Like right now, I've decided to drop the idea of getting a fountain in our backyard. It's beyond his limit. But I think we both know that we will get one eventually. Now that we've learned how, we drop issues instead of fighting about them. Something always works out in the end.

Being right and being fair are both booby prizes: when you get them, you don't get anything else: no love, no warmth, no fun.

My Spiritual Journey

The third strand of my life that led to Spiritual Partnership, in addition to my own marriage and my work with couples, is my spiritual journey.

During my years in seminary (Union Theological in New York and San Francisco Theological in Marin County) and in the ministry, both on college campuses and in congregations, I became most interested in the relationship between behavior and beliefs. In many cases, I saw little correlation. Spirituality seemed to me to be a way of approaching life, not a set of beliefs.

As I became increasingly at odds with some of the apparently immutable "beliefs" of the Christian Church, as well as with its patriarchal and hierarchical structure, I found myself in the very center of both a burgeoning feminist spirituality movement and thriving Eastern and indigenous religious groups. I eagerly explored all of them: meditating with Buddhists, celebrating in goddess circles, studying shamanism, dancing with Sufis, working with Huichol (Mexican indigenous) people, and reading widely. At a Buddhist monastery, I had a deeply moving religious experience. Because I am married to a Jew, I also learned to value Jewish traditions and rituals. Though always moderately concerned about the dangers of drawing on many religious traditions rather than settling into one, I was deeply nurtured by my spiritual explorations.

The Dearth of Spiritual Guidelines for Couples

I knew that my couples work—teaching couples to be happy and to improve areas of dissatisfaction alone rather than together—was spiritual. But as I sought corroboration for this view in my reading, I became increasingly frustrated with the lack of specific guidelines most spiritual traditions offer to intimate partners. For example, I savored *The Art of Happiness* by the Dalai Lama, eagerly anticipating the chapter titled "A New Model for Intimacy," not allowing myself to look ahead even though I couldn't wait to find out what it said.

It turned out to be a rich chapter, but it wasn't about deep intimacy between two people. It was about "realizing the importance of compassion and cultivating it" as an antidote to loneliness; developing a healthy dependence on others (as opposed to the extreme self-sufficiency our culture tends to reinforce); and expanding our definition of intimacy "to include all the other forms [of intimacy besides just that Someone Special] that surround us on a daily basis." All the Dalai Lama said about a "relationship that's characterized by a deep level of intimacy between two people" was, "Yes, I believe that kind of intimacy can be seen as something positive. I think if someone is deprived of that kind of intimacy then it can lead to problems."

So it goes in spiritual literature. No specific guidelines. Exactly how should being spiritual manifest in a love relationship?

The Vietnamese Buddhist teacher Thich Nhat Hanh wrote a book called *Teachings on Love*. It's inspiring, and all his wisdom is useful for two people who are building an intimate bond. But it's general. It offers a rich picture of a life lived from love, but few particulars about how that love works itself out on a daily basis with a beloved partner when conflicts and dissatisfactions arise.

If you are a spiritual person, exactly how does your spiritual practice affect your relationship?

I felt a strong need to lay out the answers for myself, and this book is the result. It posits the idea that a purely psychological approach to relationships has reached the limits of what it can teach us. Psychology alone, with its emphasis on pathology and on complex communication skills, simply won't carry us any further. We must turn to spirituality to uncover new levels of consciousness, to expand the reaches of what two people in love can experience together.

Right Relationship or Spiritual Partnership

Over several years, as I taught couples how to be guided, not by fairness and equality, but by spiritual principles, I sought in vain for a term that would describe this dramatically different approach. One day, in a major "Eureka!" experience, the idea of Right Relationship came to me. This was perfect, I thought! If the Buddhist precept of Right Livelihood means making a living in a way that supports other people and the planet and that harms or exploits no one, then Right Relationship would be conducting one's relationships in a way that supports other people and harms and exploits no one. The question would always be "How do I act in a manner that is consistent with Right Relationship?" rather than "How can I get my needs met?" or "How can I get across to this other person what I mean or what I want?"

In the end, I decided I could not use that term, because what I am describing, though not inconsistent with Buddhism, is not strictly Buddhist. Also, the Buddhist precepts of Right Livelihood, Right Understanding, and others are not widely known outside Buddhist circles.

Though I have been developing the ideas in this book for many years, it was when I read this passage in *The Seat of the Soul*, by Gary Zukav, that I found the name for the concepts that had been unfolding in my work:

> The archetype of marriage is no longer functional. It is being replaced with a new archetype that is designed to assist spiritual growth. This is the archetype of spiritual, or sacred, partnership.

Spiritual Partners make a sacred commitment to each other, says Zukav, to "assist each other's spiritual growth." That seemed to fit perfectly with my philosophy!

Interestingly, M. Scott Peck gave us almost exactly the same definition of love way back in 1977 in *The Road Less Traveled*. "Love," said Peck, "is the will to extend one's self for the purpose of nurturing one's own or another's spiritual growth." It is what many of us have been striving to do without realizing that we were participating in the creation of a new archetype appropriate for spiritual times. I hope the specific guidelines in this book will give new life to this emerging archetype and will help more couples become Spiritual Partners.

The Future of Spiritual Partnership

When the world is ready for an idea, that idea often will appear from a variety of independent sources at the same moment in time.

When I began suggesting to couples that they stop communicating and start behaving more kindly to each other, I had never heard of anyone else using this approach, with the single exception of psychologist George Pransky. In 1990, I began offering my innovative couples groups, in which I insisted that only one member of a couple participate in the group. I still know of no other psychologists who use this approach except for practitioners whom I have trained. However, it is interesting to see that recent work by other psychologists, though not as specific as Spiritual Partnership and Loving Actions, does corroborate these concepts and is moving in the same direction.

John Gottman, who studied couples in laboratory settings, announced that "successful conflict resolution is not what makes marriages succeed" and that couples will do better if they "nurture their admiration and fondness" and "turn toward each other instead of away." These are exactly the strategies that a spiritual approach to relationships suggests.

In a similar vein, veteran marriage therapists Andrew Christensen and the late Neil Jacobson developed an approach they call "acceptance therapy." They find that couples get along better when they work to accept each other instead of trying to change each other, also an important principle of Spiritual Partnership.

In *Relationship Rescue*, psychologist Phillip McGraw eschews "the rhetoric of traditional couples therapy" and insists that "reconnecting with your partner cannot and will not happen if you do not reconnect with yourself first." He says it is a myth to assume that you have to "straighten your partner out." These ideas, also the message of my previous book, *How One of You Can Bring the Two of You Together,* are all a radical turnaround from conventional couples work and are at the heart of Spiritual Partnership.

In his book *Soul Mates,* Thomas Moore makes the statement we have discussed before: "It is my conviction that slight shifts in imagination have more impact on living than major efforts at change." This is an outrageous statement, especially when viewed in light of the elaborate strategies aimed at communication and change that psychologists have developed in recent decades. But it is exactly the philosophy behind Spiritual Partnership.

An internal shift, a change of heart, a new understanding, *even on the part of just one partner,* will have a greater impact on you, your partner, and your relationship than any attempt at communication or change. This is a new idea, and its moment is *now.* Very soon, I predict, it will pervade relationship therapy and seem like an obvious idea that we have always known. As I write right now, however, it is still a fresh approach, right out there on the cutting edge of couples work. Most relationship strategies today are still aimed at communication and persuading one or the other partner to change.

As we've seen, Spiritual Partnership does not suggest that changes don't or shouldn't occur in relationships, only that change is more likely to occur because of a "shift in imagination" than because of an "effort at change." You are most likely to end up with the result you seek by creating an atmosphere of love and acceptance using Loving Actions.

Without question we are moving into a time when spiritual values are gaining importance in our individual and collective lives. Our approach to relationships simply had to change to keep pace with this emerging reality. It is probably not a coincidence that the new archetype of Spiritual Partnership has appeared at the beginning of a new millennium, a symbolic opportunity for renewal and regeneration.

The Wider Implications of Spiritual Partnership

When you practice Spiritual Partnership, you will find that it spills over into every aspect of your life. Through spiritual practice within your partnership, as you become increasingly aligned with your higher self, you and your partner will not be content to experience your passion only with each other; you will be compelled to share it with those around you. You will spend time not only face-to-face with each other but side by side looking out at the world together to see where your passion, born of your spiritual practice together, can best be used to benefit others.

A spiritual relationship is like a reservoir. It is fed by the streams and rivers of love, mutual support, good will, and compassion. When it becomes full, it overflows, offering its abundance to others who need it. If love were focused only on itself, it would soon shrivel up. The nature of Spiritual Partnership is that it expands, grows, spills over, and rushes out like a teaming river into the world around it, enlivening all that it comes in contact with. The peace and happiness Spiritual Partners find with each other is not something they ever keep to themselves.

As you practice Spiritual Partnership with your mate, your Loving Actions are likely to transform every relationship in your life. You will find yourself acting as if, using restraint, giving up problem solving, and approaching other people with a spirit of good will, with your children, members of your family, friends, the people in your work or professional life, and in your charitable activities.

The Impact on Your Public Life

Spiritual Partnership can be viewed as a kind of political action, because (1) our private behaviors make an impact, not only on us and our families and friends but on our greater political and social community, and (2) Spiritual Partnership is a model for the kind of political action that enlarges, rather than diminishes, human possibilities.

When you behave in accord with spiritual values in your personal life, you are contributing to the eventual shift of our self-destructing world to one that is filled with love and light. It may not be *enough* for us all to behave spiritually in our daily lives, but it is impossible to imagine widespread spiritual transformation if we don't each model love, authenticity, connection, consciousness, and surrender in our daily lives. The healing of our troubled world begins with each of us in our daily spiritual practice.

It is stunning to imagine what our world could be like if business and government were influenced by spiritual values. If everyone always acted out of love, there would be no poverty or hunger, no environmental ravaging, no inadequate education, no limited access to health care, no drug pushers, no discrimination against "minorities," no predatory capitalism, no wars. And in the world of work, there would be no unreasonable, arbitrary bosses and incompetent supervisors; no inhumane, antifamily work policies; no unfair wages; no discrimination in employment.

All these problems are a result of someone, somewhere operating from some principle other than love. Fear, greed, and the insatiable thirst for power and profit are the most common substitutes for love in our culture. Government and business leaders who make decisions that affect our lives are, for the most part, not spiritual as we have used the term in this book. Some of them may be religious, but if they were spiritual, they wouldn't be able to make decisions that flout human needs in favor of short-term financial gain. They are not in alignment with their authentic selves, not conscious, not motivated by their connection with the universe and everyone and everything in it. Their decisions move us toward separation, not connection.

The Western scientific vision of a mechanical universe has created an . . . alienation from our own inherent spiritual nature.
This has been reinforced in our daily lives by the increasing
alignment of our institutions with the monetary values of the
marketplace. The more dominant money has become in our
lives, the less place there has been for any sense of the spiritual
bond that is the foundation of community and a balanced relationship with nature. The pursuit of spiritual fulfillment has
been increasingly displaced by an all-consuming and increasingly self-destructive obsession with the pursuit of money—a
useful but wholly substanceless and intrinsically valueless human
artifact.

—David Korten

So as you experiment with Spiritual Partnership and Loving
Actions in your own family and with your friends and at work, envision each loving act you do as one tiny part of a vast movement that
is ever so gradually and certainly shifting us all to a time when love
will prevail, in our homes and on our planet.

My best wishes to you and your Spiritual Partner. May we all
blend our authentic, loving, conscious souls to help move everyone
on the planet toward connection and away from separation.

References and Further Reading

Blanton, Brad. *Radical Honesty*. New York: DTP, 1994.

Boorstein, Sylvia. *It's Easier Than You Think*. San Francisco: Harper-SanFrancisco, 1995.

Campbell, Susan M. *The Couple's Journey*. San Luis Obispo, Calif.: Impact, 1980.

Chavis, Melodie. *Altars in the Street*. New York: Harmony Books, 1993.

Chopra, Deepak. *The Path to Love*. New York: Harmony Books, 1997.

Christensen, Andres, and Neil S. Jacobson. *Reconcilable Differences*. New York: Guilford Press, 2000.

Creedon, Jeremiah. "God with a Million Faces." *Utne Reader*, July-Aug. 1998.

Dalai Lama, His Holiness, and Howard C. Cutler. *The Art of Happiness*. New York: Riverhead Books, 1998.

Gawain, Shakti. *Living in the Light*. Novato, Calif.: New World Library, 1998.

Godek, Greg. *1001 Ways to Be Romantic*. Naperville, Ill.: Casablanca Press, 1991.

Gordon, Thomas. *Parent Effectiveness Training*. New York: Three Rivers Press, 1970, 2000.

Gottman, John M., and Nan Silver. *The Seven Principles for Making Marriage Work*. New York: Crown, 1999.

Hanh, Thich Nhat. *Teachings on Love*. Berkeley, Calif.: Parallax Press, 1997.

Hendrix, Harville. *Getting the Love You Want*. New York: Henry Holt, 1988.

Hill, Julia Butterfly. *The Legacy of Luna*. New York: HarperCollins Publishers, 2000.

Hochschild, Arlie. *The Second Shift*. New York: Penguin Books, 2003.

Jung, Carl. *The Portable Jung*. New York: Penguin Books, 1971.

Kasl, Charlotte. *If the Buddha Dated*. New York: Penguin/Arkana, 1999.

Keen, Sam. *The Passionate Life: Stages of Loving*. San Francisco: Harper-SanFrancisco, 1983.

Kornfield, Jack. *A Path with Heart*. New York: Bantam Books, 1993.

Korten, David. *When Corporations Rule the World*. San Francisco: Berrett-Koehler, 1995.

Kushner, Harold S. *When Bad Things Happen to Good People*. New York: Avon Books, 1981.

Lamott, Anne. *Traveling Mercies*. New York: Pantheon Books, 1999.

Levine, Stephen, and Ondrea Levine. *Embracing the Beloved*. New York: Doubleday, 1995.

Lew, Alan, with Sherril Jaffe. *One God Clapping*. New York: Kodansha International, 1999.

McGraw, Phillip C. *Relationship Rescue*. New York: Hyperion, 2000.

Merton, Thomas. *The Intimate Merton*. New York: HarperCollins, 1999.

Millman, Dan. *The Way of the Peaceful Warrior*. Novoto, Calif.: New World Library, 1980.

Moore, Thomas. *Soul Mates*. New York: HarperCollins, 1994.

Moore, Thomas. *The Re-Enchantment of Everyday Life*. New York: Harper-Collins, 1996.

Peck, M. Scott. *The Road Less Traveled*. New York: Touchstone, 1978.

Pransky, George. *Divorce Is Not the Answer*. San Francisco: Tab Books, 1990.

Psaris, Jett, and Marlena S. Lyons. *Undefended Love*. Oakland, Calif.: New Harbinger, 2000.

Quick, Barbara. *Still Friends*. Berkeley, Calif.: Wildcat Canyon Press, 1999.

Somé, Sobonfu E. *The Spirit of Intimacy*. New York: Morrow, 1999.

Walsch, Neale Donald. *Conversations with God: An Uncommon Dialogue (Book 1)*. New York: Putnam, 1996.

Watts, Alan. *The Book: On the Taboo Against Knowing Who You Are*. New York: Random House, 1966.

Weiner-Davis, Michele. *Divorce Busting*. New York: Fireside/Simon & Schuster, 1992.

Welwood, John. *Journey of the Heart*. New York: HarperCollins, 1990.

Welwood, John. *Love and Awakening*. New York: HarperCollins, 1996.

Williamson, Marianne. *Enchanted Love*. New York: Simon & Schuster, 1999.

Zukav, Gary. *The Seat of the Soul*. New York: Fireside, 1989.

Zukav, Gary. *Soul Stories*. New York: Simon & Schuster, 2000.

About the Author

SUSAN PAGE has been conducting workshops for both singles and couples, nationally and internationally, since 1980. Her international speaking and media career has taken her to twenty-six states, Canada, Korea, Australia, and Mexico. She has appeared on the *Oprah Winfrey Show*, *Good Morning America*, CNN, and CNBC, and her work has appeared in *People* magazine, *USA Today*, *Cosmopolitan*, *Redbook*, *Glamour*, and *McCall's*.

Susan began her career as a Protestant campus minister at Washington University in St. Louis and at Columbia University in New York. She was director of women's programs at the University of California, Berkeley, where she helped found the nation's first university-based human sexuality program.

Her previous books include *How One of You Can Bring the Two of You Together*; *The Eight Essential Traits of Couples Who Thrive*; *If I'm So Wonderful, Why Am I Still Single?* and *The Shortest Distance Between You and a Published Book*.

After thirty-five years in Berkeley, California, she now lives in San Miguel de Allende, Mexico, with her husband of twenty-five years, Mayer Shacter.

Personal Coaching for Individuals and Couples by Telephone from Anywhere in the World

Susan Page and Associates offers individualized support for learning and practicing the Loving Actions presented in this book. Think of your coach as a personal trainer for your relationship. A regular, structured relationship with a professional coach will move you quickly beyond the stuck places in your relationship, guide you in creating warmth and closeness between you and your partner, and keep you focused on your own spiritual growth. Coaching will shorten your learning curve and move you more quickly to the Spiritual Partnership you seek with the person you love.

The relationship coaches at Susan Page and Associates are all therapists with at least fifteen years of experience working with couples. They are trained and seasoned in working with the principles described in this book. For information about how to acquire a personal relationship coach, call 1-510-843-2111.

Spiritual Partnership Support Groups

Susan Page trains both therapists and laypeople to conduct Spiritual Partnership Support Groups. Continuing education units are available to therapists. For information about these trainings or to join a Support Group yourself, visit Susan's Web site at

www.susanpage.com